Sport, Welfare and Social Policy in the European Union

Sport is often seen as an indicator of the civic maturity of a community, an aspect of the rights of citizens to health, education and social integration. This book examines the relationships between participation in sport and physical activity, and welfare policies across Europe.

It argues that the success of campaigns for the promotion of sport depend on the existence of dedicated welfare policies promoted by the European states and explores variations in cultural models and structures of governance across Europe. Addressing the function of supranational institutions such as the EU as well as voluntary networks, the book illuminates key issues in European societies such as migration, financial austerity and Brexit as they relate to sport policy.

This is important reading for scholars and students in the fields of European sport and physical activity, sociology, political science and organisational analysis, as well as operators and managers of the sport systems involved in advanced training programmes.

Nicola R. Porro is Full Professor in Sociology at the University of Cassino and Southern Lazio, and former President of EASS (European Association for the Sociology of Sport), Italy.

Stefano Martelli is Full Professor in the Sociology of Sport Communication at the Alma Mater Studiorum, University of Bologna, Italy.

Alberto Testa is Full Professor in Applied Criminology at Ealing Law School, University of West London, UK.

Routledge Research in Sport, Culture and Society

Social Justice in Fitness and Health
Bodies Out of Sight
Laura Azzarito

The World Anti-Doping Code
Fit for Purpose?
Lovely Dasgupta

Deleuze and the Physically Active Body
Pirkko Markula

Capitalism, Sport Mega Events and the Global South
Billy Graeff

The Nordic Model and Physical Culture
Edited by Mikkel B. Tin, Frode Telseth, Jan Ove Tangen and Richard Giulianotti

Sport and Mediatization
Kirsten Frandsen

Social Activism in Women's Tennis
Generations of Politics and Cultural Change
Kristi Tredway

Sport, Welfare and Social Policy in the European Union
Nicola R. Porro, Stefano Martelli and Alberto Testa

For more information about this series, please visit: https://www.routledge.com/sport/series/RRSCS

Sport, Welfare and Social Policy in the European Union

Edited by
Nicola R. Porro, Stefano Martelli and Alberto Testa

LONDON AND NEW YORK

First published 2020
by Routledge
2 Park Square, Milton Park, Abingdon, Oxon OX14 4RN

and by Routledge
605 Third Avenue, New York, NY 10017

Routledge is an imprint of the Taylor & Francis Group, an informa business

First issued in paperback 2021

© 2020 selection and editorial matter, Nicola R. Porro, Stefano Martelli and Alberto Testa; individual chapters, the contributors

The right of Nicola R. Porro, Stefano Martelli and Alberto Testa to be identified as the authors of the editorial material, and of the authors for their individual chapters, has been asserted in accordance with sections 77 and 78 of the Copyright, Designs and Patents Act 1988.

All rights reserved. No part of this book may be reprinted or reproduced or utilised in any form or by any electronic, mechanical, or other means, now known or hereafter invented, including photocopying and recording, or in any information storage or retrieval system, without permission in writing from the publishers.

Trademark notice: Product or corporate names may be trademarks or registered trademarks, and are used only for identification and explanation without intent to infringe.

Publisher's Note
The publisher has gone to great lengths to ensure the quality of this reprint but points out that some imperfections in the original copies may be apparent.

British Library Cataloguing-in-Publication Data
A catalogue record for this book is available from the British Library

Library of Congress Cataloging-in-Publication Data
Names: Porro, Nicola, editor. | Martelli, Stefano, editor. | Testa, Alberto, editor.
Title: Sport, welfare and social policy in the European Union / edited by Nicola Rinaldo Porro, Stefano Martelli and Alberto Testa.
Description: Abingdon, Oxon ; New York, NY : Routledge, 2020. | Series: Routledge research in sport, culture and society | Includes bibliographical references and index.
Identifiers: LCCN 2019055704 (print) | LCCN 2019055705 (ebook) | ISBN 9780815360513 (hardback) | ISBN 9781351118064 (ebook)
Subjects: LCSH: Sports--Social aspects--European Union countries. | Exercise--Social aspects--European Union countries. | Well-being--European Union countries. | Social integration--European Union countries. | Sports and state--European Union countries.
Classification: LCC GV706.5 .S73884 2020 (print) | LCC GV706.5 (ebook) | DDC 796.094--dc23
LC record available at https://lccn.loc.gov/2019055704
LC ebook record available at https://lccn.loc.gov/2019055705

ISBN 13: 978-0-8153-6051-3 (hbk)
ISBN 13: 978-1-03-223780-0 (pbk)
ISBN 13: 978-1-351-11806-4 (ebk)

DOI: 10.4324/9781351118064

Typeset in Times New Roman
by Taylor & Francis Books

Contents

List of illustrations vii
List of contributors viii

1 Introduction: sport and the citizens of a disenchanted Europe 1
NICOLA R. PORRO, STEFANO MARTELLI AND ALBERTO TESTA

PART I
Sports policies, non-profit and social issues 7

2 Migrants' social integration through movement practices? 9
STEFANO MARTELLI

3 Sport and the 'question' of Islam in Europe 29
MAHFOUD AMARA

4 European sport systems and the voluntary sector: non-profit
organisations' race for sport development 36
NICO BORTOLETTO AND ALESSANDRO PORROVECCHIO

5 Sport in jail: a sociological comparative perspective 51
MAURIZIO ESPOSITO

PART II
The sport of citizenship: an incipient Europeanisation? 67

6 The Europeanisation of sport: sociology of a new European
public action 69
WILLIAM GASPARINI

7 The organisation of sport and sports policies in Germany 75
MICHEL KOEBEL

8	Sports organisations and policies in France WILLIAM GASPARINI	86
9	Sport and welfare in Britain IVAN WADDINGTON	99
10	Welfare and sports policies in contemporary Italy NICOLA R. PORRO	110
11	Physical activity and sport in Spain JUAN ANTONIO SIMÓN SANJURJO	121
12	Sport and welfare in Central and Eastern European countries SIMONA KUSTEC AND SIMON LIČEN	132
13	In the homeland of sport for all: the Scandinavian countries IRENE MASONI	143
	Conclusion: established models of European sport revisited from a socio-politological approach JEROEN SCHEERDER	153
	Index	*169*

Illustrations

Figures

14.1	Multi-actor model of sport	158
14.2	Expanded version of the church model of sport	160

Tables

2.1	Facilitations for migrants' and refugees' social integration through sport and physical activity in an EU country	22
4.1	The five levels of the organisation of international sport according to Zintz & Winand (2013, 8)	43
8.1	Sports competences of French local authorities	95
14.1	Actors, processes and mechanisms with regard to the organisational and institutional evolution of modern sport	156

Contributors

Mahfoud Amara, Qatar University
Nico Bortoletto, University of Teramo, Italy
Maurizio Esposito, University of Cassino and Southern Lazio, Italy
William Gasparini, University of Strasbourg, France
Nicola R. Porro, University of Cassino and Southern Lazio, Italy
Michel Koebel, University of Strasbourg, France
Simona Kustec, University of Ljubljana, Slovenia
Simon Ličen, Washington State University, USA
Stefano Martelli, University of Bologna, Italy
Irene Masoni, University of Pisa, Italy
Alessandro Porrovecchio, University of Lille 2, France
Juan Antonio Simón Sanjurjo, European University of Madrid, Spain
Jeroen Scheerder, University of Leuven, Belgium
Alberto Testa, University of West London, UK
Ivan Waddington, Visiting Professor, University of Chester, UK

1 Introduction

Sport and the citizens of a disenchanted Europe

Nicola R. Porro, Stefano Martelli and Alberto Testa

On 20 June 2019, the day after the voting in the European Parliamentary elections, all European political leaders expressed their support for a politically ambitious relaunch of the so-called European model. A project to pursue without further postponements and hesitations. Brexit and the populist election advance of the previous May had highlighted its limits, delays and contradictions.

In the same days – *si parva licet componere magnis* – our transnational group was completing its research on the sport of rights and citizenship in Europe that we present in this volume. It is not a simple temporal coincidence. The boundaries of citizens' sport contain, in fact, a complex and demanding system of opportunities. Sport for all and for everyone is also called a qualitative leap induced by cultural, social and demographic change in Europe at the end of the second decade of the 2000s. The sport of the citizens constitutes in itself a challenge to be fully integrated into the political, social and institutional scenarios of the European system. A system requiring not only a simple maintenance of its original project but a courageous transformation. Work and economic growth, acceptance and reciprocity, private security and collective safeguards question not only the governance of national sports systems, which are still very different. They also cross crucial issues regarding equal opportunities, social policies and environmental sustainability. Briefly: one cannot be a citizen of sport without first being a citizen of a democratic community, founded on a shared regime of rights, duties and opportunities. However, we are convinced that sport represents a strategic sensor for measuring the breadth and depth of the crisis. It also provides a valuable vantage point to capture a cultural and relational quality that cannot be reduced to statistical sequences or, on the contrary, to mere ideological declamations. Our work describes a varied but not inconsistent picture. It does not seek an anachronistic composition of cultural, institutional and organisational models. Rather, it seeks to provide elements of knowledge and reflection, venturing in some contributions to a wider range of interpretations of the phenomenon and its recent developments. As never before since the end of the 'short century', political tensions, financial crises, social conflicts and even institutional disputes over the destiny of European construction have in fact occurred.

Some observers have wondered whether we can still reasonably describe a European model. Old conflicts and new reasons for division have generated lacerations within almost all national states, mainly in matters of equality and social opportunities. Privileged and less affluent, secured and vulnerable classes, as well as diverse age groups and cultural subsystems, have further segmented giving rise to new forms of conflict. Brexit and the May 2019 vote highlight significant aspects of the new European question. Political leaders who have become entrepreneurs of fear fuel widespread social resentment. It originates from the nightmare of social downgrading and results in mass selfishness. The wind of national particularities has begun to blow again and the feeling of belonging to the European Union on the part of the post-socialist countries has weakened. The brain drain to countries offering more job opportunities and professional success is a reliable indicator of the depletion of human capital to which one half of the continent is exposed. Despite the capacity shown by the Union in withstanding the impact of a devastating financial crisis, disenchantment seems to be the prevailing sentiment. Rather than relaunching the European construction by correcting its critical points, some governments seem worried about creating profitable positions and particular advantages through the crisis. National populism is the main political expression of this dynamic. Its return effect is represented by the growing difficulty in providing shared solutions to systemic governance problems. Problems that are real, worrying, not easy to solve and too long neglected by the community establishment.

During this period, large voluntary amateur organisations were developed to encourage the practice of sports, as in the exemplary case of the Scandinavian sports for all movements. Widespread mass organisations, often flanking the parties of the left, also took shape in France and Italy. This process interested both the countries that had known the fascist-inspired totalitarian regimes between the two wars – where regime sport had been an instrument of both nationalistic exaltation and mass political control – as well as the post-communist countries associated with the Union in the 2000s after the collapse of the socialist system. The diffusion of sporting practice was favoured by regulated market competition, welfare policies and democratic institutions. The so-called 'social democratic compromise' thus subtracted sport from the logics of propaganda, political control and social mobilisation imposed between the two world wars by totalitarianisms. An original model of activity was established (both competitive and non-competitive) that was perfectly consistent with the philosophy of social citizenship. Not a few decades have passed, however, and even the sport of citizenship appears today as an articulated and sometimes complicated system, often lagging behind the transformations of the wider globalised sports system. The contributions collected here, relating to some exemplary cases, show the profound differences which still exist in the national governance systems. They also highlight the co-existence of old problems and new critical factors, concerning both traditional social actors – the political forces, the central and peripheral administrations of the states, the networks of voluntary action – and new protagonists. Among these are the organisations for equal opportunities in the broadest sense of the term, the environmental movements and the organisations dealing with the disabled population, the elderly, the 'new citizens' of extra-European origin. In short, a system of delicate social, institutional and organisational balances revolves around sport. It cannot be dismantled and reassembled artificially by bureaucrats. As an organic part of the welfare system, moreover, since the 1990s it has undergone an aggressive campaign of de-legitimisation both by liberal thought and by populist movements.

It cannot, therefore, be surprising that the same Eurozone has created a unified area for the market and the circulation of money, but did not encroach on the powers of nation states in the welfare regime: the same that generated and fuelled the sport of citizens. Over two centuries ago, Europe first developed the idea of shared responses, inspired by social solidarity, to cope with the risks of ageing, illness, unemployment, loss of self-sufficiency. It was a question of bringing together, in the incipient time of industrialisation, democratisation, nation-building and the formation of mass markets and rights societies. It is the same challenge that awaits the EU in the 21st century and that our research intends to interpret and question, dealing with that demand for well-being, quality of life, health promotion and cultural and value promotion that is associated here with the sport of citizens. We therefore need to focus on the specifics of sport in relation to the policies of the nation states, trying to reconstruct the challenges that await sport and the trajectories it is following.

The main stimulus to this collective reflection among scholars of different European nationalities is represented by the need to analyse the developments and the transformations of the European sports system 12 years after the publication of the *White Paper on Sport*, elaborated on in 2007 by the EU Commission. The paper, chronologically situated between the first expansion towards Eastern Europe (2004 and 2007) and the Lisbon Treaty (2007),[1] although presenting heuristic and scientific limitations, had, however, the merit of undertaking sport as an issue requiring new attention and, indeed, connected to the wider issue of social integration. It is therefore symptomatic of a significant phase of the Union in the presence of new challenges and opposing forces. On one hand, the need for a more gradual and patient harmonisation of sport regulations after the entry of the post-socialist countries to the Union; on the other hand, the urgency of more convincing forms of EU policy regulations. The issue of integration, its normative meaning and its politico-cultural management, thus reappears in the form of the long-neglected 'sport issue'. Legislative and social policy legitimisation of sport appear, however, closely interactive and intertwined. Partially moving away from the conceptual deceit of monolithic European sport is necessary but not sufficient for effective action in the presence of restrictions and resistance for innovation still present and active.[2] These include organisational heritage and the existing forms of institutional legitimacy of sport in different national contexts. Even before the expansion towards Eastern Europe, there were different and, in some cases, antagonistic ideas of the institutionalisation of sport organisations. Twenty-five years later, it is still impossible to find a unique model of institutional regulation of sport systems. We cannot therefore either renounce the reasons for the resistance to integration, nor ignore interesting and little-known experiences of contamination between organisational models and normative principles. The review presents examples of both cases.

The research has temporally superimposed itself on the tormented events of Brexit. A political crisis that cannot be limited to the country directly concerned, although so important, and which presents significant meanings for sport at large. Great Britain was in fact the land of choice for the voluntary sports movement and has shaped the cultural paradigm of sport in late modernity. The break with the 27 countries of the European Union has symbolic implications that have not yet been fully investigated. In May 2019, moreover, the European Union parliamentary elections registered an advance of populist and nationalist forces that were particularly critical – when not openly opposed – to the processes of European integration. Their success did not have sufficient dimensions to induce a crisis in the integration process, already exposed to various challenges. However, it had the effect of cracking the construction of a European 'we', as mentioned by Gasparini in his contribution dedicated to the Europeanisation of sport which introduces the second section of this research. Sport is a construct of identity that reverberates in that 'we'. It draws nourishment and legitimacy from a philosophy inspired by social inclusion, solidarity and communication between different cultures. Precisely these values represent the privileged targets of the nationalist and anti-Europe insurgencies that have burst onto the political agenda of almost all EU countries, albeit with different electoral outcomes.

The Europeanisation of sport, like that of other crucial experiences in public life, therefore witnesses a critical passage in this historical and political phase. Social scientists must strive to develop a more courageous and less conventional analysis than those entrusted with the mere comparison of the institutional mechanisms regulating the sports systems in different countries. Assuming this perspective, Scheerder's considerations, inspired by the idea of the *societalisation* of sport, conclude our work in continuity with the reflections dedicated by Gasparini to its *Europeanisation*. Both are problematic concepts with results that are not obvious and are still largely unforeseeable. Only through the comparison of national cases and specific experiences of voluntary action through sport, however, can we try to compose a multi-coloured but meaningful panorama.

We cannot limit ourselves to updating the excellent pioneering analyses proposed, between the 1990s and 2000, by the Club of Cologne under the guidance of Klaus Heinemann.[3] Produced in other temporal contexts and in an incipient phase of Europeanisation, that research gives us a representation of the European sports system that is unrecognisable at the end of the second decade of the 2000s, despite the fact that just 20 years have passed. Thanks to the advanced vision of those scholars, the sports issue was settled strength of the most important sociological issue. The sports phenomenon, however, has experienced in recent decades a radical metamorphosis, becoming more and more conditioned by marketing, individualisation and hyper-mediatisation logics. Scientific inquiry has therefore focused on the relationship between sports, entertainment and old and new media. This trend has of course been accompanied by a growing attention to the phenomena of financial globalisation and the functional specialisation of the infinite subsystems that orbit sports. The integration between its many varied systems and subsystems has thus often been reduced to questions of tax regime, media promotion or commercial incentives, inevitably favouring the territories of spectacular professional sport.

It is therefore necessary to return to the original civic inspiration of the sport of citizenship and strive to update the analysis of the European model without prejudice. This requires overcoming an abstract and romantic representation of sport for all, but at the same time requires a renewed intellectual tension and the experimentation of original analytical tools. Not by chance Scheerder, in the pages that conclude this work, proposes a straight-to-the-point and useful analysis on the main sociological representations of the phenomenon. A reading that is in perfect harmony with that of us as editors, convinced as we are that innovation *in* sport and Europeanisation *of* sport constitute two sides of the same coin. On the condition, however, that both researchers and political decision-makers, as well as sports managers, strive to intercept changing cultural questions and to devise an organisational experiment capable of interpreting them.

We have therefore allowed ourselves, as a working method, to move away from a recognition of some exemplary experiences. We have thus tried to isolate, in the first section of the volume, some cases of sports activities oriented towards social inclusion, socialisation and representation of migration processes as a resource for the host communities rather than as a problem capable of arousing social alarm. Stefano Martelli and Mahfoud Amara propose updated reflections of the phenomenon from an original analysis perspective. The first investigates the significant traits of the question as they reverberate in concrete public policies. The second examines the socio-cultural dimension focusing on the experience of migrant communities of Islamic faith. Nico Bortoletto and Alessandro Porrovecchio, on the other hand, observe through the lens of sport the transformations affecting the universe of the voluntary action movement in the European context. Maurizio Esposito investigates comparatively the experiences of sport in the context of a total institution, such as prison, highlighting its potential as a socialisation and integration strategy rather than as a mere rehabilitation tool.

The second section of our research is devoted to a number of national and supranational contexts. In his contribution, which opens the section, William Gasparini convincingly illustrates the direction of what we mean as *Europeanisation* of sport in the years of Brexit and the disenchantment fuelled by the offsetting of new populisms against the 'European establishment'.

The researchers have illustrated the main national cases investigating the relationship between sports movement, social institutions and welfare policies in the demographic 'big five': Germany (Michel Koebel), France (William Gasparini), the United Kingdom (Ivan Waddington and Andy Smith), Italy (Nicola R. Porro) and Spain (Juan Antonio Simón Sanjurio). Other authors have analysed the Scandinavian area (Irene Masoni), particularly significant for a comparative reading of the relationship between widespread sports practice and welfare policies, and that of the post-socialist countries (Simona Kustec and Simon Ličen). We have necessarily had to sacrifice some important national contexts. None of them is automatically attributable to the models traditionally adopted and all show characteristics that would deserve an accurate treatment. The hope is to be able to devote to these national cases a specific and more adequate medium-range analysis that we cannot carry out here.[4]

Finally, Jeroen Scheerder suggests a broader reading of how the European sports system – if one can analyse it in a unitary dimension – succeeds (or fails) in intercepting new cultural questions and widespread needs emerging from social change at large.

The research involved 15 scholars from 7 different countries. Each of them used tools and categories of analysis reflecting differentiated schools of thought and various national traditions. However, the need for an update of classical theoretical models, to which a social phenomenon so widespread and culturally relevant as the sport of citizens, was widely shared. The reference to scholars such as Titmuss, Esping-Andersen and Ferrera, to mention only the authors of the most known and organic models of classification of welfare systems, remains valuable. However, it inevitably requires theories to be verified, as they were elaborated in the post-war decades: a period that experienced the gestation, the birth and the progressive consolidation of the Welfare State in Western Europe. Seventy years later, the very idea of sport for all has to face new challenges and undergo a non-trivial and non-obvious verification of its own foundations. The work we are proposing will have reached its most ambitious goal if it will succeed in encouraging and mobilising ideas and energies among scholars, public policy operators and sports opinion leaders in our countries.

Notes

1 A more ambitious European constitution project was rejected in 2005 by popular referendums in France and the Netherlands.
2 B. García-García (2009), Sport governance after the White Paper: The demise of the European model? *International Journal of Sport Policy*, 1: 267–284.
3 K. Heinemann (editor), 1999, *Sport Clubs in Various European Countries*. Schorndorf und Stuttgart: Hofmann Verlag-Schattauer; K. Heinemann (editor), 2003, *Sport and Welfare Policies: Six European Case Studies*. Schorndorf und Stuttgart: Hofmann Verlag-Schattauer.
4 On the contrary, in her article Irene Masoni associates the Norwegian case, despite the fact that the country does not belong to the EU, to those of Denmark and Sweden. This differentiates the properly Scandinavian area from the Nordic one, which includes Finland and Iceland (the first is a partner of the Union, the second is not a EU member).

Part I
Sports policies, non-profit and social issues

2 Migrants' social integration through movement practices?

Stefano Martelli

Introduction

In 2018, around 150,000 irregular arrivals were detected across EU external borders, a 25% decrease compared to 2017. This was the lowest level in five years and over 90% below the peak year for the migratory crisis in 2015. EU action has contributed to almost 730,000 rescues at sea since 2015. Millions of asylum seekers, refugees and displaced people have benefited from programmes financed by the EU Emergency Trust Fund for Africa2 – with over 5,3 millions vulnerable people receiving basic support, almost a million being reached by communication campaigns, and over 60,000 helped with reintegration after return. The Trust Fund for Africa has also been key to the voluntary humanitarian return of over 37,000 vulnerable migrants from Libya to their countries of origin since the start of 2017. A total of 34,710 people in need of international protection have been relocated from Italy and Greece. Since 2015, more than 50,000 people in need of international protection have been resettled to the EU. Over EUR 140 millions was provided under the Asylum, Migration and Integration Fund to support measures on integration and legal migration between 2015 and 2017. (EC 2019: 1, box: 'Key progress under the European Agenda on Migration')

Much more data could be reported, but the quote above should be sufficient to draw the material framework of European society in recent years. The positive climate of the 1990s, which ended with optimism and pride for the progress of the modern society in the world (Fukuyama 1992), at the beginning of the Third Millennium left its place at a dark period. Negative attitudes – e.g. fear, resentment and social discomfort – prevailed among the people, especially within the middle classes which, more than the other strata social classes, were fearful of losing the welfare they had enjoyed until now. This socially negative climate strenghthens populism in politics and feeds racism and other negative rejections of immigrants and refugees in European societies.

In my opinion it is important to keep this scenario always in mind when one reads these pages, so that everyone can easily recognise that the issue of migrants' and refugees' integration through sport and physical activity has an amplitude, is much more than appears at first glance; indeed this issue is located in a complex process of changes from modern to 'post'-modern society. So the question, if sport and physical activity could be, or not be, resources for migrants' and refugees' social integration, can have its answer only if it is seen from the inside of the network of social policies and welfare tools of the European host societies.

Section 1: Socially integrated / included / excluded: which is the right concept?

Social integration: a complex and diversified process

Can sport and physical activity be resources for migrants' and refugees' integration in Europe? One might think that this topic has to be absorbed inside a wider issue, such as 'social integration of ethnic minorities'; and the one and other topics would (should?) tend to assure the social cohesion inside a European society.

Indeed 'social integration' is a term used in sociology and in several other social sciences which means the process to insert persons or groups (e.g. handicapped people, those addicted to drugs or alcohol, old people, immigrants searching for work and better opportunities, political refugees, members of the underprivileged strata of society, ethnic or religious minorities, etc.) into the social mainstreams, and to make themselves able to have the same opportunities, rights and services offered by the welfare society.

Integration of minorities is an indispensable socio-political aim of governments and civil societies, pursuing human rights and values, and this one aim is substantial in the project of 'late' or 'post'-modernity (see Touraine 2015, 2018; Taylor 2007; et al. 1994; Kymlicka 1995, 2015; Portes 1995; Portes, Rumbaut 2001; deWind, 2007).

Social integration is a long-lasting and very differentiated process of joining together and growing together. It needs convergence, argumentation, communication, finding agreements, identification of differences, assumption of common responsibilities.

In contrary to 'assimilation' (total conformity), 'integration' does not ask a migrant individual or a refugee to surrender his/her own cultural identity; further, it demands of everybody, who was born in the host society from native-born parents, not to see its own society as an unchangeable and untouchable one. Moreover, in a migrant's or a refugee's eyes, integration is neither to shut him/herself in an ethnic network, nor to cultivate independence; genuine integration is to acknowledge the culture of the receiving country as a 'guiding culture' (Alexander 2001). Furthermore, the existence and setting up of parallel social circles – both within the migrants' and refugees' people, and inside the European host society – is counteracting the process of social integration, so that it may lead to opposite outcomes, such as isolation or social exclusion: so everybody – not only a migrant or a refugee in a European country but also a European citizen who was born from autochthonous parents – could be excluded by the mainstream society.

Migrants' social integration 11

In short, in my opinion, social integration is a multi-dimensional process which aims at peaceful co-existence within a socio-historical reality, among individuals and groups, which are different culturally and/or ethnically; it is founded on mutual respect for ethno-cultural diversities, which do not harm basic human rights and do not put democratic institutions at risk.

Integration always consists of a process, which takes time; it is a goal which is not acquired once and for all, but which is constantly pursued and declined at the economic, cultural, social and political levels. Moreover, it should be borne in mind that integration has two directions, so it concerns not only immigrants and refugees but also and jointly affects the citizens of the receiving country.

From social cohesion / assimilation / acculturation, to integration / inclusion / exclusion

Further considerations have to be offered, in order to fully understand the clearest definition of social integration of immigrants and refugees; but the limits of space, assigned to this chapter, prevent me from doing so. Briefly, I would suggest my readers bear in mind the following two perspectives:

i *A diachronic look* at the sociological studies shows that 'assimilation' and 'acculturation' were the main concepts, used by 'classic' sociologists in Europe and in America (Thomas and Znaniecki 1918; Redfield et al. 1936; Gordon 1964), who led their studies inside the Durkheimian overview of 'social cohesion' (Durkheim 1897). In recent times the concept of 'social integration' prevailed, as well as the correlate ones of 'social inclusion' and 'exclusion' (Castles, Davidson 2000; Sniderman et al. 2000; Kivisto 2005; Heath, Cheung 2007; Lewitt, Jaworsky 2007; Carmel, Cerami, Papadopoulos, 2011; Fleischmann, Phalet, 2012). This substitution in the leading concepts denotes a change in social policies, which nowadays refuse to assimilate immigrants to white middle class, or to 'force' their behaviours towards specific forms of occidental culture or national identity.

ii Indeed, today European social policies have as their main goal the 'social inclusion' of immigrants and refugees in the host country, offering them the *minimum* conditions for a good life (Alexander 2001). The concept of 'social inclusion' has to be used with great caution and critical shrewdness, because it takes for granted that the host country is the best one, and that a migrant or a refugee has only to adapt him/herself to the local culture. For a sociologist, this shift is incorrect, because it hides a peril, i.e. the unconfessed passage from a descriptive to a normative level.

iii *Descriptive vs. normative perspective*: In every study or research, led by one of the above concepts, one can note a polar tension between a descriptive analysis and a normative perspective – i.e. if a person, or a group, *is* or *is not* socially *aligned* (descriptive analysis), or if he/she/a group *has to respect* human rights, democratic institutions, and so on. The undeclared shift in social studies or researches from the description of the reality to a normative perspective often makes controversial their attempt to define and measure the process of integration of migrants and refugees in the host country (Sciortino 2012).

Other perspectives and methodologies were adopted by social scientists, such as the comparative analyses among two or more countries, e.g. in Europe (Castles 1984; Brubaker et al. 1992), or between the USA and Canada (Lee, Boyd 2008), or elsewhere (Eisenstadt 2019). Moreover, many scholars observed the integration of the 'second generation' of immigrants more frequently if a fundamentalist religious factor or an ethnic one seems to explain their behaviours (Portes, Rumbaut 2001; MacDonald, Marsh 2005; Kasinitz et al. 2008).

In recent years, too, sport and physical activity were observed, questioning if they can or cannot be resources for social integration of migrants and refugees, as I will try to debate further on. Indeed, the next paragraph will show that in Europe the answer to the many perspectives about 'social integration' has been *not* a theoretical solution, but only *an administrative praxis*: i.e. the way to manage immigrants and refugees, which in recent years the European Union is promoting and steering in its member states, is a collection of 'good practices', suggested by many recent official documents and sustained by EU finalised funds.

European Union and the efforts to remove obstacles to social integration: a short diary

In recent times in Europe, 'social integration' has been seen as a complex process; moreover, in it one can distinguish three dimensions – a socio-economic one, a legal-political one, and a sociocultural one, and each of them has a certain degree of autonomy from the others (Entzinger, Biezeveld 2003). For the first time, the most influential European countries have given more significance to the first dimension, so that the solution to the social integration of migrants was reduced to a question about jobs or to material conditions (housing, transportation, etc.); to these solutions the European Community policies gave a strong response.

The beginning of European policy on migrants' integration can be traced back to the Tampere Programme (1999) focusing, among other issues, on the closely related topics of migration and social acceptance.

In June 2003, following a request (2002) of the Justice and Home Affairs Council to establish National Contact Points on Integration, the European Council invited the European Commission to publish annual reports on migration and integration.

The Brussels European Council conclusions of November 2004 on The Hague Programme and the Thessaloniki European Council called upon the importance of establishing common basic principles for immigrant integration policies.

In 2005, the European Commission adopted the communication: *A Common Agenda for Integration – Framework for the Integration of Third-Country Nationals in the European Union*, with the aim of providing its first response to the European Council's request of establishing a coherent European framework to integrate immigrants (CEC 2005). The cornerstones of this document were proposals for concrete measures with a view to putting in place the *Common Basic Principles* through a series of supportive EU procedures.

The 2009 Stockholm Programme for the period 2010–2014 embraced the development of core indicators for monitoring the results of integration policies in a limited number of relevant policy areas (e.g. employment, education and social inclusion).

The Zaragoza Declaration, adopted in 2010 by the European Ministerial Conference on Integration, held in that Spanish city, identified a number of policy areas relevant to migrant integration and agreed on a set of common indicators to monitor the situation of immigrants and the outcomes of integration policies.

In 2011, the European Institute for Statistics, in its pilot study, *Indicators of immigrant integration*, examined proposals for common integration indicators and reported on the availability and quality of the data; in order to be able to carry out comparative analyses, Eurostat highlighted the importance of having available harmonised and agreed sources (EC-Eurostat 2011a). Its subsequent report, *Migrants in Europe: A statistical portrait of the first and second generation*, offered relevant outcomes of a broad analysis about immigrant people in the EU and EFTA countries (EC-Eurostat 2011b). These pilot studies were further developed and elaborated in the report, *Using EU indicators of immigrant integration* (EC-DG Home Affairs 2013). The project's objectives were to boost the monitoring and assessment of the situation of migrants, along with the relative outcomes of integration policies.

Briefly, the Zaragoza Declaration promoted a multi-dimensional approach for studies on immigrant people's social integration, which was maintained by the European Institute for Statistics in more recent publications, such as *Migrant integration*, and *Migrant integration statistics* (EC-Eurostat 2017, 2019). Indeed, a multi-dimensional approach was adopted both by the Organisation for Economic Co-operation and Development in its reports of the series *Settling In* (OECD 2012 and following editions: 2015, 2018), and by the Migrant Integration Policy Index (MIPEX) (Huddleston et al. 2015).

Section 2: Which indicators for what dimensions of social integration?

Today, more than ever, the 'Zaragoza indicators' are relevant to achieve the goals of European Union politics and to monitor its derived strategies and benchmarks. In order to illustrate the main lines of the EU's policies about immigrants' social integration – above briefly named 'the administrative approach' – I have below summarised the main outcomes obtained from existing quantitative and qualitative social researches; these outcomes compare immigrants and autochthonous citizens of the receiving country, thus better showing the unequal opportunities and the urgency to intervene with targeted social policies.

Evidence about European policies on migrants' and refugees' social integration

The main evidence about the effects of European policies for migrants' and refugees' social integration, collected by Eurostat periodical surveys, are the following eight (see EC-DG 2013: 5):

1. *About time of residence:* Integration is a long-term process. Immigrants show better outcomes the longer they are in the country. Just as for non-immigrants of working age, outcomes show that it improves generally with age.
2. *About gender:* Across all 'Zaragoza indicators', foreign-born women and mothers are among the most vulnerable groups, in particular those born in non-EU countries.
3. *About country of origin*: Compared to immigrants from EU or highly-developed countries, immigrants from non-EU countries, in particular less developed countries, have more frequently many reasons to leave their native places, different aspirations for their own futures, and different types of problems. Non-EU immigrants face greater challenges in the labour market, the housing market and in schools. They are more likely to be affected by poverty and over-qualification. Immigrants from less developed countries are also more likely to naturalise.
4. *About socio-economic background*: Social mobility remains modest for immigrants. Employment and education outcomes still largely depend on the parents' socio-economic status. Immigrants are more likely to be concentrated in lower track, low-performing schools with a low average socio-economic status. Children of immigrants with low socio-economic status face much greater difficulties advancing into higher education.
5. *About quality*: Social integration is more than a matter of obtaining a job, finding a house and having a basic education in the receiving country. More often than native citizens, immigrants find a part-time job, or a temporary one, which more frequently is below their qualifications and with a wage which is not sufficient to protect them from poverty. They are more likely to live in overcrowded housing and to pay more of their income on rent. Foreign qualifications are often devalued within the labour market or not formally recognised.
6. *About discrimination*: Unequal treatment hampers integration. Immigrants are less likely to be hired, even when their qualifications are similar to those of native citizens. Immigrant students are less likely to be referred to higher track education, even when their grades are similar to the performance of non-immigrants. In countries with larger

gaps between immigrants and native citizens, the general public is more likely to say that discrimination against migrants is a problem.
7   *About social context*: Structures of society shape integration. Immigrants from the same country of origin and with a similar social background perform differently in different EU countries. Immigrants tend to have better labour market outcomes, to perform better in schools and to take part in politics more frequently in countries in which the majority of people obtain higher outcomes. Some European welfare systems protect immigrants from poverty better than others in Europe, and some education systems are more favourable for low-performing immigrants than those of other European systems. Briefly, more research is needed about the direct impact on integration outcomes of immigrants of the welfare system, the education system, housing and general labour market structures of each receiving European country.
8   *About policy effects*: 'There is a lack of rigorous impact evaluations of policy effects in the EU. There is evidence that policies are directly relevant for some EU integration indicators. For example, employment rates tend to be higher in countries with a larger share of work migration. Welfare systems in some countries were more successful in reducing poverty than others. Richer, more equal countries tend to adopt more ambitious integration policies. More immigrants naturalise in countries where naturalisation policies are more open. While there is a better understanding of which countries adopt policies and which outcomes seem to be associated with which policies, very little is known about the causal effects of specific policies or programmes' (EC-DG Home Affairs 2013: 5, col. II).

Four dimensions of migrants' social integration

If many social factors influence migrants' integration in a European country, which are the most relevant ones? This question is pertinent in the overview to steer integration policies at various levels of governance; with this goal in mind, the 'Zaragoza indicators' (EC-Eurostat 2011a,b) outline a fruitful approach, which stimulates social scientists to propose some additional ones.

I would like to make a contribution to this collective effort so, here, I will offer a redistribution of social indicators on immigration by a multi-dimensional tool: the AGIL scheme, which is a 'pivotal' interpretative key, usually adopted by many studies and researches (Parsons 1970: 26–50; Münch 1987; Donati 2013). By this useful and powerful tool, one can place the numerous outcomes of European social policies according to the following four dimensions, which every social phenomenon fulfils: the adaptive function (A), the political function (G), the social integrative function (I), and the latent values function (L). And the the outputs of social policy interventions to support immigrants' and refugees' integration, generated by the 'Zaragoza indicators', are distributed according to those four dimensions, with their difficulties also highlighted:

(A) Employment

A.1) Immigrants face severe discrimination in the labour market. More accessible and coherent anti-discrimination legislation, stronger equality bodies, more teacher and public sector training as well as anonymous job applications could enhance the situation.

A.2) Highly-qualified immigrants are most likely to be overqualified for the job which they have in the host country. Easier and more accessible identification procedures, equivalence courses and European co-operation could facilitate the recognition of qualifications and skills.

A.3) Immigrants and their descendants are under-represented in the public sector, which is a major share of the job market in many EU countries. Public sector employment targets and targeted information campaigns can increase application rates of eligible immigrants.

A.4) Little is known about the impact of legal restrictions for employment on some migrant groups and their participation in labour market programmes on immigrants' employment outcomes.

(L) Education

L.1) Education outcomes still largely depend on the parents' social background, so that a child may suffer by its parents' low level of education and insufficient ability to speak the language of the receiving European country. There is evidence that decreasing socio-economic segregation in schools, increasing the hours spent in school, improving the quality of teaching, delaying the age of tracking and supporting students before and during the transition into higher education can reduce that link. Smaller classes and more parental involvement have proven to be effective for improving immigrant children's outcomes.

L.2) Quality early childhood education and care is associated with better education outcomes for immigrants at the age of 15 years. Access and quality of early childhood education and care can have an impact on immigrants' long-term education and careers.

L.3) Education outcomes improve over time. General education policies can accommodate recent immigrants by providing homework and other general school support for younger ones, language tuition for everybody, equivalence classes and access to lifelong learning for adult immigrants. Targeted policies can tackle longer settled groups with lower achievement.

L.4) Foreign-trained immigrants' qualifications are often not recognised in the receiving European country, or the foreign skills and qualifications do not fit current labour demand in the new society. Opportunities for adult migrant learners to upgrade or equalise their qualifications, including by providing easier access to lifelong learning, can help to enhance employability of immigrants.

L.5) Immigrant students with good potential face obstacles of discrimination in schools. A way to tackle this is by providing discrimination awareness training and support for teachers to deal with second language issues.

(I) Social integration

I.1) Basic knowledge of the receiving European country, such as its language, history and social institutions is an important resource. Enabling immigrants to acquire this basic knowledge, by training courses or other educational programmes, is essential to successful social integration.
I.2) Immigrants are more likely to live in bigger families and overcrowded housing. However, not enough is known about how housing policies affect integration outcomes. Evidence is needed on accessing the housing market and its impact on the situation of immigrants.
I.3) More frequently, immigrant women in large households are affected by poverty. There is a good reason for reviewing compliance with and implementation of gender equality legislation and the effects of family and unemployment benefits on migrant families.

(G) Active citizenship

G.1) Citizenship and long-term residence are only two elements of active citizenship. Indicators of other forms of civic participation of migrants such as voting, membership of organisations, running for or holding a political office, protesting or volunteering are needed to capture immigrants' political and civic involvement.
G.2) The interaction between access to citizenship and social integration is complex. Naturalisation is both a final step in the process and a tool to further improve integration in several areas of life. Citizenship is a societal outcome indicator, a policy indicator and a measure of openness of receiving societies, all at the same time.
G.3) In many European countries, a large number of immigrants, living in it for more than ten years, have not naturalised. These people are still seen as foreigners and largely excluded from the democratic process.
G.4) Immigrants become citizens and long-term residents more often in countries where the process is more inclusive and where dual citizenship is accepted in both the country of origin and destination. Beyond legal changes in order to facilitate naturalisation, support to pay naturalisation fees and minor changes of administrative procedures could facilitate acquisition of citizenship.
G.5) Naturalised immigrants have on average better integration outcomes than non-naturalised in most countries, regardless of whether naturalisation policies are inclusive or restrictive. It remains unclear whether this 'citizenship premium' is greater or lesser in certain European countries due to their policies or to other factors. More research is needed about who benefits more frequently from naturalisation.

Indeed, social integration indicators are rarely part of the debate on migrant integration, despite the fact that low income, poverty, problems of health and overcrowded housing largely affect other areas of the migrant's life, such as education and employment. Some evidence suggests that immigrants actually are less likely to use social benefits than non-immigrants, if several factors are accounted for. Some studies have begun to make assessment of these policies (Di Bartolomeo et al. 2017; Weinar et al. 2017), but much more research is needed about the impact of social benefits on migrant people's integration.

Section 3: What is the place of sport and physical activity in European social policies in integrating migrants and refugees?

The integration of migrants and refugees into European societies nowadays is one of the greatest challenges facing the European Union at the present time. One can note a growing interest towards sport and physical activity as resources to support social policies in the fields of education, employment, health, social cohesion, etc., both in recent documents by the European Commission, and in civil society.

The *White Paper on Sport* stated that, 'Sport can ... facilitate the integration into society of migrants and persons of foreign origin, as well as support intercultural dialogue' (CEC 2007: 7).

'The Lisbon Treaty, in force since December 2009, introduced a specific article, namely Article 165 TFEU, which gave the EU a new supporting competence for sport. This article entails provisions for promoting European sporting issues and calls for EU action to develop the European dimension in sport.

In 2011, the European Commission adopted a communication, entitled *Developing the European Dimension in Sport*, providing for specific actions regarding the societal functions of sport, its economic relevance and its organisation. Furthermore, the Council adopted the resolution *EU Work Plan for Sport 2011–2014*, which further strengthened European co-operation on sport by setting priorities for European level work engaging the EU member states and the Commission.

In 2012, the European Council adopted conclusions in order to promote health-enhancing physical activity and to strengthen the evidence base for sport policymaking, calling on the Commission to issue regular surveys on sport and physical activity. Following a proposal from the Commission, financial support for sport is now included in the form of a specific chapter in *Erasmus+*, the EU programme for education, training, youth and sport (period 2014–2020).

A new *EU Work Plan for Sport* came into force in July 2017 (CEU 2017). It sets out the key topics that EU member states and the Commission should prioritise, up to 2020:

a   Integrity of sport will focus on good governance, safeguarding minors, fighting match-fixing, doping and corruption;

b   The economic dimension, focusing on innovation in sport, and the links between sport and the digital single market;
c   Sport and society, focusing on social inclusion, coaches, media, environment, health, education and sport diplomacy.

In the meantime, outcomes about the effects of the first programmes, which use sports and physical activities to integrate immigrants, have been collected and debated (Elmose-Østerlund 2016; Østerlund, Ibsen et al. 2017; Marivoet 2017; Piątkowska et al. 2017).

Evidence about sport and physical activity in European social policies

The growing focus, recently put on sport and physical activity as social resources to integrate migrants and refugees in receiving European countries, indeed risks increasing excessive expectations. Really, these movement practices, if they act alone, will not be able to solve either social problems, or the migration crisis; conversely, if sport and physical activity is to be seen as one of many components of good social politics, the movement practices could be effective resources in order to achieve a positive social integration for immigrant people.

What the movement practices can offer is a 'universal language', which is able to transcend social, cultural and national boundaries; at best, they can bring people together, no matter what their origin, social background, religious beliefs or economic status (UN 2003). Sport and physical activity may be an inclusive, universal and safe arena for cultural exchanges and for individual and community developments, in order to facilitate migrants' integration in the receiving European society (Collins, with Kay 2003; Spaaij, et al. 2014).

It is on this premise that EU politicians, policymakers and professionals are now looking to sport and physical activity for inspiration, recognising that there are some lessons and good practice examples which can be taken from them, in particular from grassroots sport initiatives and programmes across various member states. This topic was at the top of the agenda at the EU Sport Forum 2016, held in The Hague (the Netherlands), where leading representatives from international and European sport federations, officials and managers of the Olympic movement in European national sport umbrella organisations and other sport-related associations came together to discuss how to facilitate the social integration of migrants and refugees through sport and physical activity, and mainly what answers European grassroots sport can provide (EC-DG for Education and Culture 2016).

In some European countries, such as Germany, Italy and the United Kingdom, there are numerous examples of targeted sports initiatives and programmes, which have demonstrated how sport can connect communities and contribute to the integration of migrants and refugees (SPIN 2012). The types of projects can take many forms, from organisations running sports days within the local community, with a range of sporting activities involved, to more structured approaches, such as the development of local football leagues involving migrants in local and mixed teams. The majority of these targeted initiatives are delivered by support organisations for migrants and refugees, community organisations, local sports clubs, or representative bodies of particular sports. A key driver, especially in Germany, is the provision of targeted government funding for the implementation of *Integration durch Sport* (Integration through Sport), highlighting the positive attitude and the political significance and weight given to this issue (Elmose-Østerlund, Ibsen, 2016; ESPIN 2017).

There are also a range of transnational projects and networks across Europe, many of which are funded by the EU Commission through the *Erasmus+* Sport Programme and other ways, which facilitate the exchange of good practices for the integration of migrants by collaborative partnerships, and not-for-profit events and actions, which strengthen the evidence base for social policymaking (Steinbach, Elmose-Østerlund, 2017).

It is beyond the scope of this chapter to consider, in any detail, the wide-ranging academic literature which looks at the ability of social policies to contrast the causes of social exclusion, and in them the movement practices as resources to migrants' and refugees' inclusion. It is recognised, however, that while poverty is at the core of social exclusion, it is often exacerbated by prejudices and discriminations, which follow on from differences of class, gender, age, ethnicity, disability, and social location – for instance: natives versus outsiders (Haudenhuyse, Theeboom 2015; Haudenhuyse 2017). It is also recognised that social integration has a close connection with anti-discrimination efforts, as both aim to create a more inclusive society and to ensure equal participation for everybody in a European receiving country (FRA 2017).

Previous research has highlighted that sport and physical activity as resources for social integration need to take account of the complexity of the structural issues underlying exclusionary processes; specific social outcomes can be achieved through movement practices, only if certain social conditions are present and if successful processes are realised. So, rather than putting stress on sport contributing to social integration, it is more effective that various aspects of social integration may precede such participation. Aside from the obvious relevance of sport clubs and associations, strategic partners in such inclusive activities can be schools, youth and community groups, health and welfare bodies, churches and religious groups, trades unions, voluntary associations and other social realities (Collins, with Kay 2003; Spaaij, et al., 2014).

A theoretical and methodological framework to deepen the facilitation function of sport and physical activity as resources to integrate migrants and refugees

A map of good practices relating to social integration of migrants in a European country could be developed, drawing on previous researches which highlight effective processes to engage youth in sports such as football, athletics or

Migrants' social integration 21

swimming (Levermore, 2013; EC-DG for Education and Culture 2017). Sport and physical activity function more frequently as a hook to attract disadvantaged and marginalised young people, without attaching to them the stigma commonly associated with social interventions. The key change processes, which associate sport and physical activity to social policies for migrants' and refugees' integration, may be explained according to the known AGIL scheme:

(A) *Employability support*: sport attracts individuals into youth/social work-type programmes, which include a package of employability support, ranging from careers advice and guidance, through to life skills coaching, placements, internships and even jobs brokerage.

(G)*Education and vocational training*: sports programmes may provide people with specific
educational opportunities leading to a qualification (or further level of study) which, in turn,
enhances employability and earning prospects (Schwenzer 2016).

(I)*Personal and social development*: well-structured sports activities help to improve life skills such as confidence, motivation, self-esteem, communication and team-working, and to improve health and access to social capital networks. Alongside other support, indirectly this may help individuals into employment, through developing some of the essential characteristics associated with retention in school, improved employability and/or improved productivity.

(L)*Volunteering in sport*: through taking up the opportunity to volunteer as a sports coach, or other project role, individuals develop vital skills and experience to enhance their employability (and may even lead to employment in the sports sector itself) (Tomlinson 2016).

In detail, the social indicators which can measure these four functions, fulfilled by sport and physical activity, and their positive effects on migrants' and refugees' integration are shown in Table 2.1 below. A further distribution, according to micro-/meso-/macro-sociology (Alexander et al. 1987), will specify the indicators to measure the social integration of immigrant people in European sporting clubs or in associations' sport-for-all, and indirectly in a European country.

An opening conclusion

Are these social indicators able to measure migrants' and refugees' social integration through sport and physical activity, or not? Necessarily the answer will be given only by further social researches; therefore, this chapter pauses here, leaving to the following ones, both in this part of the book, and in the second part of it, the task to develop the common issue further.

Indeed, this chapter is only the first step of an intellectual journey, which this book will take further; so:

Table 2.1 Facilitations for migrants' and refugees' social integration through sport and physical activity in an EU country

AGIL scheme (the four functions, which sport & physical activity perform at the level specified on the side)	Micro-sociological level (individual migrants or refugees, and their families or networks)	Meso-sociological level (sport clubs or voluntary sport associations in the EU host country)	Macro-sociological level (an EU host country, the whole EU as a social system)
(A)	Migrant's or refugee's abilities to earn his/her own sustenance legally	Offering a job to a migrant or to a refugee, e.g. as player, coach, functionary, clerk, etc.	Legal and administrative facilitations in sport & physical activity to improve migrants' and refugees' adaptation to their host societies
(G)	Migrants' engage in political form of activism, such as anti-racism campaigns, etc.	Promoting political activities, such as anti-racism campaigns, etc.	Realising most advanced forms of political participation through formal and informal relationships in sport & physical activity
(I)	Bolstering the migrant's or refugee's belonging to a community by involving him/herself in sporting services and festivities	Adopting statutes and rules, free of racism and discrimination norms	Contrasting any discriminations or social exclusions as a mandatory duty for public authorities
(L)	Facilitating the migrant's or refugee's interiorisation of universal values through sport & physical activity	Promoting the intercultural openness of the sports club or voluntary sports association in public relations activities Developing a mission statement, based on diversity and respect of minority groups	Promoting sporting forms and activities according to a perspective of homogeneisation among cultures

a The short literature review, offered in section 1, keeps open the theoretical overview about migration processes: the insights offered on the concept of 'social integration', as with other concepts used by social scientists, may keep the intellectual horizon open about the current reality. Not always does the administrative perspective, de facto legitimised both by the EU declarations and by other official documents of its agencies, do this. Really, the pluralism is a European value, and sociology has the duty to keep it live;
b The synthesis of most important outputs, collected by Eurostat surveys – see section 2 – summarises the main social barriers, which migrants and refugees face in their efforts to live in a European country. It can help always to keep in mind the various causes of social exclusion, and to avoid the risk of reducing this complex problem to one social cause;
c This multi-dimensional approach is at the preliminary stages of discussion, both theoretical and methodological, about the use of sport and physical activity as resources for migrants' and refugees' social integration, conducted in section 3;
d This discussion cannot be conclusive because currently there are not sufficient evaluations of the programmes, supported by European funds, or by other social entities or foundations. Therefore, the last section of this chapter presents a table (Table 2.1) of the social indicators which probably better measure the effectiveness of sport and physical activity on migrants' and refugees' social integration.

Before closing this chapter it is worth noting that the list of social indicators in Table 2.1 is not exhaustive; the work of social scientists about the effectiveness of sport and physical activity to facilitate the social integration of migrants and refugees is yet *sub judice*. Indeed the relevant work, produced in the last 30 years by Eurostat and by other national statistical institutes to evaluate EU and regional policies for social integration in terms of their valuable impact, has not yet been carried out for sport and physical activity.

More exactly, today it is possible to say if a policy is functional, or not, for the social integration of migrants and refugees in a receiving European country because there is a sufficiently solid and legitimised evidence-based formalisation of the requirements of a 'good' policy (or practice) (Rinne 2012; Jain, Sabirianova 2017).

Instead, in the field of sport and physical activity, until now there has been no formalisation of these requirements; therefore, evaluations in this field may have an exploratory function, but not be conclusive. Indeed, the social scientist tries to understand how a social policy (or a practice) has been implemented and, then, which is its social context. So his/her final evaluation is not an 'impact evaluation' (a judgement on the effects of the considered social policy, or practice), it is simply an attempt to understand if this social policy (or practice) is 'good'. And this sentence is not a real evaluation, because there is no evidence of the reasons to increase the actual level of social integration in a

European host country. Indeed this second type of evaluation has yet to clarify how the social context is modified in the presence of a social policy (or practice), which uses sport and physical activity as a tool as the main goal to integrate migrant people in a European society.

Briefly, nowadays there is no sufficient formalisation in the field of sport and physical activity so that it is not possible to respect the *ceteris paribus* rule, and therefore a correct comparative analysis cannot be carried out (Smelser 2013). The following chapters of this book will try to show if, in some sports, social groups or European countries the social scientists have been able to realise an evaluative analysis.

Bibliography

Alexander, J.C., 2001. Theorizing the 'Modes of incorporation': Assimilation, hyphenation and multiculturalism as varieties of civil participation. *Sociological Theory*, 19 (3), 237–249.

Alexander, J., Giesen, B., Münch, R., Smelser, S.N., eds., 1987. *The Micro-Macro Link*. Berkeley – Los Angeles – London: California University Press.

Brubaker, R., 1992. *Citizenship and Nationhood in France and Germany*. Cambridge, MA: Harvard University Press.

Carmel, E., Cerami, A., Papadopoulos, T., 2011. *Migration and Welfare in the New Europe: Social Protection and the Challenges of Integration*. Bristol: The Policy Press.

Castles, S., 1984. *The Age of Migration: International Population Movements in the Modern World*. Basingstoke: Palgrave Macmillan.

Castles, S., Davidson, A., 2000. *Citizenship and Migration: Globalization and the Politics of Belonging*. Basingstoke: Macmillan.

CEC–Commission of the European Communities, 2005. A common agenda for integration. framework for the integration of third-country nationals in the European Union. Brussels: Publications Office of the European Union. Retrieved from: https://eur-lex.europa.eu/legal-content/EN/TXT/PDF/?uri=CELEX:52005DC0389&from=FR, 17. 3. 2019.

CEC–Commission of the European Communities, 2007. White Paper on sport. Brussels: Publications Office of the European Union. Retrieved from: https://eur-lex.europa.eu/legal-content/EN/TXT/PDF/?uri=CELEX:52007DC0391&qid=1552992282618&from=EN, 20. 03.2019.

CEU-Council of the European Union, 2017. Resolution of the Council and of the Representatives of the Governments of the Member States, meeting within the Council, on the European Union Work Plan for Sport (1 July 2017–31 December 2020). Retrieved from: http://data.consilium.europa.eu/ doc/document/ST-9639-2017-INIT/en/pdf, 25. 3. 2019.

Collins, M.F., with Kay, T., 2003. *Sport and Social Exclusion*. London: Routledge.

Di Bartolomeo, A., Kalantaryan, S., Salamonska, J., Fargues, P., eds., 2017. *Migrant Integration between Homeland and Host Society, Vol. 2: How Countries of Origin Impact Migrant Integration Outcomes: An Analysis*. Cham: Springer.

Donati, P., 2013. Relational Sociology and the Globalized Society. In F. Dépelteau, C. Powell (eds.), *Applying Relational Sociology: Relations, Networks, and Society*. New York: Palgrave Macmillan, pp. 1–24.

Durkheim, E., 1897. *Suicide: A Study in Sociology* (Simpson, G., ed.; Spaulding, J.A., Simpson, G., tr. 1951). New York: The Free Press.

EC-European Commission, 2019. Communication from the Commission to the European Parliament, the European Council and the Council: Progress Report on the Implementation of the European Agenda on Migration. Brussels: Publications Office of the European Union. Retrieved from: https://ec.europa.eu/home-affairs/sites/homeaffairs/files/what-we-do/policies/european-agenda-migration/20190306_com-2019-126-report_en.pdf, 6. 3. 2019.

EC-European Commission, DG-Directorate General for Education and Culture, 2011. Developing the European dimension in sport. Brussels: Publications Office of the European Union. Retrieved from: https://publications.europa.eu/en/publication-detail/-/publication/db29f.162-d754-49bc-b07c-786ded813f.71, 25. 7. 2019.

EC-European Commission, DG-Directorate General for Education and Culture, 2016. Mapping of good practices relating to social inclusion of migrants through sport. Final report. Brussels: Publications Office of the European Union. Retrieved from: https://publications.europa.eu/it/publication-detail/-/publication/f1174f.30-7975-11e6-b076-01aa75ed71a1, 23. 3. 2019.

EC-European Commission, DG for Education and Culture, 2017. Study on the contribution of sport to the employability of young people in the context of the Europe 2020 Strategy. Luxembourg: Publications Office of the European Union. Retrieved from: https://publications.europa.eu/en/publication-detail/-/publication/e189cc96-b543-11e7-837e-01aa75ed71a1/language-en, 23. 3. 2019.

EC-European Commission, DG-Directorate General for Home Affairs, 2013. Using EU indicators of immigrant integration. Luxembourg: Publications Office of the European Union. Retrieved from: https://ec.europa.eu/home-affairs/sites/homeaffairs/files/e-library/documents/policies/legal-migration/general/docs/ final_report_on_using_eu_indicators_of_immigrant_integration_june_2013_en.pdf, 15. 1. 2019.

EC-European Commission, Eurostat, 2011a. Zaragoza pilot study: Indicators of immigrant integration. Luxembourg: Publications Office of the European Union. Retrieved from: www.fondazioneleonemoressa.org/newsite/wp-content/uploads/2011/05/Eurostat_indicatori-di-integrazione.pdf, 17. 3. 2019.

EC-European Commission, Eurostat, 2011b. Migrants in Europe: A statistical portrait of the first and second generation. Luxembourg: Publications Office of the European Union. Retrieved from: https://ec.europa.eu/eurostat/web/products-statistical-books/-/KS-31-10-539, 19. 3. 2019.

EC-European Commission, Eurostat, 2017. Migrant integration. Luxembourg: Publications Office of the European Union. Retrieved from: https://ec.europa.eu/eurostat/documents/3217494/8787947/KS-05-17-100-EN-N.pdf/f6c45af2-6c4f.-4ca0-b547-d25e6ef9c359, 17. 3. 2019.

EC-European Commission, Eurostat online, 2019. Migrant integration statistics. Luxembourg: Publications Office of the European Union. Retrieved from: https://ec.europa.eu/eurostat/statistics-explained/index.php? title=Migrant_integration_statistics_-_at_risk_of_poverty_and_social_exclusion, 25. 7. 2019.

Eisenstadt, S.N., 1975. *The Absorption of Immigrants: A Comparative Study Based Mainly on the Jewish Community in Palestine and the State of Israel*. Westport, CT: Greenwood Press.

Eisenstadt, S.N., 2019. *The Transformation of Israeli Society: An Essay in Interpretation*. London: Routledge.

Elmose-Østerlund, K., Ibsen B., 2016. Introduction to the project 'Social Inclusion and Volunteering in Sports Clubs in Europe', Sivsce report n. 1. Odense: Sdu-University of Southern Denmark.

Elmose-Østerlund, K., Ibsen B., Nagel S., Scheerder J., eds. 2017. Explaining similarities and differences between European sports clubs. An overview of the main similarities and differences between sports clubs in ten European countries and the potential explanations, Sivsce report n. 4. Odense: Sdu-University of Southern Denmark.

Entzinger, H., Biezeveld, R., 2003. *Benchmarking in Immigrant Integration*. Rotterdam: Erasmus University.

ESPIN-European Sport Inclusion Network, 2017. *Promoting Equal Opportunities of Migrants and Minorities through Volunteering in Sport*. Vienna: VDC.

Eurostat, 2017. Migrant integration. Vienna: Eurostat. Retrieved from: https://ec.europa.eu/eurostat/ documents/3217494/8787947/KS-05-17-100-EN-N.pdf/f6c45af2-6c4f.-4ca0-b547-d25e6ef9c359, 15. 1. 2019.

Eurostat, 2019. Migrant integration statistics. Eurostat dataware. Retrieved from: https://ec.europa.eu/eurostat/statistics-explained/index.php/Migrant_integration_statistics, last change seen on 25 February 2019.

Fleischmann, F., Phalet, K., 2012. Integration and religiosity among the Turkish second generation in Europe: A comparative analysis across four capital cities. *Ethnic and Racial Studies*, 35 (2), 320–341.

FRA-European Union Agency for Fundamental Rights, 2017. *Together in the EU: Promoting the Participation of Migrants and Their Descendants*. Luxembourg: Publications Office of the European Union.

Fukuyama, F., 1992. *The End of History and the Last Man*. New York: The Free Press.

Gordon, M., 1964. *Assimilation in American Life: The Role of Race, Religion and National Origins*. New York: Oxford University Press.

Haudenhuyse, R., ed., 2017. Sport for social inclusion: Questioning policy, practice and research. Special issue of *Social Inclusion*, 5 (2).

Haudenhuyse, R.P., Theeboom, M., eds., 2015. Sport for Social inclusion: Critical analyses and future challenges. Special issue of *Social Inclusion*, 3 (3).

Heath, A., Cheung, S., 2007. *Unequal Chances: Ethnic Minorities in Western Labour Markets*. Oxford: Oxford University Press.

Huddleston, T., Bilgili, Ö., Joki, A.-L., Vankova, Z., 2015. Migrant integration policy index (MIPEX) 2015. Barcelona – Brussels: Cidob and Mpg. Retrieved from: https://ec.europa.eu/migrant-integration/index.cfm?action= media.download, 18. 3. 2019.

Jain, A., Sabirianova Peter, K., 2017. Limits to wage growth: Understanding the wage divergence between immigrants and natives. IZA DP No. 10891. Bonn: Institut of Labor Economics. Retrieved from: http://ftp.iza.org/dp10891.pdf, 23. 3. 2019.

Kasinitz, P., Mollenkopf, J.H., Waters, M.C., Holdaway, J., 2008, *Inheriting the City: The Children of Immigrants Come of Age*. New York: Russell Sage Foundation.

Kivisto, P., 2005. *Incorporating Diversity: Rethinking Assimilation in a Multicultural Age*. Boulder, CO: Paradigm.

Kymlicka, W., 1995. *Multicultural Citizenship*. Oxford: Oxford University Press.

Kymlicka, W., 2015. Solidarity in diverse societies: Beyond neoliberal multiculturalism and welfare chauvinism. *Comparative Migration Studies*, 3 (1) (https://doi.org/10.1186/s40878-015-0017-4).

Lee, S.M., Boyd, M., 2008. Marrying out: Comparing the marital and social integration of Asians in the US and Canada. *Social Science Research*, 37(1), 311–329.

Levermore, R., 2013. Sport in International Development: Facilitating Improved Standards of Living? In B. Houlihan and M. Green (eds), *Routledge Handbook of Sports Development*. London –New York: Routledge, pp. 285–307.

Lewitt, P., Jaworsky, B.N., 2007. Transnational migration studies: Past developments and future trends. *Annual Review of Sociology*, 33, 129–156.

Li, M., 2018. Integration of migrant women: A key challenge with limited policy resources, EWSI-European web site on integration. Retrieved from: https://ec.europa.eu/migrant-integration/feature/integration-of-migrant-women, 17. 3. 2019.

MacDonald, R., Marsh, J., 2005. *Disconnected Youth?: Growing up in Britain's Poor Neighbourhoods*. Basingstoke – New York: Palgrave Macmillan.

Marivoet, S., 2017. Final evaluation report for the European Sport Inclusion Network (ESPIN). Vienna: VIDC-Vienna Institute for International Dialogue and Cooperation.

Müller, F., van Zoonen, L., de Roode, L., 2008. The integrative power of sport: Imagined and real effects of sport events on multicultural integration. *Sociology of Sport Journal*, 25 (3), 387–401.

Münch, R., 1987. *Theory of Action: Towards a New Synthesis Going beyond Parsons*. London: Routledge & Kegan Paul.

Organisation for Economic Co-operation and Development, 2012. Settling in: OECD indicators of immigrant integration 2012. Directorate for Employment, Labour and Social Affairs, Paris. Retrieved from: https://www.oecd-ilibrary.org/social-issues-migration-health/settling-in-oecd-indicators-of-immigrant-integration-2012_9789264171534-en, 18. 3. 2019.

Parsons, T., 1970. *The Social System*. London: Routledge & Kegan Paul.

Piątkowska, M., Perényi, S., Elmose-Østerlund, K., eds., 2017. Promoting social integration and volunteering in sports clubs. Lessons from practice. Sivsce report no. 3. Odense: Sdu-University of Southern Denmark.

Portes, A., ed., 1995. *The Economic Sociology of Immigration: Essays on Networks, Ethnicity, and Entrepreneurship*. New York: Russell Sage Foundation.

Portes, A., Rumbaut, G.R., 2001. *Legacies: The Story of the Immigrant Second Generation*. Berkeley: University of California Press.

Portes, A., deWind, J., eds., 2007. *Rethinking Migration: New Theoretical and Empirical Perspectives*. New York – Oxford: Berghahn Books.

Redfield, R., Linton, R., Herskovits, M.J., 1936. A memorandum for the study of acculturation. *American Anthropologist*, 38, 149–152.

Rinne, U., 2012. The evaluation of immigration policies. IZA DP No. 6369. Bonn: Institute of Labor Economics.

Schwenzer, V., 2016. Equal access for migrant volunteers to sports clubs in Europe: A baseline study. Berlin: Camino ESPIN partner. Retrieved from: www.footballforequality.org/fileadmin/mediapool/pdf/spin/ ESPIN_Baseline_Study_Equal_access_for_migrant_volunteers_to_sports.pdf, 26. 10. 2018.

Sciortino, G., 2012. Ethnicity, Race, Nationhood, Foreignness and Many Other Things: Prolegomena to a Cultural Sociology of Difference-Based Interactions. In J. C. Alexander, R.N. Jacobs, P. Smith (eds), *The Oxford Handbook of Cultural Sociology*. Oxford: Oxford University Press, pp. 365–389.

Smelser, N.J., 2013. *Comparative Methods in the Social Sciences*. Upper Saddle River, NJ: Prentice Hall.

Sniderman, P.M., Peri, P., de Figueiredo, R.J.P.Jr., Piazza, T.L., 2000. *The Outsider: Prejudice and Politics in Italy*. Princeton, NJ: Princeton University Press.

Spaaij, R., Magee, J., Jeanes, R., 2014. *Sport and Social Exclusion in Global Society.* London – New York: Routledge.

SPIN-Sport Inclusion Network, 2012. Inclusion of migrants in and through sport: A guide to good practice. Vienna: VIDC-Vienna Institute for International Dialogue and Cooperation. Retrieved from: www.sportinclusion.net, 23. 3. 2013.

Steinbach, D., Elmose-Østerlund, K., 2017. European cooperation in sports club research: The SIVSCE-project in a nutshell. Odense: SDU-University of Southern Denmark.

Taylor, C., 2007. *The Secular Age.* Cambridge, MA: Harvard University Press.

Taylor, C.*et al.*, 1994. *Multiculturalism: Examining the Politics of Recognition.* Princeton, NJ: Princeton University Press.

Thomas, W.I., Znaniecki, F., 1918. *The Polish Peasant in Europe and America.* Chicago: The University of Chicago Press.

Tomlinson, D., ed., 2016. Handbook on volunteering of migrants in sport clubs and organisations. Vienna: VIDC & FAI ESPIN partners. Retrieved from: www.footballforequality.org/fileadmin/ediapool/pdf/spin/2016_Migrants_Booklet__3_.pdf, 20. 11. 2018.

Touraine, A., 2015. *Nous, Sujets Humains.* Paris: Seuil.

Touraine, A., 2018. *Défense de la modernité.* Paris: Seuil.

UN-United Nations General Assembly, 2003. Resolution 58/5: Sport as a means to promote education, health, development and peace. New York: United Nations Office. Retrieved from: https://www.un.org/sport2005/resources/un_resolutions/engl_58_5.pdf, 23. 3. 2019.

Weinar, A., Unterreiner, A., Fargues, P., eds., 2017. *Migrant Integration between Homeland and Host Society, Vol. 1: Where Does the Country of Origin Fit?*Cham: Springer.

3 Sport and the 'question' of Islam in Europe

Mahfoud Amara

Introduction

The question of religion in Europe, particularly Islam, has been defined to a certain extent around the following dichotomies: homogeneity *versus* cultural diversity, private *versus* public spheres, and belief *versus* disbelief. The question of sport and religion (including Islam) is also shaped by these discourses such as accommodating sport to religious needs (or *vice versa*), and access to public funding and sport facilities by Muslim communities. There have been a number of questions raised in Europe around the use of tax revenue to fund sports projects targeting Muslim communities only, especially over the expression of religiosity, for instance wearing the veil (and burqa) in leisure centres, and the issue of sport and PE in schools in a mixed gender environment. With the phenomenon of so-called radicalisation of Muslim youth, the visibility of Muslims and the expression of Islamic faith are being put under more scrutiny by states' security apparatus and the media.

Muslims in the West are facing multiple dilemmas concerning the complexity of combining multiple identities: a sense of belonging to Islamic Ummah (community of Muslim believers) and a sense of belonging to host societies or countries of birth. They are under pressure more than ever before to demonstrate their loyalty to their European nationality/citizenship. The complex, and for some contradictory, layers of identity are being felt in the domain of sport. Demands are being made by Muslim communities – in the name of democracy, citizenship and rights to cultural and religious differences – to accommodate specific times for Muslim women and young girls at local leisure centres, to allow men to wear long swimming trunks in public swimming pools, and to allocate specific training/nutrition programmes for professional athletes to meet their religious duty of, for instance, fasting during the month of Ramadan (Silverstein, 2002; Walseth, 2006). For the majority of Muslim Europeans (or European Muslims) not necessarily holding any political agenda, sport is another field to reconcile their multiple identities, including that of being Muslim in a dominantly secular environment. For conservative-nationalist movements and some states' authorities in Europe, sport is another public (secular) space to safeguard from the over-expression and/ or over-visibility (to different degrees), of religion and particularly, more recently at least, Islamic faith, which for some is equated with 'political Islam' or 'Islamist ideology'.

In terms of structure, the chapter first discusses the question of religious phenomenon in Europe in relation to the debate of cultural diversity, ethnicity and citizenship rights. The second part examines the question of Islam and Muslims in the West. The last part of the chapter provides examples of tensions around Islam and Muslim communities in the domain of sport.

Religious phenomenon in Europe

According to Pew Research data on religion in Europe, the number of Muslims in Europe (the 28 countries presently in the European Union, plus Norway and Switzerland) as of mid-2016, was estimated at 25.8 million (4.9% of the overall population) – up from 19.5 million (3.8%) in 2010. The Muslim population of Europe would be further expected to rise from the current level of 4.9% to 7.4% by the year 2050 (Pew Research Centre, 2017).

Notwithstanding the dominance of secular discourse in science, politics and the media, many commentators agree that there is a global resurgence or revitalisation of religious movements, including Islam, which started according to Riesebrodt (2000) in the 1970s. Habermas (2010) recognises that we are in a 'post-secular' epoch. In his article, 'notes on a post-secular society', he asks about the current place of religion in Europe, how we should see ourselves as members of a post-secular society and what we must reciprocally expect from one another in order to ensure that in firmly entrenched nation-states, social relations remain civil despite the growth of a plurality of cultures and religious world views.

One can argue that, despite the apparent triumph of secularism, the division between the transcendent and the temporal is not always explicit. Sometimes the Judeo-Christian tradition of Europe is used as an argument to justify the incompatibility between Islam and European culture, for example, debate around the question of the integration of Turkey into the EU. It is worth noting here that Turkey is accepted as part of the European space in sport but not (yet or fully) in cultural spaces. Secularism means different things in different national contexts. The same is true for the relation between the state and religion (including Islam). Regarding this point, Cesari (1998, 2004) asserts that the relationship of the government to religion in Europe, and thus the institutionalisation of Islam, tends to pattern itself on one of the three principles: co-operation between church and state (e.g. Austria, Belgium, Italy, Spain and Germany); the existence of state-sponsored religion (e.g. Great Britain, Denmark and Greece); or the 'total' separation of religion and politics (the case of France).

The otherness of the 'others' (i.e., Islamic faith and Muslim culture) lies in what Edward Said refers to as Orientalism. The construction of Islam, in the Western/collective imagination, is argued to be a product of opposition between, or in contrast to, the East/Orient/Islam on one side, and the West/ the Occident/Christendom on the other. As a result of this antagonistic differentiation, Islam and the 'Orient' as depicted in the West have been reduced to a set of references and characteristics, linked to 'a collective fiction' which sees the 'Orient', including neighbourhoods in European cities where the majority of Muslim communities live, as places of 'violence', 'superstition' and 'irrationality'. The example of the outskirts cities of France (named in banlieues) (Bronner, 2011) are usually depicted as places outside central state rule and authority, with dominant anti-Semitic sentiments, and a place to recruit jihadists; although in fact, 'the profiles of French jihadists do not track closely with class. Many of them have come from bourgeois families' (Pracker, 2015). As suggested by Cesari (2012: 1), due to securitisation processes in all European countries, laws have expanded the powers of the state to deal more harshly with potential threats associated with Muslim citizens or immigrants. It involves 'constructing Islam as an existential threat that requires extraordinary and emergency procedures outside the bounds of regular political procedure'.

Notwithstanding the European tradition of tolerance and respect, the growing discourse of exclusion, fuelled by fear from increasing immigration, has been used by nationalist parties across Europe to portray the foreign 'others' (ethnic minorities, religious communities, refugees and asylum seekers) not only as guilty by virtue of their 'foreignness' but also by their cultural (Muslim) heritage. As rightly highlighted by Pascoët (2018) for *EUobserver* to explain the raise of Islamophobia sentiments even within mainstream politics and the media, 'Public discourses across Europe hammering that Muslims are a problem are currently justifying the adoption of policies, legislation and practices that are putting our core democratic and fundamental rights principles at risk'.

Sport and Muslims in Europe

In Britain, Amara and Henry (2010, 2012) show that Muslim organisations offering sports activities to their members have become a common phenomenon, particularly in cities with substantial Muslim populations such as London, Leicester and Birmingham. Muslim organisations in these cities offer a range of sports activities from karate and badminton to fitness and swimming as well as recreational activities for the elderly. In Norway, Walseth (2015; 2016) shows that Muslim organisations offer sports as a way of gathering Muslim youth together. Both studies reveal that the selection of sports activities tends to be dictated by the availability of sports facilities and not necessarily by the literal interpretation of the Islamic texts. However, most of the time these activities are organised in non-mixed gender environments. Generally, policymakers in European countries are reluctant to perceive religion or Muslims as a target group, and there are few examples of co-operation between sports policymakers and representatives from Muslim organisations. In Germany, according to Burrmann and Mutz (2015) through sports clubs, immigrants are supposed to have the opportunity to develop social relationships and make friends, acquire linguistic competence and familiarise themselves with the cultural norms within German society; however, the reality is that ethnic minorities, in particular among Muslim communities (dominated by Turkish), are under-represented in German sports clubs. It is estimated that roughly two-thirds of youths without a migration background are involved in a sports club – 67% of boys and 63% of girls. Muslim boys are also frequently involved in sports clubs (69%). It is not the case with Muslim girls, among whom only 16% are members of a sports club. Sports clubs thus reach Muslim boys very well, while girls of the same religious confession are strongly under-represented.

Living in between

> In the eyes of Grindel [German Football Association] and his supporters, I am German when we win, but I am an immigrant when we lose ... I feel unwanted and think that what I have achieved since my international debut in 2009 has been forgotten. Despite paying taxes in Germany, donating facilities to German schools and winning the World Cup with Germany in 2014, I am still not accepted into society. I am treated as being 'different' ... Mesut Özil. (Pearson, 2018)

For some European citizens of immigrant origin, sport (particularly soccer) is an occasion to celebrate their double sense of belonging to a 'hybrid' identity – that is, an amalgam of aspects of migrant culture and citizenship, expressed neither in terms of fully belonging to 'European culture' nor in terms of belonging to 'culture of origin'. However, due to the sentiment of being marginalised in their country of birth or to improve their international career, other athletes from immigrant descent choose to represent their country of origin in the international sporting arena. This is evident in the steady increase in the number of third-generation young players from immigrant communities in North African national teams (Tunisia, Morocco and Algeria). If we take the example of Algeria, the number of players with an immigrant background participating in the Algerian national football team has increased. This increase has been facilitated by the new FIFA rules on nationality and national team eligibility, 'article 6.1, a player must either be born in a country, have biological ties to the country or have lived in the country for a certain period of time'. These players are principally from France, Belgium, Holland and Denmark, which are known for their high concentrations of residents with North African, Sub-Saharan African and Turkish origins. One can argue that, for these athletes, participating with the national team of their country of origin represents a unique opportunity to compete at international level.

Top athletes who choose to compete for their country of birth are still celebrated as 'ambassadors' of their country of origin, and their performance is explained as a direct product of the creativity, courage and intelligence they inherited from their culture. When winning a medal in the Olympics and helping their teams to victory in the UEFA Champions League or in other sports, they are praised usually in the media for their natural 'North African'

'Sub-Saharan' or 'Turkish or Albanian' ability to run or skills and products of (Western) discipline, rational and strategic thinking and socialisation (de-culturation) in schools.

Islamophobia in sport

The question of Islam in sport in Europe and elsewhere has been confronted in a number of ways. The demand by Muslims to accommodate sport to their culture and religious beliefs is perceived as a sign of disintegration or non-assimilation of European values of citizenship and community cohesion, even more, as a defiance to national (secular) values of universalism, social cohesion and national unity.

Muslim communities and athletes have recently been facing a number of Islamophobic incidences in sport. On 25 August 2019, ESPN Major League Baseball (MLB) analyst Curt Schilling, a former player himself, issued a tweet that compared 'Muslim extremists' to 'Nazis'. The tweet inserted the vilification of Muslims into the world of sport (Beydoun, 2015). In an effort to capitalise on the growing market of Muslim consumers globally, Nike, following the trends of big designers brands, started their 'Nike Sport Hijab' products targeting Muslim women athletes and non-athletes who want to be part of the sporting experience while keeping their hijab, as a symbol of their Islamic faith. Their advertisements have been, according to Nuraan Davids, 'welcomed by some – mostly Muslim women. But it's also been criticised harshly for endorsing the oppression of women. Criticism on social media has promoted tweets of dissent with the hashtag #BoycottNike' (*The Conversation*, 2017). The French sport retailer Decathlon had to simply cancel its plan to launch sports hijab products in France, with the motto, 'make sport accessible to all women in the world'. On the day of the announcement it was reported that the company received more than 500 calls and emails and that staff in its stores had 'been insulted and threatened, sometimes physically' (Dixon, 2019). The company was criticised for promoting 'sexual apartheid'. Even the government represented by Minister of Health Agnès Buzyn had to intervene in the debate stating that such a product is 'not forbidden by law', but 'it is a vision of women that I do not share. I would have preferred that a French brand not promote the veil'.

More recently the star of Liverpool, Mohamed Salah, has had to face Islamophobic chanting because of his religion by Chelsea FC and West Ham fans, singing 'Salah is a bomber'. A number of players of Muslim faith and culture received similar abuses in European stadia, following a general trend of racism and xenophobia in European football, as revealed by Kick It Out. A total of 111 incidents from England's top four leagues had been reported to the anti-racism body by the midway stage of the 2018 season, with 64 coming from the Premier League (Lovett, 2018).

Arab-Muslim investments in the global sports arena, represented by bidding for/and staging of major football tournaments, sponsorship and even direct ownership of European football clubs (e.g. Manchester City; Paris Saint-

Germain, aka PSG; FC Barcelona), are welcomed as they boost the global economy of sport. For others it is also perceived as a threat to the identity (and hegemony) of European football clubs. Identity would also include 'Christian' values of European football clubs. As with the case of Real Madrid which made a decision to remove the traditional Christian cross from its logo, after signing a three-year contract with the National Bank of Abu Dhabi.

Conclusion

Sport is at the centre of the debate on integration and national identity of immigrant communities in Europe, centred today around Muslim faith or culture. Sport is becoming a contested terrain to defend the expression of diversity and pluralism, for some, and for the protection of Western European secular values from 'Islamism'.

Adapting sports brands and logos to meet Islamic cultural and religious requirements is perceived as a way to surrender to 'Islamist ideology'. Accepting investment from Middle Eastern wealthy funds (including in sport) is being put under severe scrutiny due to security and sovereignty concerns, and can even be subject to parliamentary debate, as with the case of Qatar's investment in sport in France.

For Muslim athletes, sport, and particularly football, is a terrain for identity-making and resistance against stigma. The incidents in sport involving Muslim athletes are an occasion for the supporters of 'clash of cultures' and 'final solution' to exacerbate existing ethnic tensions, thus mixing in their interpretation aspects of 'violence, Islam, and masculinity'.

Sport is becoming the space to test the success of 'integration' policies of minorities into the host society and to question the loyalty of Muslim minorities to the 'host' nation. Muslims of immigrant origin are caught between affirming their (multiple) identities while avoiding and combating stigmatisation both in their country of birth and country of origin.

Bibliography

Amara, M. and Henry, I. P., (2010) Sport, Muslim identities and cultures in the UK, an emerging policy issue: Case studies of Leicester and Birmingham. *European Sport Management Quarterly* 10, 419–443. doi:10.1080/16184742.2010.502743.

Amara, M. and Henry, I. P., (2012) Deconstructing the Debate around Sport and the 'Question' of 'Muslim Minorities' in the West'. In Farrar, M., Robinson, S., Vallic, Y. and Wetherly, P. (eds.), *Islam in the West: Key Issues in Multiculturalism*. London: Palgrave, pp. 138–153.

Beydoun, K., (*Aljazeera*, 2 September 2015) The vilification of Muslims in world sport. Retrieved from www.aljazeera.com/indepth/opinion/2015/08/vilification-muslims-world-sport-150830110323002.html (accessed 30 September 2015).

Bronner, L., (*Le Monde*, 4 October 2011) La place croissante de l'islam en banlieue. Retrieved from www.lemonde.fr/societe/article/2011/10/04/banlieues-de-la-republique_1581976_3224.html (accessed 10 September 2012).

Burman, U. and Mutz, M., (2015) Sport Participation of Muslim Youths in Germany. In Testa, A. and Amara, M. (eds), *Sport in Islam and in Muslim Communities*. Routledge: London (33–49).

Burrmann, U., Brandmann, K., Mutz, M. and Zender, U. (2017) Ethnic identities, sense of belonging and the significance of sport: stories from immigrant youths in Germany. *European Journal for Sport and Society* 14 (3), 186–204.

Cesari, J., (2004) *When Islam and Democracy Meet: Muslims in Europe and in the United States*. New York: Palgrave.

Cesari, J., (1998) *Musulmans et Républicain: Les Jeunes, l'Islam et la France*. Paris: Editions Complexe.

Cesari, J., (2012) Securitization of Islam in Europe, *Die Welt des Islams* 52, 430–449.

Dixon, F., (27 February 2019) 'Gendered Islamophobia': Muslim women slam Decathlon's backtrack over sports hijab. Retrieved from www.alaraby.co.uk/english/news/2019/2/27/women-slam-decathlons-backtrack-over-sports-hijab (accessed 30 November 2019).

Habermas, J., (18 June 2008) Notes on a post-secular society. Signandsight.com. Retrieved from www.signandsight.com/features/1714.html (accessed 1 September 2010).

Lovett, S., (*The Independent*, 7 February 2018) Kick it out reports 38% increase in discrimination across Premier League and EFL. Retrieved from www.independent.co.uk/sport/football/news-and-comment/kick-it-out-38-increase-in-discrimination-racism-homophobia-premier-league-efl-a8198966.html (accessed 17 January 2019).

Pascoët, J., (*EUobserver*, 21 September 2018) Wake-up call on European Day against Islamophobia. Retrieved from https://euobserver.com/opinion/142921 (20 March 2019).

Pearson, M., (*DW*, 22 July 2018) Mesut Özil quits Germany over Erdogan controversy. Retrieved from www.dw.com/en/mesut-%C3%B6zil-quits-germany-over-erdogan-controversy/a-44777380 (accessed 23 July 2018).

Pew Research Centre, (29 November 2017) Europe's growing Muslim population. Retrieved from www.pewforum.org/2017/11/29/europes-growing-muslim-population/ (accessed 25 March 2018).

Pracker, G., (*The New Yorker*, 24 August 2015) The other France: Are the suburbs of Paris incubators of terrorism? Retrieved from www.newyorker.com/magazine/2015/08/31/the-other-france (1 May 2019).

Riesebrodt, M., (2000) Religions in the disenchanted world. *Numen* 47 (3), 266–287.

Silverstein, P.A., (2002) Stadium Politics: Sport, Islam and Amazigh Consciousness in France and North Africa. In Magdalinski, T. (ed.) *With God on their Side: Sport in the Service of Religion*. London: Routledge, pp. 37–54.

The Conversation, (3 November 2017) How Nike's hijab sports gear is taking on Islamophobia and patriarchy. Retrieved from http://theconversation.com/how-nikes-hijab-sports-gear-is-taking-on-islamophobia-and-patriarchy-86700 (accessed 4 November 2017).

Walseth, K., (2006) Young Muslim women and sport: The impact of identity work. *Leisure Studies* 25, 74–94.

Walseth, K., (2015) Muslim girls' experiences in physical education in Norway: What role does religiosity play?. *Sport, Education and Society* 20, 3, 304–322.

Walseth, K., (2016) Sport within Muslim organizations in Norway: ethnic segregated activities as arena for integration. *Leisure Studies* 35, 1, 78–99.

4 European sport systems and the voluntary sector

Non-profit organisations' race for sport development

Nico Bortoletto and Alessandro Porrovecchio

Introduction

Sport is the largest social and voluntary activity in Europe. Sport and recreation volunteerism are among the largest simple categories of benevolent work: any other form of volunteerism involves fewer volunteers than sport and recreation.

Sport plays an important role in bringing together people from different backgrounds, helping to develop a sense of belonging hard to reach elsewhere. In the 21st century, European societies are permanently facing challenges to remain inclusive and to renew their welfare model. Volunteering in sport, as an engagement in society, may support social integration, it can contribute to active citizenship and can be used to tackle social exclusion.

Volunteering in sport contributes to the production of a stronger sense of belonging to society for its more vulnerable members. This can help to promote a real active citizenship. It can reach people at international, national, regional and local levels. It can also be a powerful social tool in many areas of public and social policies, being used to help the increasing migrant population to integrate, to fight against social exclusion as well as to contribute to gender equality (Bortoletto, Porrovecchio, 2018). It plays an important role in creating social cohesion and inclusive communities. Local authorities, in co-operation with sport clubs, associations and other entities play a crucial role in the creation of such forms of social integration.

For seniors, for instance, volunteering in sport represents an important and growing part of European society's economy, culture and lives. This social group could be affected by loneliness, and sport involvement could push them to share their experience, creating benefits for an inter-generational dialogue too (Gard, Dionigi, 2016).

Volunteering in sport allows young people to develop a variety of skills and competences; it contributes, moreover, to a positive social attitude based on values developed through sport. It could act as a safety net for young people who are out of education or employment and on the margins of society.

It plays a relevant role in including people within a community by increasing employability, promoting values and – eventually – inter-cultural dialogue. Voluntary activities in sport can take different forms and can be performed in many ways (for example, the preparation and organisation of local, regional, national and international sporting events) or on a more regular day-to-day basis (for example, activities carried out in running various sports bodies or associations active in the field of sport). Organised sport is the actual base of volunteer work and in many countries sport volunteers represent the largest category of volunteers who offer their free time in formal organisational settings.

Section 1: Defining the field

Defining volunteering seems to be relatively simple but, in the field of sport, it's quite complex. Although the word 'volunteer' may seem to have a commonly shared meaning, there is no universal consensus about the meaning of the term. In any case we are speaking about 'unpaid work' (Donnelly, Harvey, 2011), about time, skills, social abilities given freely by individuals. olunteerism is – especially in the case of sport – embedded in the values of amateurism, related especially to a previous sporting activity. The dual origin of the current spread of volunteering (reduction of state welfare and search for new forms of social cohesion) seems to lead directly towards a form of social interaction, which is able to fill the lack of social cohesion and reciprocal confidence that seems to affect the majority of Western societies.

Sport England, a British organisation that performed a national survey on sport volunteering, defines sports volunteers as people who give up 'their time for the benefit of the environment, individuals or groups other than, or in addition to, close relatives without being paid for it' (Sport England, 2018).

Moreover, the Eurostat, our main reference for the data in this chapter, provides this definition that, especially for sport volunteerism, stresses the organisational dimension of the phenomenon: 'Formal volunteering is defined [here] as activities that are structured through an organisation, a formal group or a club, including unpaid work for charitable or religious organisations ...'

These definitions show that the key element of volunteering is the unpaid 'work'. And, at the end, this work – especially in sport volunteerism – must be performed in an organisational framework. Very little is known about informal volunteerism in sport, despite the relatively huge number of people that, in the national and European surveys, declare to be a volunteer outside of an organisational framework.

Cnaan, Handy and Wadsworth (1996: 371) interestingly identified four key dimensions of volunteerism based on:

- free choice;
- remuneration;
- structure (the context within which the volunteer activity is performed);
- the beneficiaries.

Given these dimensions and combining previous existing definitions, widely considered in their seminal work, the authors performed a content analysis where they stressed the continuity of the 'volunteerism' definition from a status of 'pure' volunteering to a broader status of volunteering. The authors stress that being a member of this community relies on the one hand on the absence of retribution and, on the other hand, looks at an activity which by its very definition is uncoerced. Volunteering, therefore, can take place within or outside an organisation but is carried out for no monetary gain by an individual who is not coercively engaged.

Mike Collins (2008), by looking at the English history of sport policies, shows us that the present situation began a long time ago, with modern sport games, requiring places, structures, organisations, norms and many other elements that push the whole movement to modernise. In the final part of his work he focused on the pillars of every policy approach in sport policies (2008, 80):

- wise use of symbols to improve sport practice among people;
- re-thinking the social division of time (gender gap);
- investment in sport facilities and in their maintenance;
- sport for health promotion;
- lack of personal time devoted to sport.

The ultimate sense of all these elements is based on the drive towards the involvement of civil society in the frame of active citizenship. The ability of a public authority to form a path in this framework could contribute to re-define, with a bottom-up approach, the whole agenda of the 21st century's sport policies. At the end, the aim of the whole process will be the construction of an agenda which is able to recover the lack of personal involvement in the broader society (Big society, suggests Morgan using a well-known Giddensian concept). This – after all – should be the ultimate end of sporting public policies. The elements that identify the basics of a voluntary action (non-coercion, availability of leisure time, non-remuneration) could be boosted by an adequate political approach.

Section 2: EU governance

The general action

Only since the Lisbon Treaty came into force in December 2009 has sport become a new area of expertise for the European Union. Although there is no specific legal jurisdiction over sport in the former Treaties, since the 1970s the EU has always been active in promoting participation in sport and its educational and social values. The European Sport for All Charter, ratified in 1975, was the first sports policy initiative of the EU, and the European Year of Education through Sport in 2004 was a significant action which also involved the volunteer sector. After this, the Commission outlined a European sport policy through the 2007 White Paper on Sport (WPS) and the 2008 'Pierre de Coubertin' Action Plan, which exemplifies the strong link with the world of the Olympics.

At the present time, the EU is responsible for defining a policy based on evidence, to encourage co-operation and to manage initiatives that promote physical activity and sport in Europe. For the 2014–2020 period, for the first time, a specific budget has been created under the *Erasmus+* programme[1] to support projects and networks in the field of sport, that affects the volunteer sector too.

With the Lisbon Treaty, the Union has acquired a specific competence in the field of sport, integrating it within a pyramidal model of governance. Article 6 (e) of the Treaty on the Functioning of the European Union (TFEU) empowers the Union to take measures to support or supplement the action of the member states in the field of justice, while Article 165, paragraph 1, of the TFEU details the elements of sport policies, stating that the Union contributes to the promotion of the European world of sport, taking into account its specificities, its volunteering and its social and educational functions. The second paragraph states that the Union aims to develop the European dimension of sport by promoting fairness and transparency in sporting competitions and co-operation between the bodies which are responsible for sport, as well as by protecting the physical and moral integrity of the athletes, especially the younger ones.

The Union now has a legal basis to support sport in a structural way through the *Erasmus+* programme and it tries to speak with one voice in international bodies and non-EU countries. EU sports ministers also meet at the Education, Youth, Culture and Sport (EYCS) council meetings. In addition, the Union's competences, with regard to the single market, have already had a considerable impact on sport. For instance, the Court of Justice of the European Union (CJEU) has developed considerable case laws which have had important consequences for the world of sport (e.g. the Bosman ruling).[2] Many of the appeals were based on the principle of free movement of trade, as advocated by the European Union. In each case, the CJEU confirmed that sport is governed by Community law, provided that it constitutes an economic activity. The decisions of the CJEU in sport led the sports authorities to review their rules, but also confirmed the legitimacy of sports rules and the specificity of sport. These disputes led to a European awareness of the need for European sports legislation, recognising the specificity of sport and the organisations and associations that govern it. In the meantime, the Union exercised its non-binding legislative powers in related areas such as education, health and social inclusion through its respective funding programmes. In these areas, the importance of voluntary action is fundamental.

As for sport financing, in a statement on EU funding for sport, the European Non-Governmental Sports Organisation (ENGSO, www.engso.eu/) – the main sports governance institution in the EU – emphasised the need for adequate pre-financing. That is a form of European funding which is not modelled on private resources, and operating grants for grass-roots sport promotion organisations active at European level, whose programme is in line with the priorities of the EU's sport chapter.

The ENGSO also recommends the inclusion of small-scale projects and the recognition of volunteer activity as a contribution in kind. Having consulted with many stakeholders concerning local sporting opportunities, and given the limited number of local clubs involved in the projects selected in the first year of the *Erasmus+* Sports programme, the Representative Office of the European Olympic Committees in the EU proposed some amendments to the implementation of the sports chapter to increase the presence of mass sport. In particular, it recommended supporting projects with fewer partners and/or smaller budgets, allowing volunteering as a contribution to the project budget, and reducing the administrative and financial burden, for example by simplifying procedures, candidacy and allocation, given the limited financial and human resources available to local sports.

On volunteering

As anticipated, an awareness of the importance of sports and of the voluntary action appears to be meaningfully present in the European White Paper on Sport; this in turn opened the debate on three main dimensional levels: the social role of sport, its economic dimension and its organisation. The first part deals with issues that directly affect citizens. Its priorities are related to the regular practice of physical activities, social inclusion, the promotion of equality between men and women through sport, the promotion of a wider level of practice of physical activity through the educational system, the fight against doping, racism and xenophobia, and the support for the dual careers of athletes (i.e. access to university and professional education during their sports career). The second deals with the economic aspects of sport, its objectives of monitoring and forecasting sports data, the economic potential of sport, the support of anti-trust policies, and the granting of state aid in accordance with European competition laws. The third component focuses on the political and legislative framework of sport. The toughening of governance requirements in the sports sector, the fight against match-fixing, the promotion of a fair regulation at all levels, the guarantee of the free movement of amateur and professional sportsmen and women and – to conclude – the development of rules to preserve the integrity of, and to prevent the exploitation of, the players during their transfer.

Focusing on the WPS, which represents the main core of the EU's sports philosophy, we can find, among many others, some items related to the social policies:

> The Commission believes that better use can be made of the potential of sport as an instrument for social inclusion in the policies, actions and programmes of the European Union and of Member States. This includes the contribution of sport to job creation and to economic growth and revitalisation, particularly in disadvantaged areas. Non-profit sports activities contributing to social cohesion and social inclusion of vulnerable groups can be considered as social services of general interest. (European White Paper on Sport: 7).

Moreover, in the WPS we can find elements related to the support of sustainable development policies and the economic growth related to the sports sector: all elements that the European Union take into consideration for promoting its own values using its own policies.

The quote below is in relation to the WPS advocate:

> 2.4.1. The EU is putting increasing emphasis on objectives and policies which create solidarity within the EU and secure opportunities for all citizens. The Commission has defined its overall strategic objectives accordingly. Voluntary activities in the sport sector strengthen social cohesion and inclusion and promote local democracy and active citizenship. Voluntary activities in sport also have a socio-economic value in terms of GDP and if converted in e.g. full-time employment. There is also an implicit economic value: without volunteers sport activities would come at a much higher cost and many of the social activities related to sport would disappear.

And, again:

> 2.5.1. [At the same time] there is a need to better use the potential of sport as an instrument for social inclusion in the policies, actions and programmes of the European Union and Member States. This includes the potential of sport as an employment creation factor, particularly in disadvantaged areas. Also in this light, sport activities contributing to social cohesion and to social inclusion of vulnerable groups can be considered as social services of general interest.

National and European policies unavoidably encompass different dimensional levels. Within these levels there are transversal concepts like social capital, strictly related both to the level of social regulation in a given society and on the normative side. In this framework, the massification of sport has gradually justified the creation of macro-structures for its management. The modern sports movement happened as a consequence of the need to regulate sport for the organisation of sports competitions, first at a national level, and then at an international one (Gasparini 1999).

Sports governance in the EU: a short overview

The sports movement has given rise to the birth of a large number of international non-governmental organisations which are strongly interconnected and involved with the world of volunteering. International sports competitions and the creation of universal sporting rules resulted in a need for harmonisation between countries, which has resulted in supranational sports associations/institutions such as the International Olympic Committee (IOC) and international sports federations (Zintz, Winand, 2013, p. 7). At the same time, continental institutions that interface with public or private structures developed. According to Zintz and Winand, the IOC, responsible for the organisation of the Olympic Games, as we know them today, is the emblematic representative of the world sports movement. This global sports system implements a general network of sports activities around the world and exerts a relatively strong supervision over them. Moreover, the world sports institutions want to guarantee the retention of sports' values, sports' rules and sportsmanship in general. The national proliferation of these rules and values is achieved by the associations established in the countries: the National Sports federations and the National Olympic Committees.

Table 4.1, elaborated from Zintz and Winand's model (2013, 8), helps us to frame, resume and complete what we just described. It represents the five levels of the organisation of international sport, from the international to the local one. This model distinguishes three elements. First of all, the Olympic and Sports Movement, made up of sports organisations/associations such as the International Sports Federations and the IOC. Secondly, the public authorities. Lastly, the regulatory bodies, including the Court of Arbitration for Sport (CAS) and the World Anti-Doping Agency (WADA). All of these organisations/associations are related to the worlds of athletes and volunteers.

Zintz and Winand (2013, p. 8) explain that some other organisations, which are indirectly related to sport, have a large influence on the activities of athletes, volunteers and their representative bodies. These are, for one, associations that include commercial enterprises producing goods and sports equipment (for example, the World Federation of the Sporting Goods Industry, WFSGI, and the Federation of the European Sporting Goods Industry, FESI), sponsors (European Sponsorship Association, ESA) or advertising agencies (World Federation of Advertisers, WFA) and, also, the International Chamber of Commerce (ICC) and its European, national and regional counterparts, which regulate and inform on commercial transactions.

As we have seen, the activities of the European Union in sporting matters aim at promoting fairness and equal opportunities in sports competitions, supporting co-operation between bodies responsible for sport and protecting the physical and moral integrity of athletes, in particular among younger demographics. For example, doping and related problems are condemned by the European Union, and managed by the European Anti-Doping Regional Office.

Even if it generally supports the regulatory bodies, the wording of Article 165 of the Treaty remains vague and leaves much room for interpretation. It's important to know that the European Union does not intend to harmonise sports legislation and regulations in member countries: Article 165 of the Lisbon Treaty explicitly excludes such a scenario. As a result, although the EU developed a position related to sport, the responsibility for sport remains in the hands of the member states and national sports organisations, according to the subsidiarity principle: each country has its own culture and peculiarities related to sport, including the influence of the national stakeholders and the national sports system of regulation put in place, which contribute to the concept of national sports systems.

Table 4.1 The five levels of the organisation of international sport according to Zintz and Winand (2013, 8)

Level	Olympic movement		Public authorities	Regulatory authorities
International	Sport Accord (GAISF) International Sport Federations	International Olympic Committee International Paralympic Committee Association of National Olympic Committees	United Nations Office on Sport for Development and Peace, UNOSDP UNESCO-MINEPS	CAS
	ASOIF – AIOWF – ARISF			
European	ENGSO European Sport Federations	EOC – EPC	Council of Europe – Sport Unit Commission Directorate General – Internal Market and Services Directorate General for Competition	
National	National sport federations professional leagues	National Olympic committees national paralympic committees	Sport ministries Sport directorates/ offices	
Regional	Regional leagues	Regional Olympic committees	Regional sport services	
Local	Sports clubs		Local sport services	
		Athletes		

Source: T. Zintz and M. Winand, 2013, Les fédérations sportives. *Courrier hebdomadaire du CRISP*, 2179 (14), 5–52.

Section 3: Sports associations in the EU: some elements from a blurred reality

The pyramidal structure of European sports relies considerably on voluntary work. According to Andreff, Dutoya and Montel (2009), in Europe volunteering is strongly linked to the effectiveness of sport development in general and 'sport for all' in particular.

Donnelly and Harvey (2011) stressed the difficulty of quantifying the monetary value of volunteers' work, highlighting the strain to identify the so-called 'replacement costs' and eventually suggesting that the value of the contribution of sport volunteerism is invariably greater than the total of dedicated public funding. For instance, Orlowski and Wicker (2015), among others, propose a couple of economic approaches for estimating the monetary value of voluntary work based in the subjective perception of the value of the work performed, and in an alternative-employment wage approach. The results, even in the work of different authors (Davies, 2004; Vos et al., 2012), show that volunteers replace workers in many cases (10%, following the latter study), with a really different perception (self and measured) of the equivalent value of volunteer workload.

According to the last European Special Barometer Survey (472/2018) within the EU's 28 countries, 6% of respondents (1480; n=26693) claim to perform some sport-related voluntary activity. Among this percentage we find 8% of men and 4% of women from the entire sample, performing these types of activities. When analysing briefly some other socio-demographic aspects, we can stress that this type of volunteering is preferred among young people (14% of the whole sample was born after 1980), and those who have a higher educational level (14% of the whole sample).

Among those that declare that they volunteer, the main activities are related to coaching or training tasks (27%), administrative tasks (19%), board membership (21%), day-to-day club activities (21%), refereeing (12%), helping to run sports events (34%): very often people are carrying out several activities within the same involvement.

These percentages are slightly decreased if compared with the previous survey (EBS 412/2013), where 7% of respondents (2033; n=27919) were involved in sport volunteering. In 2013 the percentages in the different domains of volunteer involvement were similar: coaching or training tasks (29%), administrative tasks (16%), board membership (22%), day- to-day club activities (20%), refereeing (9%), helping to run sports events (35%). The time that volunteers spend undertaking these activities is relevant: 31% spent between one and five hours/month and another 30% spent between six and 20 hours/month; 9% spent more than 21 hours/month. Respondents in the Netherlands, Sweden (both 19%) and Denmark (18%) are the most likely to engage in voluntary work.

There have been numerous attempts to quantify the work of volunteers (Taylor et al. 2003; Andreff, 2009; Le Roux et al. 2010) in terms of full-time equivalent employees. Andreff's study, for instance, reported some data for Western European countries: Germany 210,000; Italy 125,000; France 271,000; Denmark 42,000).[3] The problem is the lack of a real standardisation and the difficulty in the field of definition of what sports volunteering is. Generally speaking, the EBS adopts this definition '... any voluntary work or activity for which you do not receive any payment except to cover expenses, for example organising or helping to run events, campaigning or raising money, providing transport or driving, taking part in a sponsored event, coaching, tuition, mentoring, etc.' (EBS, 2017). The definition is really clear from the financial point of view (only the expenses are covered), but rather indefinite in an attempt to qualify the voluntary activity that encompasses, in that way, different personal perceptions of volunteer work that is possible.

In any case, exactly in the same way that happens for other voluntary activities, the status of volunteering is more appreciated among people who are involved in the same activity (most sports volunteers practise a few times a week) and feel as though they belong to the upper middle class (12%) or even to the upper class (7%).

What we can draw from this data are different types of motivation and different forms of sport volunteering. According to the existing literature, we can identify three main types: volunteering for grass-roots (community sports); volunteering for high-level sport and volunteering for major (or mega) sport events. This last type of volunteering is frequently analysed (Solberg, 2003; Guala et al., 2006; Baum, Lockstone, 2007; Doherty, 2009; Dansero, Putilli, 2010; among others). It's usually recognised as relevant in terms of contribution to the social legacy and major event perception but, strictly speaking, with very short-term effects for volunteering: partly for different motivations (event attendance, personal skills improvement, networking), partly for different forms of organisational characteristics, partly for the very different impact in the involved communities. For these reasons this form of volunteering is not frequently associated with sport (and personal) development which is, at the end, the real aim of sport volunteering.

The most frequent form of volunteering in sport is substantially connected to sport development: we can find it at the grass-roots level and there the volunteering is mainly characterised by the organisational aspects mentioned above (coaching, fundraising, refereeing, driving, event planning, etc.).

Section 4: Volunteerism as social practice

Data and literature suggest that sport volunteerism is one of the meaningful fields of the volunteer sector in European societies (Fairley et al., 2015; Salamon, Sokolowski, 2014). Eventually, the network of non-profit associations gathers the archipelago of clubs, circles and societies that make up the structural backbone of the system, performing relational and charitable functions. It monopolises the social performance of the activities (Porro, 2013a).

Volunteerism, as Godbout (2002) for instance stresses, is clearly related to the 'gift' theory. We can find in volunteering the giving of time and energy and civil engagement among individuals. So, on one side we can face, trying to consider volunteering solely through quantitative indicators, the reductionist scenario that leads us into an arid neo-liberal perspective. On the other side, the quantification of the phenomena is relevant to an adequate implementation of the European policies aiming to enhance solidarity among citizens.

We can face the phenomena in relational terms too, considering the volunteer turnover problem: which is the element that boosts or retains volunteers in their service? According to Rhyne (1995) this element seems to be primarily the amount of free time and secondly the economic status of the volunteers. The decreasing of both these elements boosts the departure of volunteers. This is why the growth of volunteerism relies on the search for new forms of social innovation: abilities to combine the use of time with a perceived personal and societal advantage. Organisational factors that may enhance volunteers' contributions to social innovations include a decentralised organisational structure, the 'scaling up' of ideas, the provision of training and giving volunteers a sense of ownership. (De Wit et al., 2017, 16).

Doherty (2005) suggests, indeed, that the co-occurrence of personal barriers (lack of skills, time, family, etc.) and organisational barriers (poor management, lack of sense of belonging, lack of training, etc.) are crucial. Volunteers may work as initiators of a social innovation process. For this role, developing a decentralised organisational structure is likely to be beneficial both for volunteers and the whole organisation (Porro, 2013a).

In general it's widely accepted that volunteerism performs a meaningful action in the construction of social capital (Harvey, 2007; Kay, Bradbury, 2009; Zhuang, Girginov, 2012; Morgan, 2013; among others). The core idea of this statement relies on the construction of different forms of social capital, all referring to various social and moral relations capable of building the ultimate bonds within a community. Following the father of social capital in terms of civic engagement, we must consider the fact that the presence of the features related to social capital (trust, norms, networks, etc.) improves the efficiency of society by smoothing the way for co-ordinate action (Putnam, 2000). According to Harvey et al. (2007) it's possible to identify a strong correlation between social capital and volunteerism in sport. Becoming a volunteer in sport is likely to produce higher levels of social capital. Volunteers provide for their communities a relevant mix of resources in terms of time, expertise and materials. The concept of 'restitution' is fundamental to understanding the multi-dimensional role of social capital in the formation of the sense of identity or belonging (paradoxically even in negative terms) in a sports club.

Finally, Nicola R. Porro pointed out that: 'The composite universe of new practices is – on the contrary – crowded with initiatives inspired by inclusion, communication between differences and/or innovation of practices. Paraphrasing Putnam (2000), it seems that the old competitive bonding system, dominated by the imperatives of social cohesion and by the symbolic reasons of nationalisation, is flanked a century later by a bridging model, born of globalisation and fed by post-materialistic attitudes' (Porro, 2013b, 6).

Conclusion

We can consider volunteerism as one of the main determinants of sport development. We have already stressed that volunteers are involved in every level of almost every sport, from the grass-roots to high-level performance activities.

An important part of the literature converges on the idea that a limited proportion of volunteers carry out the majority of countable and uncountable work (Wicker, 2017). In Europe we find a problem of retention and adequate training of volunteers in a general framework of increasing complexification of the volunteer work in terms of safety issues, required technical skills and reductions of public resources. The result is an increasing need for professionalisation with a relevant percentage of paid staff employed to respond to the formal and legal environment in which the organisation works (Wicker, Hallman, 2013).

The formal and political recognition of sports associations must, however, be followed by the implementation of political actions that embrace two levels of intervention: one driven by the state, the other by the sports system. In the first case, it is necessary to rethink the strategies for integrating sports associations into social policies, with the state implementing a more systemic involvement of sport players and implementing/encouraging synergistic actions within and between the concerned systems (e.g. education and training). The sports system, in turn, is called upon to redirect its policies and to reshuffle the distribution of its resources in order to renew its agenda: this must be able to provide significant support for that part of the association that is committed to promoting the practice of sport as a tool for social intervention (De Gennaro, 2013).

The guiding idea behind the working hypothesis of this research is that sport and physical-motor activity constitute a powerful sensor of cultural change and at the same time represent a developing right to belong to a community. Sport, as a social construction, is always the product of the activation of symbolic systems, able to evoke cultural representations ingrained in the public imagination. The symbolic construction of Europe is therefore a key factor in the integration process (Porro, 2013c). Volunteerism in sport, as we have tried to highlight, could be a sensible indicator both of the involvement of citizens in general volunteerism – of which it reproduces most of the characteristics – and the specific forms of sport volunteerism that are perhaps the reason that lead the White Paper on Sport to declare: 'The European institutions have recognised the specificity of the role sport plays in European society, based on volunteer-driven structures, in terms of health, education, social integration, and culture'. The non-formal education provided by sport volunteering had to be recognised and enhanced to become attractive for young people's engagement in VSO. Participation in a team, compliance with the rules of the game, respect for others, solidarity and discipline as well as the organisation of amateur sport which involves non-profit clubs and volunteering, reinforce active citizenship. (WPS, 2007).

Notes

1 See one of the related pages: https://eacea.ec.europa.eu/erasmus-plus/actions/sport_en.
2 The Bosman ruling was an important decision on the free movement of labour and had a profound effect on the transfers of sport professionals within the EU.
3 Cited in Donnelly and Harvey, 2011.

Bibliography

Andreff, W., Dutoya, J. & Montel, J. 2009, A European model of sports financing: Under threat. *Revue Juridique et Économique du Sport*, 90, 75–85.

Baum, T.G., Lockstone, L., 2007, Volunteers and mega sporting events: Developing a research framework. *International Journal of Event Management Research*, 3(1), 29–41.

Bortoletto N., Porrovecchio A., 2018, Social inclusion through sports: A short comparison of Italy and France. *Society Register*, 2(1), 39–58.

Cnaan, R.A., Handy, F. & Wadsworth, M., 1996, Defining who is a volunteer: Conceptual and empirical considerations. *Nonprofit and Voluntary Sector Quarterly*, 25(3), 364–383.

Collins, M., 2008, Public policies on sports development: Can mass and elite sport hold together? In V. Girginov (ed.) *Management of Sports Development* (pp. 73–102). New York: Routledge.

Cuskelly, G., Hoye, R. & Auld, C., 2006, *Working with Volunteers in Sport: Theory and Practice*. New York: Routledge.

Dansero, E., Puttilli, M., 2010, Mega-events tourism legacies: The case of the Torino 2006 Winter Olympic Games: a territorialisation approach. *Leisure Studies*, 29(3), 321–341.

Davies, L.E., 2004, Valuing the voluntary sector in sport: Rethinking economic analysis. *Leisure Studies*, 23(4), 347–364.

De Gennaro, S., 2013, Le istituzioni sportive tra politiche europee e nuovi diritti di cittadinanza. In N. Porro, A.M. Pioletti (eds), *Lo sport degli europei. Cittadinanza, attività, motivazioni*. Milano: FrancoAngeli.

De Wit, A., Mensink, W., Einarsson, T. & Bekkers, R., 2017, Beyond service production: Volunteering for social innovation. *Nonprofit and Voluntary Sector Quarterly*, 48 (2), 52S-71S.

Doherty, A.J., 2005, *A Profile of Community Sport Volunteers / Volunteer Management in Community Sport Clubs*. Toronto: Parks and Recreation Ontario / Sport Alliance of Ontario. Retrieved from: http://wm.p80.ca/Org/Org185/Images/Resource%20Documents/Volunteer%20Resources/Phase1_finalReport.pdf.

Doherty, A.J., 2009, The volunteer legacy of a major sport event. *Journal of Policy Research in Tourism, Leisure and Events*, 1(3), 185–207.

Donnelly, P., Harvey, J., 2011, Volunteering and sport. In B. Houlihan & M. Green (eds), *Routledge Handbook of Sports Development*. New York: Taylor & Francis, 55–71.

EBS (Special Eurobarometer), 2017, December, 472, Sport and physical activity. 978-92-79-80242-3. doi:10.2766/483047.

Fairley, S., Green, B.C., O'Brien, D. & Chalip, L., 2015, Pioneer volunteers: The role identity of continuous volunteers at sport events. *Journal of Sport & Tourism*, 19(3-4), 233–255.

Gard, M., Dionigi, R.A., 2016, The world turned upside down: Sport, policy and ageing. *International Journal of Sport Policy and Politics*, 8(4), 737–743.

Gasparini, W., 1999, *Sociologie de l'organisation sportive*, Paris: La Découverte.

Godbout, J., 2002, Le bénévolat n'est pas un produit. *Nouvelles pratiques sociales*, 15(2), 42–52.

Guala, C., Bondonio, P., Dansero, E., Mela, A. & Scamuzzi, S. (eds), 2007, *A Giochi fatti: le eredità di Torino 2006*. Roma: Carocci.

Harvey, J., Lévesque, M. & Donnelly, P., 2007, Sport volunteerism and social capital. *Sociology of Sport Journal*, 24, 206–223.

Kay, T., Bradbury, S., 2009, Youth sport volunteering: Developing social capital? *Sport, Education and Society*, 14(1), 121–140.

Kim, M., Chelladurai, P. & Trail, G.T., 2007, A model of volunteer retention in youth sport. *Journal of Sport Management*, 21, 151–171.

LeRoux, N., Camy, J., Chantelat, P., Froberg, K. & Madella, A. 2000, *Sports Employment in Europe*. Lyon: European Observatoire of Sports Employment.

Morgan, H., 2013, Sport volunteering, active citizenship and social capital enhancement: What role in the 'Big Society'? *International Journal of Sport Policy and Politics*, 5(3), 381–395.

Orlowski, J., Wicker, P., 2015, The monetary value of voluntary work conceptual and empirical comparisons. *Voluntas*, 26(6), 2671–2693.

Porro, N., 2013a, *Movimenti collettivi e culture sociali nello sport europeo*. Catania: Bonanno.

Porro, N., 2013b, Lo sport Europeo tra welfare e performance. Rivista di Scienza *dell'Amministrazione*, 1, 2013, 5–28.

Porro, N., 2013c, Europa, sistemi sportivi e integrazione comunitaria. In N. Porro, A. M. Pioletti (eds), *Lo sport degli europei. Cittadinanza, attività, motivazioni*. Milano: FrancoAngeli.

Putnam, R., 2000, *Bowling Alone: The Collapse and Revival of American Community*. New York: Simon & Schuster.

Rhyne, D. 1995, *Volunteerism in Sport, Fitness and Recreation in Ontario*. Toronto: Recreation Policy Branch, Ontario Ministry of Culture, Tourism and Recreation.

Salamon, L., Sokolowski, W., 2014, The third sector in Europe: Towards a consensus conceptualization. Retrieved from: http://thirdsectorimpact.eu/site/assets/uploads/documentations/tsi-working-paper-no-2-third-sector-europe-towards-consensus-conceptualization/Conceptualiza-Wrkg-Ppr-Fnl-LMS-12-20-14.pdf.

Solberg, H.A., 2003, Major sporting events: assessing the value of volunteers' work. *Managing Leisure*, 8(1), 17–27.

Taylor, P., Nichols, G., Holmes, K., James, M., Gratton, C., Garrett, R., Kokolakakis, T., Mulder, C. & King, L. 2003, *Sports Volunteering in England*. London: Sport England.

Vos, S., Breesch, D. & Scheerder, J., 2012, Undeclared work in non-profit sports clubs: A mixed method approach for assessing the size and motives. *Voluntas*, 23, 846–869.

Wicker, P., 2017, Volunteerism and volunteer management in sport. *Sport Management Review*, 20(4), 325–337.

Wicker, P., Hallmann, K., 2013, A multi-level framework for investigating the engagement of sport volunteers. *European Sport Management Quarterly*, 13(1), 110–139. doi:10.1080/16184742.2012.744768.

Zhuang, J., Girginov, V., 2012, Volunteer selection and social, human and political capital: A case study of the Beijing 2008 Olympic Games. *Managing Leisure*, 17, 239–256.

Zintz, T., Winand, M., 2013, Les fédérations sportives. *Courrier hebdomadaire du CRISP*, 2179(14), 5–52. doi:10.3917/cris.2179.0005.

Web resources

Commission Staff Working Document. *The EU and Sport: Background and Context*. Accompanying document to the White Paper on Sport. Available at: https://eur-lex.europa.eu/legal-content/EN/TXT/?uri=celex:52007SC0935/.

European Olympic Committees. Available at: www.euoffice.eurolympic.org/.
European Non-Governmental Sports Organization (ENGSO). Available at: www.engso.eu/.
Italian Institute of Statistics. Page on Non Profit Organization permanent survey. Available at: www.istat.it/it/archivio/207807/.
Sport England 2018. Available at: https://www.sportengland.org/media/13782/sirc-se-sports-club-volunteers-report.pdf/.
White Paper on Sport Available at: https://eur-lex.europa.eu/legal-content/EN/TXT/?uri=celex:52007DC0391/.

5 Sport in jail

A sociological comparative perspective

Maurizio Esposito

Introduction

Expiation of a sentence is never an inert, neutral and silent process. The advent of prisons, in the modern sense, is the result of development of a capitalistic society and it does not transcend the public policies and welfare system of the state that inflicts the punishment: that is why philosophers and legal sociologists refer to prisons as a kind of social extractor (see Wacquant 2004), or dare to state that 'law borrows something from the violence that it fights against' (Ost 2007: 88. My translation). Serving time in jail often means colliding with violent and unknown social worlds, characterised by contradictory elements: punishment ineluctably generates hatred and conflict (see Cartabia, Violante 2018).

Based on the announcement made by the UN 'Universal Declaration of Human Rights' in 1948, several scientific studies and political movements addressed issues related to punishment: it needs to be 'human', depriving of freedom without additional punishments; and it needs to be educational, favouring the social and professional reintegration of the prisoner.

From this point of view, the inmate needs to be considered as a dynamic subject of treatment: it must focus on social reintegration, returning to society a better person than the one deprived of his freedom.

For example, the Dutch prison system regulations, dating back to 1951, state, 'Without prejudice to the type of penalty or measure, enforcement must also contribute to preparing the prisoner to reintegrate the society' (art.26). Similarly, art.188 of the French code of penal procedure defines the position (role) of penitentiary administration to ensure enforcement of judicial decisions that give rise to a custodial sentence or an order for temporary detention and ensure the custody of persons who, in the cases established by law, must be supervised, as required by art.189, 'the regime of the establishments devoted to the execution of the penalties is instituted to favour the amendment of the convicts, and to facilitate their social reintegration …'.

The thesis of the rehabilitative purpose of imprisonment is also asserted in England: in 1895, with the Gladstone Committee, the principle, according to which imprisonment must focus on re-education of the convict, is established

(Ancel, Chemithe 1981); and the first one of the 'Prisons rules' of 1964, regulating the English prison services, states that, 'the purpose of training and treatment of convicts shall be to encourage and assist them to lead a good and useful life'.

Recent years have provided a propensity to implement measures that are 'alternative' to detention, as in Italy, with the Gozzini law of 1986; or in Denmark and Sweden, where it is possible to use the various establishments in order to organise the most appropriate treatment in relation to the different categories of prisoners, in a so-called *en douceur* style (see Foucault 1975); or in Norway, where the application of pecuniary penalties seems preferable to the loss of freedom (Ancel, Chemithe 1981).

The need to consider punishment in terms of not only restriction and security but also re-education and treatment is widely underlined on an international level: in Italy, Law 354/1975 finally embraces the treatment paradigm, to the point that the first article is entitled 'treatment and re-education'. Until the Seventies, the prison protocol usually referred to the fascist prison system, with specifically restrictive and punitive characteristics. The reformist will of this law is evident in the fourth paragraph of art.1, which says, 'The prisoners and the internees are called or indicated by their name'. This assumption highlights, even on a metaphorical level, the will to humanise and personalise the treatment, which must focus on social reintegration of the prisoners and is to be implemented according to the criteria of individualisation, established in relation to the specific conditions of the subjects and in agreement with art.27 of the Italian Constitution.

In France, the Loi pénitentiaire of 24 November 2009, art.1 establishes that:

> Le régime d'exécution de la peine de privation de liberté concilie la protection de la société, la sanction du condamné et les intérêts de la victime avec la nécessité de préparer l'insertion ou la réinsertion de la personne détenue afin de lui permettre de mener une vie responsable et de prévenir la commission de nouvelles infractions.

In England, The Prison Act dates back to 1952 (1952 c.52). It specifies the conditions in which prisoners must be kept. Article 14 refers to the cells and the need for them to be adequate, in order to guarantee the health of prisoners, and therefore:

> 14 Cells
> (1) The Secretary of State shall satisfy himself from time to time that in every prison sufficient accommodation is provided for all prisoners.
> (2) No cell shall be used for the confinement of a prisoner unless it is certified by an inspector that its size, lighting, heating, ventilation and fittings are adequate for health and that it allows the prisoner to communicate at any time with a prison officer.

All the above is theoretically confirmed in thoughts and paradigms of various origins, which are well explained by the following assumption by the philosopher Paul Ricoeur (1984) who reminds us that a person is undoubtedly and always capable of something other than his crimes and his mistakes. More recently, Martha Nussbaum reinforces this position by stating that the suffering of the guilty does not return the damaged asset back to the victims and society (See Nussbaum 2016). In the same way, referring to the Book of Genesis, Marta Cartabia and Luciano Violante (2018) remind us that Cain became the constructor of a city after he had killed his brother. Many opinions support the growing need for restorative justice, which reconstructs the broken ties, so that the offender 're-pays the *malum actionis* not so much through suffering (the *malum passionis*) but through reparation, with the *bonum actionis*. Evil is not doubled, but elided' (see Fassone 2015: 208. My translation).

International rules concerning physical activity and sport in prison

International rules repeatedly express the essentiality for the prisoner to spend a good part of his time outdoors, and where possible to carry out physical and sports activities. Due to the soft law nature of these rules, they often have an eminently directing and guiding role (*vis directiva*), and not a binding or sanctioning role (*vis coactiva*); therefore, the effective implementation of these recommendations is systematically delegated to national regulations, and sometimes even to the will of personnel responsible for ensuring that actions do not only remain abstract intentions but become real rehabilitative efforts.

In a more general sense, the Preamble of 'International Charter of Physical Education, Physical Activity and Sport' (1978), by UNESCO, states that:

> 4 ... resources, authority and responsibility for physical education, physical activity and sport must be allocated without discrimination on the basis of gender, age, disability or any other basis, to overcome the exclusion experienced by vulnerable or marginalized groups;
> 7 ... the provision of quality physical education, physical activity and sport is essential, to realize their full potential to promote values such as fair play, equality, honesty, excellence, commitment, courage, teamwork, respect for rules and laws, respect for self and others, community spirit and solidarity, as well as fun and enjoyment;
> 10 ... physical education, physical activity and sport should seek to promote stronger bonds between people, solidarity, mutual respect and understanding, and respect for the integrity and dignity of every human being;

In the same Charter, explicit reference is made to the preventive and rehabilitative value of sport:

2.5 Physical education, physical activity and sport may contribute to prevention and the rehabilitation of those at risk of drug addiction, alcohol and tobacco abuse, delinquency, exploitation and abject poverty.

Furthermore, the need for adequate spaces for sport in every public facility is reiterated:

8.1 Adequate and safe spaces, facilities, equipment, and dress-options must be provided and maintained to meet the needs of participants in physical education, physical activity and sport mindful of different needs associated with climate, culture, gender, age, and disability.
9.1 Physical education, physical activity and sport must take place in a safe environment that protects the dignity, rights and health of all participants.

On an international level, the value of sport as a driver of social inclusion is repeated more than once. In the 'Council of 18 November 2010 on the role of sports as a source of and a driver for active social inclusion' (2010/C 326/04), the social value of sports practice is attested by the EU: sport plays an important role in the lives of many EU citizens, with a powerful potential for social inclusion through sport, meaning that participation in sport or in physical activity in many ways contributes to inclusion into society; whereby inclusion in sport involves a combination of 'sport for all', equal access to sport, equal opportunities in sport, and varied demand-oriented sporting opportunities and sports facilities, and whereby social inclusion through sport involves inclusive participation in society, community development and strengthened social cohesion. All of this in order to encourage and promote participation in sport of people from disadvantaged backgrounds, at the same time as ensuring their inclusion into society through sport by introducing them to new social networks and equipping them with new skills.

More specifically, as exercise and physical activity in jails are concerned, it is important to remember the *European Prison Rules*, published by the Council of Europe (2006), which includes the following articles:

Exercise and recreation
27.1 Every prisoner shall be provided with the opportunity of at least one hour of exercise every day in the open air, if the weather permits.
27.2 When the weather is inclement alternative arrangements shall be made to allow prisoners to exercise.
27.3 Properly organised activities to promote physical fitness and provide for adequate exercise and recreational opportunities shall form an integral part of prison regimes.
27.4 Prison authorities shall facilitate such activities by providing appropriate installations and equipment.
27.5 Prison authorities shall make arrangements to organise special activities for those prisoners who need them.

27.6 Recreational opportunities, which include sport, games, cultural activities, hobbies and other leisure pursuits, shall be provided and, as far as possible, prisoners shall be allowed to organise them.
27.7 Prisoners shall be allowed to associate with each other during exercise and in order to take part in recreational activities.
Specialist staff
89.1 As far as possible, the staff shall include a sufficient number of specialists such as psychiatrists, psychologists, social and welfare workers, teachers and vocational, physical education and sports instructors.

Another fundamental cornerstone in this sense are the United Nations 'Standard Minimum Rules for the Treatment of Prisoners (the Mandela Rules)', adopted by the United Nations General Assembly on 17 December 2015 after a five-year revision process. The right to physical activity and sport is ruled in the following articles:

Exercise and sport
Rule 23
1 Every prisoner who is not employed in outdoor work shall have at least one hour of suitable exercise in the open air daily if the weather permits.
2. Young prisoners, and others of suitable age and physique, shall receive physical and recreational training during the period of exercise. To this end, space, installations and equipment should be provided.

What emerges strongly from these articles is the clear will that physical and sporting activity in prison is not just a mere solipsistic exercise, nor a sort of 'onanistic' pastime, but rather a right and an opportunity to create, renew and strengthen social relationships, contacts with the outside world, empowerment, a sense of autonomy; in accordance with the aforementioned principle of humanisation and personalisation of the penalty.

Sports activity in prison: an international look

The advantages of practising physical activity and sport in prison can be considered under two aspects: one is subjective and individual, the other is social and relational. From the first point of view, doing sports in prison means combating diseases related to inactivity and unbalanced lifestyles, but also reducing aggression and risks of self-harm behaviour. From the second point of view, sport in prison supports the prisoner in his acquisition of fundamental values in the process of socio-relational growth: respect for others, integration within a group, acceptance of limits, loyalty, acceptance of defeat, but also contact with the outside world aimed at social and professional reintegration.

Although at times literature has spoken of the 'pre-selection effect' (see Sugden, Yannakis 1982), for which sporting activities mainly involve people and groups generally oriented at respect for rules and socialisation, an enormous number of results, backing a positive and socialising function of practising sport in reclusive contexts, seems difficult to falsify.

Moreover, much of the scientific literature has shown how sporting activity in prisons is essential in achieving objectives not directly linked to sport: these include the possibility of offering social networks as an alternative to those usually experienced, access to positive models, the possibility of experimenting with 'virtuous roles' and social identities, the probability of improving one's self-esteem, self-determination, tolerance, co-operation, and finally the ability to work in groups and to mediate conflicts (see Coalter 2002).

The growth of the population detained in prisons has produced over the years a large number of scientific studies on the paradigms of security and treatment and their operational declinations in the area of punishment. In particular, as far as sport is concerned, there are mainly three areas investigated: the relationship between physical activity and health of prisoners; the sports rehabilitation function; and, finally, participation in physical and sporting activities.

Regarding the first area, most of the literature has favoured experimental approaches and the use of control groups, and the main findings have generally shown how constraint, promiscuity and prison overcrowding are factors of high risk to human health (see Courtenay, Sabo 2001). From an individual point of view, sport in prison has been studied above all as a virtuous alternative to inactivity, and therefore as a protection factor in terms of risks of obesity, hypertension, diabetes, cardiovascular diseases and even mortality (Jebb, Moore 1999). Therefore, in a complementary way, it has been shown that physical activity in prison not only produces a better state of health by significantly reducing the possibility of contracting diseases, but it also leads to a reduction in stress and anxiety and an increase in self-esteem and sense of trust and self-determination (Cashin, Potter 2008). Other studies have shown that participating in sport-type treatment activities has reduced aggressive behaviour, both verbal and physical (Wagner, McBride, Crouse 1999).

With regards to the second area, concerning the purely rehabilitative function of sport, it has been widely demonstrated how physical activity in prison is useful and necessary in many ways: it can help to combat boredom (Grayzel 1978), to handle time spent in prison in the best possible way (Sabo 2001), to mediate conflicts of power and problems related to the semantics of one's own body and prison '*machismo*'. Ultimately, and as a final completion of this point, sport can help to deal with the fundamental phase of 'critical review' of one's personal experience: an epitomic phase for the treatment of activities to be successful and effective, because through this phase prisoners can succeed not only in avoiding the degrading conditions imposed by the prison institute but can also rebuild their personal image. The meaning attributed to sports practices in prison is therefore not stable but evolutionary, guided by the complex intertwining of penal conditions and personal motivations (Gras 2003).

Lastly, with regards to the third area of our interest, namely the one concerning participation in sports, scientific studies have mainly focused on an analysis of how the most important results in the implementation of these activities are not so much related to psychological aspects, but rather to virtuous circuits activated in terms of social relations and in terms of sense of belonging (Frey, Delaney 1996). There are other researches that (see Balibrea, Santos 2011), along the same line, focus mainly on the pedagogical function of sport, which in this context is supportive and may contribute to the creation of an ethical sense in the prisoner (self-discipline), allowing him to undertake different roles other than that of 'deviant' and helping him develop respect for the opponent.

Political positions regarding sport in prison vary considerably in the different countries of the EU, even with regard to their welfare systems: in Denmark, whose welfare system has been identified as institutional-redistributive, the penitentiary system offers inmates the opportunity to practise many sports, some of which are also considered 'niche' such as golf and spinning, and implements contacts and relationships with sports clubs outside the institute. On the contrary, in the United States, with a more markedly residual welfare model, the strengths of practising sports are held back by prejudicial hypotheses on possible factors of danger and disorder, such as the possible use of the physical strength of prisoners against prison officers (Amtmann 2001). In the United Kingdom, whose welfare model has been defined as universalist (it is not by chance the homeland of the Beveridge model and the National Health Service), physical and sporting activities have been part of the justice policies for a long time, and sport is recognised as having a very important role, in particular for health promotion and the reduction of recidivism. Sport is of considerable importance in prison, and it is an activity included in the planning of health promotion actions, 'by health promotion we mean any activities, programmes and initiatives aiming to raise awareness and to develop skills in preventing and promoting physical, emotional, mental and social health of individuals and groups in custody. This includes a wide range of health promotion aspects that can be addressed in custody, varying from regular sports to informative sessions for young offenders on alcohol, tobacco and drug use' (Szabo, Nistor 2014: 571). Very often, however, prisoners do not have access to the activities that constitute a valid factor of protection against the contraction of diseases; these include: 'drinkable water, hot water, heating, healthy food, fresh air in the room, regular sport activities, prompt and qualitative medical care, family contact' (ibid.: 572).

In England and Wales, the so-called *whole prison approach* has been favoured for some years, a holistic approach that takes into account the response to the multiple needs of prisoners in order to improve their physical and mental health (Meek, Lewis 2012: 118). Prison healthcare therefore passed in 2006 from Her Majesty's Prison Service to the National Health Service, a transition that would take place in Italy two years later, in 2008, with the transfer of functions and duties related to the health of prisoners from the Ministry of Justice to the National Health Service.

Physical education programmes play a very important role in the UK:

Prison gym departments are increasingly seen as having a role to play in delivering such provision and this is made evident in the physical education (PE) instruction (Ministry of Justice, 2011) which stipulates that PE programmes must incorporate access to remedial PE and should promote healthy living and dietary opportunities as well as activities that boost self-esteem to improve psychological wellbeing. (Ibid.)

In an interesting piece of research on health promotion involving seven European countries (Bulgaria, Czech Republic, England and Wales, Estonia, Germany, Latvia and Romania), health promotion activities are described as a protective factor in relation to self-injurious and deviant behaviour. Among these activities, physical and sporting activities seem to have a significant importance as a protection factor especially regarding mental illnesses. Indeed:

> a number of prison experts highlighted that young prisoners experience a wide range of stressful circumstances related to the prison environment. These include problems with adaptation, violence, lack of regular contact with their families and partners, boredom and lack of activities including frequent physical activities and sports, over-crowding and lack of social space leading to mental health problems. This was echoed by many prisoners expressing that their mental health had deteriorated due to sleeping problems, homesickness, boredom, loneliness, over-crowding, lack of fresh air, lack of sport opportunities, lack of access to frequent showers/baths and a stressful environment. (MacDonald, Rabiee, Weilandt 2013, 158)

In particular, the study shows that the lack of physical activities is felt and registered above all by prisoners, while other types of concerns regarding security, are mainly registered from the response of prison staff from the countries investigated: 'although there were similarities between prisoners and staff's views about health promotion issues in prison including lack of social space, mental health issues, staff had more concerns about potential security issues, infection diseases and drugs, whereas prisoners are more concerned about food, physical activity, bullying, etc.' (ibid., 160).

Furthermore, an area of great interest for these activities to be effective refers to contacts with the outside world and concern for everything that will happen after the release in terms of social reintegration and, above all, of job reintegration:

> in order to provide appropriate health promotion activities to young prisoners in key areas of mental health, education, employment and social relationships (Chitsabesan et al. 2007), an assessment of the needs and accessible services is necessary. Activities also need to be able to motivate and involve young people through participatory approaches, with a view to developing their life skills and preparing them for a crime-free life after their release. (Ibid.: 162)

Moving from theoretical studies and research to a concrete analysis of existing programmes in prisons, many activities and projects are found which are linked to the public policies of the countries in which they are implemented. The international panorama offers a series of virtuous examples of application of sports activities in penal institutions. Let us consider some of them in a comparative sense.

The Prisoners' Education Trust (PET) is a charity working across every prison in England and Wales to help prisoners achieve their potential through learning. Its mission is: *every prisoner a learner, every prison a place to learn*. In 2012, it published 'Fit for Release',[1] a research project conducted in collaboration with the University of Teesside that examines the value of sport as a rehabilitative tool in prison settings, specifically in relation to educational and employment opportunities. This report brings together a compelling set of evidence from prisoner learners and other stakeholders to demonstrate the value of sport as a rehabilitative tool in prison settings, specifically in relation to educational and employment opportunities. Whilst sport alone will not necessarily prevent reoffending, it offers an effective and powerful way in which to embed numeracy and literacy, promote higher level learning and motivate prisoners who may be difficult to engage in other resettlement, educational or psychological interventions.

More specifically, among the projects related to the practice of rugby, we can identify those conducted in a maximum-security prison in Buenos Aires, Argentina, where a team consisting of prisoners with good behaviour was formed, followed by professional coaches (Deges 2010). In Georgia, rugby was used to promote the health of younger prisoners and to develop values such as respect, discipline, friendship and teamwork; this project has the vital objective of community reintegration through relations with local rugby clubs. Projects in prison have also been carried out in Venezuela: these include the Alcatraz project involving young prisoners in a programme that includes agricultural work, psychological counselling and rugby, with the aim of reducing crime rates in the region and reducing at the same time recurrence rates (Morsbach 2011).

As we know, football is undoubtedly the most followed and practised sport in the world. Rosie Meek (2014) offers an interesting description of the projects in this sense, with reference to the Anglo-Saxon world: the Cardiff club, for example, offers a six-week programme to teach football techniques, especially in the area of sports communication. The formal participation of the club provides prisoners with an external contact that can be used even after termination of the sentence. Even the Chelsea club uses its staff to visit some prisons in London organising games, tournaments and courses, with the aim of creating skills among prisoners to be used in sports associations even after their release. This project has an eminently social value, as it foresees that these prisoners, once released, can become in turn 'peer educators' for people at risk in suburban areas of the city.

The Bristol prison, in England, mainly consists of prisoners with addiction problems. It proposes programmes, also based on sport, aimed at reducing the use of drugs. The activities carried out for these purposes are mainly of a low intensity, such as walks, bowls and group games. Inmates also learn about healthy eating lifestyles and techniques for cooking healthy dishes. The actions are designed to involve inmates and help them to focus their lives away from drugs, improving physical health, promoting communication and teamwork skills, increasing self-esteem and supporting healthy lifestyles.

In this sense, in the Correctional Institute of Parc some projects combine theoretical lectures on healthy lifestyles (food, diet and fitness) with low impact physical activities. The participants in these projects are mainly prisoners with specific needs, such as those belonging to the most vulnerable and older categories. The activities are dedicated to this type of population and are mainly based on low intensity actions, such as bowls and sitting exercises. Moreover, speaking of low intensity, it is worth mentioning a very recent experiment carried out in the maximum-security prison Naivasha GK Prison, in Kenya, where a session of *Mindfulness*, a technique of Buddhist origin which aims to train the mind to focus on the *here-and-now*, born in the United States during the 1970s, was successfully tested. In this prison, there are many prisoners sentenced to death or life imprisonment. One of them, as reported in the Italian newspaper *La Repubblica* on 26 April 2018, states: 'the relationship with the guards was hell. Today they are like brothers to me, we talk, and we laugh. They give me hope'. Of the approximately 2,000 inmates, 90% reported being less angry, more relaxed and having given up on drugs and alcohol.

Finally, some programmes have an objective in terms of sustainability: in this sense, an interesting project is implemented in the Santa Rita do Sapucaí prison, in Brazil, where the prisoners, pedalling on their bikes connected to electric generators, produce green energy to illuminate street lamps; those who participate in this activity have two types of benefits, the first linked to their physical state of health and the second consisting in a real possibility of reducing the penalty: for every 16 hours of pedalling, they are rewarded with a one-day penalty discount (Bevins 2012).

These practices would remain examples of empty fragments if they did not have sustainable objectives and a clear and precise mission, which can be summarised in the following points:

- creating completely autonomous and structured opportunities for meeting and relationships, forcing prisons to request or carry out directly cultural, recreational and sports activities, encouraging the implementation of a social dimension of sport;
- managing social sports activities aimed at integrating a segment of prison life with the outside world;
- projecting and implementing initiatives that bring the external environment into contact with the prison reality, favouring the overcoming of

mutual distrust and the creation of a solid relationship between the outside world and prisoners;
- soliciting acceptance of training opportunities, also in sports, as a connecting tool with the Third Sector, the world of work and society of the outside world;
- establishing the strengthening of soft skills, empowerment, autonomy and self-esteem;
- fostering the growth of a community capable of enhancing the diversity and originality of each person, planning initiatives that can respond as widely as possible to the needs of everyone from a recreational, cultural, sporting and training point of view in the detention phase and in the social reintegration phase.

Conclusion: Sport is not enough!

In conclusion, the sense of practising of sports in prisons depends on numerous *macro* and *micro* factors. A fundamental determinant is the welfare system but also, on a more specific basis, the type of penitentiary institution and penalty to be served: prisons are a polymorphic and poly-semantic reality, which cannot be considered as an amorphous and immutable 'magma'.

The value of sports practice in prison also depends on personal motivations and characteristics: life in prison determines the deprivation of the most important forms of relationship that the person normally has with the outside world. By creating a break with the outside world, the shock of incarceration is often evoked to explain the interruption of sports practices and the abandonment of expectations. However, the individual perception resulting from this 'dispossession' is not the same for everyone. The importance given to this forced deprivation is the more intense the more prestigious the social position occupied before incarceration, and the greater the ease of access to goods and services, in line with the concept of 'relative deprivation' elaborated by Merton and Lazarfeld in 1950 (in Gras 2003: 198).

The psychosocial difficulty linked to incarceration does not therefore only depend on the quantity of goods and services granted by the prison institution, but also on what the individual possessed before his incarceration. Following the same model, the sportiest inmates have difficulty in experiencing the impossibility of not being able to practise a sport in the same way as before incarceration. However we consider it, a cross-cutting advantage of practising sport in prison can be identified in the possibility of fighting the so-called 'imprisonment' syndrome (Clemmer 1940, Thomas 1977), a process of progressive depersonalisation that can change the identity of the prisoner: a process by which the prisoner acquires the informal traditions, habits, rules and values of the new prison society. Thus, the detainee is not only deprived of his freedom, but also experiences what has been well-defined as 'biographical plunder' ('*dépouillement biographique*', Gras 2003: 199), developing a form of dependence and subjection to a system of values which causes a process of infantilisation. Thanks to sports activities, the prisoner can recover his self, becoming a new person, trying to build a new job position and therefore social:

> D'une logique de résistance physique envers l'institution, le sens des pratiques sportives suit ensuite de manière progressive une logique d'apprentissage au cours duquel l'individu parvient à se détacher de l'identité de reclus qui lui est imposée pour finalement retrouver une image de lui-même plus valorisante. Enfin, si l'appréciation relativement complexe des effets de ces carrières sportives sur la réinsertion et l'ambiguïté de leur interprétation (conversion réelle ou stratégie d'adaptation?) demeurent, l'existence de carrières sportives en prison permet de montrer que la durée des peines ne peut pas être systématiquement associée à un temps perdu mais peut parfaitement être envisagée de manière constructive. (Ibid.: 209–210)

However, that is not enough! Sports in prison must not, and cannot, be considered as a panacea, especially if conducted in a monotonous, autonomous or self-managed manner, as occurs in many cases; in fact, the risk is incurring narcissistic or, worse, 'male chauvinist' and self-referential drifts of relations between prisoners. As confirmed by numerous studies, 'sport does not seem capable of pursuing the goal of integration on its own but it needs to be included in a wider network working together with other socialisation agencies such as school and family' (see Falese 2008: 129). Moreover, for many years now, the hypothesis has been made that physical activity itself would not lead to an improvement in conduct and social relations, but rather the context within which these activities take place, and above all the programming process in which they are inserted (see Coalter 1996).

It seems rather *naïve* to consider sport as an all-in cure, and it is also quite convenient to keep prisoners 'engaged' in activities without a real *ex ante* programming of intervention and, above all, without *ex post* assessment of their effects and impacts. International research (see Crosnoe 2002) anodically calls into question the assumption that sport is dogmatically a protective factor against deviant behaviour, and studies conducted in Italy by associations such as Antigone (2018) specify how the possibility of practising physical activity and sports in prisons is continually put at risk by structural elements such as: the conditions of wear and tear of sports facilities, the unhealthy nature of the environments, the inadequacy of the premises, the lack of contact with the outside world and limited resources; to the point that too often programming of sports activities in the prison is entrusted to Third Sector agencies and sports associations, that become a kind of 'life preserver' for short-sighted and self-referential policies of a now emptied welfare.

The risk, therefore, is that sports practice in prison can become more a form of social control than a cathartic, regenerating and re-socialising activity: keeping the prisoner 'involved' in routine activities, without evaluating the expected effects and their social and relational impacts, could lead to a sort of modern, and more subtle, reformulation of the model of the panopticon, elaborated by Bentham: a place where formal social control is concealed by small short-lived freedom and *simulacra* of spaces only fictitiously open to traces of self-autonomy.

The political implications of our considerations are not limited only to a sociological level of analysis, but also involve other aspects of public policies, such as project management and the architecture and planning of penitentiary structures, which must be designed to facilitate access to physical and sporting activities, really integrated into the prisoner's living environment.

It is therefore necessary to radically change the way of thinking around sport and start to reinterpret it beyond the *cliché* of playful pastimes, but also beyond the ideal type of professionalism that thrills the masses only in passive terms of *audience*; to reconsider it no longer as 'controlled excitement' and 'behavioural reserve' (Elias, Dunning 1986), or as a shred of emotional involvement that ordinary social life has the obligation to control; to reinterpret it no longer as a 'reproduction of dominant social values' (Bourdieu 1979) and therefore as *conspicuous consumption*; on the contrary, to rethink it as an activity and instrument of direct expression of one's personality, as a revolutionary agent of change and, above all, as a human right.[2]

Notes

1 https://www.prisonerseducation.org.uk/resources/fit-for-release-how-sports-based-learning-can-help-prisoners-engage-in-education-gain-employment-and-desist-from-crime.
2 As defined by UNESCO in 1978 in the 'International Charter of Physical Education, Physical Activity and Sport'.

Bibliography

Amtmann, J., 2001, Physical activity and inmate health. *Corrections Compendium*, 26 (11), 6–7.

Anastasia, S., 2014, Carcere, giustizia e società nell'Italia contemporanea. Un'introduzione. *Democrazia e diritto*, 3, 7–16.

Ancel, M., Chemithe, P., 1981, *Les systémes pénitentiaires en Europe occidentale*. Paris: La Documentation française.

Antigone, 2018, *Un anno di carcere. XIV Rapporto sulle condizioni di detenzione*. Roma: Associazione Antigone.

Baccaro, L., Mosconi, G., 2003, Il girone dei dannati, ovvero il fenomeno della recidiva. *Dei Delitti e delle Pene*, X, 1–3.

Balibrea, K., Santos, A., 2011, *Deporte en los barrios: ¿integración o control social?* Valencia: Editorial Universidad Politecnica de Valencia.

Bevins, V., 2012, Brazil prisoners ride bikes toward prison reform. *Los Angeles Times*, 5 September.

Bourdieu, P., 1978, Sport and social class. *Information (International Social Science Council)*, 17(6), 819–840.

Bourdieu, P., 1979, *La distinction. Critique sociale du Jugement*. Paris: Minuit.

Buckaloo, B.J., Krug, K.S., Nelson, K.B., 2009, Exercise and the low-security inmate: Changes in depression, stress, and anxiety. *The Prison Journal*, 89(3), 328–343.
Cartabia, M., Violante, L., 2018, *Giustizia e mito*. Bologna: Il Mulino.
Cashin, A., Potter, E., Butler, T., 2008, The relationship between exercise and hopelessness in prison. *Journal of Psychiatric and Mental Health Nursing*, 15, 66–71.
Chalat, A., 2012, Hope behind bars. *The Junket*, 18 October.
Chitsabesan, P., Bailey, S., Williams, R., Kroll, L., Kenning, C., Talbot, L., 2007, Learning disabilities and educational needs of juvenile offenders. *Journal of Children's Services*, 2(4), 4–17.
Cipolla, C., 1997, *Epistemologia della tolleranza*. Milano: FrancoAngeli.
Clemmer, D., 1940, *The Prison Community*. New York: Holt, Rinehart and Winston.
Coalter, F., 1996, *Sport and Anti-social Behaviour: A Policy-related Review*. Edinburgh: Scottish Sports Council.
Coalter, F., 2002, *Community Sports Development Manual*. Edinburgh: Sports Scotland.
Commission of the European Communities, 2007, *White Paper on Sport*. Brussels.
Condon, L., Hek, G., Harris, F., 2008, Choosing health in prison: Prisoners' views on making healthy choices in English prisons. *Health Education Journal*, 67, 155–166.
Conley, D., 2004, *The Pecking Order*. New York: Pantheon.
Cooper, C., 2011, Disability – the next equality challenge. *Prison Service Journal*, 195, 16–21.
Courtenay, W.H., Sabo, D., 2001, Preventive health strategies for men in prison. In Sabo, D., Kupers, T.A. & London, W. (eds), *Prison Masculinities*, 157–172. Philadelphia: Temple University Press.
Crosnoe, R., 2002, Academic and health-related trajectories in adolescence: The intersection of gender and athletics. *Health and Social Behaviour*, 43, 317–335.
Deges, F., 2010, Scaling the wall. *Rugby World*, May, 116–119.
Durcan, G., 2008, *From the Inside: Experiences of Prison Mental Health Care*. Sainsbury Centre for Mental Health.
Elias, N., Dunning, E., 1986, *Quest for Excitement: Sport and Leisure in the Civilizing Process*. Oxford: Basil Blackwell.
Esposito, M., 2010, The health of Italian prison inmates today: A critical approach. *Journal of Correctional Health Care*, 16(3), 230–238.
Esposito, M., 2012, 'Double burden': A qualitative study of HIV positive prisoners in Italy. *International Journal of Prisoner Health*, 8(1), 35–44.
European Commission, 2011, *Developing the European Dimension in Sport*. Brussels.
Falese, L., 2008, Il peso delle disuguaglianze socio-economiche sulla pratica di attività fisica e sulla salute. Il caso italiano. In Porro, N., Raimondo, S. (eds), *Sport e Salute. Salute e Società*, anno VII, 2.
Fassone, E., 2015, *Fine pena: ora*. Palermo: Sellerio.
Foucault, M., 1975, *Suveiller et punir*. Paris: Gallimard.
Francis, P., 2012, Sport and harm. *Criminal Justice Matters*, 88(1), 14–15.
Frey, J.H., Delaney, T., 1996, The role of leisure participation in prison: A report from consumers. *Journal of Offender Rehabilitation*, 23(1/2), 79–89.
Garland, D., 1985, *Punishment and Welfare*. Aldershot: Gower.
Gentleman, A., 2012, Inside Halden, the most humane prison in the world. *The Guardian*, 19 May.
Goffman, E., 1961, *Asylums: Essays on the Social Situation of Mental Patients and Other Inmates*. New York: Doubleday.

Gonin, D., 1991, *La Santé incarcérée; médecine et conditions de vie en détention*. Paris: l'Archipel.
Gras, L., 2003, Carrieres sportives en milieu carceral: l'apprentissage d'un nouveau rapport a soi. *Sociétés Contemporaines*, 49–50, 191–213.
Grayzel, J., 1978, The functions of play and the play motif at a State penitentiary. In M. Salter (ed.), *Play Anthropological Perspectives*. New York: Leisure Press.
Hsu, L., 2004, Moral thinking, sport rules and education. *Sport, Education and Society*, 9(1), 143–154.
Jebb, S., Moore, M., 1999, Contribution of a sedentary lifestyle and inactivity to the aetiology of overweight and obesity. *Medicine and Science in Sports and Exercise*, 31 (11), 534–541.
Johnsen, B., 2001, Sport, masculinities and power relations in prison. Unpublished Master Thesis. The Norwegian University of Sport and Physical Education, Oslo (Norway).
Lewis, G., Meek, R., 2012, Sport and physical education across the secure estate: An exploration of policy and practice. *Criminal Justice Matters*, 90, 32–34.
MacDonald, M., Rabiee, F., Weilandt, C., 2013, Health promotion and young prisoners: A European perspective. *International Journal of Prisoner Health*, 9(3), 151–164.
Meek, R., 2014, *Sport in Prison: Exploring the Role of Physical Activity in Correctional Settings*. London: Routledge.
Meek, R., Champion, N., Klier, S., 2012, *Fit for Release: How Sports-based Learning Can Help Prisoners Engage in Education, Gain Employment and Desist from Crime*. London: Prisoners Education Trust.
Meek, R., Lewis, G., 2012, The role of sport in promoting prisoner health. *International Journal of Prisoner Health*, 8(3–4), 117–130.
Morris, L., Sallybanks, J., Willis, K., Makkai, T., 2004, Sport, physical activity and antisocial behaviour in youth. *Trends and Issues in Crime and Criminal justice*, 249, 1–6.
Morsbach, G., 2011, A very different Alcatraz. Retrieved from: http://news.bbc.co.uk/1/hi/world/americas/4854506.stm.
Nelson, M., Specian, V.L., Campbell, N., DeMello, J.J., 2006, Effects of moderate physical activity on offenders in a rehabilitative program. *Journal of Correctional Education*, 57(4), 276–285.
Nussbaum, M., 2016, *Anger and Forgiveness: Resentment, Generosity, Justice*. New York: Oxford University Press.
Ost, F., 2007, *Mosè, Eschilo, Sofocle. All'origine dell'immaginario giuridico*. Bologna: Il Mulino.
Ozano, K.A., 2008, The role of physical education, sport and exercise in a Female Prison. Unpublished MSc dissertation. University of Chester.
Porro, N., 2006, *L'attore Sportivo*. Bari: La Meridiana.
Ricoeur, P., 1984, *Time and Narrative*. Chicago: Chicago University Press.
Rios, M., 2004, La educacion fisica en los establecimientos penitenciarios de Catalunya. *Tándem, Didáctica de la Educación Física*, 15, 69–82.
Sabo, D., 2001, Doing time, doing masculinity: Sports and prison. In Sabo, D., Kupers, T. A. & London, W. (eds), *Prison Masculinities*. Philadelphia: Temple University Press.
Stidder, G., Hayes, S., 2012, *Equity and Inclusion in Physical Education and Sport*. London: Routledge.
Sugden, J., Yannakis, A., 1982, Sport and juvenile delinquency: A theoretical base. *Journal of Sport and Social Issues*, 6(1), 22–30.
Sykes, G., 1958, *The Society of Captives*. Princeton, NJ: Princeton University Press.

Szabo, A., Nistor, G., 2014, Training prison staff on issues of young prisoners' health needs. *Procedia – Social and Behavioral Sciences*, 142, 570–577.

Thomas, C.W., 1977, Theoretical perspectives on prisonization: A comparison of the importation and deprivation models. *Journal of Criminal Law and Criminology*, 68, 135–145.

UNICEF, 2011, Rugby as a tool for rehabilitation and reintegration. Retrieved from: www.unicef.org/georgia/media_18249.html.

Vaiciulis, V., Kavaliauskas, S., Radisauskas, R., 2011, Inmates' physical activity as part of the health ecology. *Central European Journal of Medicine*, 6(5), 679–684.

Wacquant, L., 2004, *Punir les pauvres*. Marseille: Agone.

Wagner, M., McBride, R.E., Crouse, S.F., 1999, Effects of weight-training exercise on aggression variables in adult male inmates. *Prison Journal*, 79(1), 72–89.

Wellard, I., 2009, *Sport, Masculinities and the Body*. London: Routledge.

World Health Organization, 2007, *Health in Prisons: A WHO Guide to the Essentials in Prison Health*. Copenhagen: Organization Regional Office for Europe.

Part II
The sport of citizenship
An incipient Europeanisation?

6 The Europeanisation of sport

Sociology of a new European public action

William Gasparini

Introduction

The Eurobarometer survey on sport and physical activity indicates that 40% of the European Union citizens engage in a sport activity on a regular basis (with one-third of them engaging in the competitive practice of sport in a club) and almost 15 million people work in the sports industry. The social, economic, media and cultural importance of sport is indisputably recognised in every European country, in all 27 countries of the European Union and all 47 member countries of the Council of Europe. In this respect, it is the number one non-governmental and volunteer-organised activity in Europe. It gathers more participants and volunteers than any other activity. Consequently, for the European Commission, 'sport is one of the fundamental aspects of the life of millions of European citizens'. Article 165 of the Treaty of Lisbon of 1 December 2009, states that 'the Union shall contribute to the promotion of European sporting issues, while taking account of the specific nature of sport, its structures based on voluntary activity and its social and educational function'. Following the European cultural convention, the Council of Europe took an interest in sport in the early 1960s and passed its first resolution on this matter in 1967. However, despite the intervention of the European institutions in some relatively consensual aspects of sport,[1] sport still falls within the abilities of each Member State, since it pertains to their national interests.

Therefore, whether in sport or education policy, the European Union only provides support to its Member States, at least in principle. However, sport generates an economic activity, which means that its stakeholders are subjected to European regulations. Consequently, as early as the 1990s, and more precisely in 1995 with the Bosman judgment, EU law entered the world of sport despite the reluctance of the European spheres of professional sport. In response to the unease induced by this essentially economic approach to sport, and at the request of the sports world that the European sport specificity be taken into account, the Commission initiated another – more 'societal' – dimension of community intervention as early as the 2000s. In keeping with the principle of subsidiarity, the Member States are still in charge of sports affairs, but article 165 of the TFUE allows and invites the European Union to use political instruments such as recommendations, calls to 'best practices' and incentives (*Erasmus+* funding programmes dedicated to sport, for instance). In this way, European sports policy tends to progressively establish itself in the European space beyond its mere supportive capability. Then, can one deduce that after the nationalisation and municipalisation periods analysed by numerous researchers and experts, a new step would follow, that of the Europeanisation of sport? Does the European construction contribute to the emergence of a political process of development of a European 'us' through sport?

Issues of the analysis of European sport practices

In many fields, the 'founding fathers' of the European institutions and studies have often managed to impose their political and scientific view of Europe, through a double transfer of the political categories to the scientific and scholarly issues within political discourses.[2] For instance, as early as the 1990s, the 'scholarly' study of European football was mostly carried out by economists, jurists and European experts, who spread the idea of a naturalisation of the categories of law, in order to analyse the changes in football after the Bosman judgment. Thinking of sport in Europe through the prism of the categories of European institutions amounts to contributing to the construction of Europe rather than analysing it.[3] The challenge raised by the empirical analysis of the Europeanisation of sport is yet linked to the development of new theoretical approaches that would allow for the study of new political 'interstices' resulting from the transnationalisation of political issues. As a whole, studies on the European Union focus on highly Europeanised sectors such as the monetary union, agriculture or environment. However, the contours of this new political European area could be better defined, by analysing such a recent field of international co-operation as sports policies. Actually, since the early 20th century, these policies have mostly fallen within the competence of national governments. Virtually all of these public policies have been elaborated by national policy makers who wanted to protect national sovereignty and identity. Relying both on the identification of the people with their national team and champions, and on the delegate sport organisations, high-level sport was widely used by nation states to create and strengthen the national sense of 'belonging'.

This text proposes to explore the role played by the Europeanisation agents in the European public sport action, from a socio-political perspective. After a reminder of the two forms of the Europeanisation of sport, we propose to focus on those who 'make' the Europe of sport, and more specifically on the MEPs. Beyond their political and national divergences, these 'makers of Europe' consider sport as a medium for the European identity.

The dual Europeanisation of sport

As a whole, Europeanisation refers to the processes of construction, circulation and institutionalisation of formal and informal rules, procedures, policy paradigms, styles, 'ways of doing things' and shared beliefs and norms, which are first defined and consolidated in the making of EU decisions and then incorporated into the logic of the domestic discourses, identities, political structures and public policies at the national level.[4] Quite common in social sciences since the mid 1990s, the term 'Europeanisation' was more recently used in the field of sport to refer to the effects of integration and of the European standards on the functioning of sport in Europe.[5] To understand the sport policy of the European Union, one has to analyse a dual process of Europeanisation. Firstly, the 'formal' Europeanisation is carried out by imposing the EU laws on the Member States and sport organisations. This process first concerned sports that caught the media attention the most and resulted in the late 1970s in sport being commodified and turned into a show with the privatisation of television channels across Europe. Consequently, in professional football, the creation of the Champions League, together with the exceptional increase in television incomes and the Bosman judgement, have strengthened the European dimension and the market orientation of an increasingly denationalised and professionalised event. The second process refers to an 'informal' Europeanisation operated through a set of recommendations and Europeanised discourses which tend to impose the idea that sport possesses a European identity or dimension. A 'soft' regulation (or 'soft power'), this policy has facilitated the elaboration of a genuine body of rules, conducts and practices which are accepted or promoted in sport across the EU Member States.

'The European identity through sport': political genesis of a European imagination

Aware of the process of identification with sports teams and sense of belonging to a territory through sport, the European Commission and the European Parliament have gradually resorted to sport in order to facilitate the emergence of a 'European identity'. On 25–26 June 1984, the Council of Europe of Fontainebleau, which led to heads of state and governments of the Europe of Ten declaring that they wanted to strengthen the identity and image of Europe among its citizens and throughout the world, established an ad hoc committee for the Europe of citizens. Headed by Italian Pietro Adonnino, a former MEP, this group of experts is responsible for the proposal of measures to strengthen the identity of the EU and facilitate the emergence of a Europe without borders. Approved by the Council of Europe in Milan in 1985, the 'Adonnino Report' is the first EU document to recognise the importance of sport in European society. It enshrines the idea that sport can be regarded as an important tool in the development and consolidation of a European identity. Via public-awareness campaigns on the sport-induced sense of belonging to the EU, this report has paved the way to a new form of informal Europeanisation, with a view to spreading the idea of 'a European citizenship through sport'. The efforts of the European Commission and the European Parliament have since converged on this issue. The 2007 White Paper on Sport, together with the entry into force of the 2009 Treaty of Lisbon and the introduction in 2014 of a chapter dedicated to sport in the *Erasmus+* programme, are as many steps toward the promotion of the European dimension of sport.

The process of Europeanisation of sport is yet relatively complex, inasmuch as it is the product of a variety of stakeholders and sport areas, of a system of formal and informal rules, of a plurality of decision-making centres, but also of anti-Europeanism phenomena through the sports-related nationalism of states and their citizens. Whether they are EU institutions, such as the European Court of Justice and the European Commission, or intergovernmental institutions, especially the Council of Europe, or private institutions such as sport federations, associations or NGOs, each and every one of these stakeholders eventually contributes to the Europeanisation process and tries to gain influence according to their interests, national habitus and own systems of beliefs.

Sports entrepreneurs of Europe

In this new European political field developing since the 1990s, various kinds of stakeholders take action to various degrees, co-ordinate or oppose each other.[6] They are mainly stakeholders from the field of European professional sport (athletes, managers of clubs and federations, spokespersons of players' unions, referees, European supporters' clubs). However, there are also private and public stakeholders involved: ministers for sport and officials from the EU and the Council of Europe Member States, the MEPs and European Commission officials, the lobbyists and think tanks of the civil society advocating a 'sport cause' and committed to fighting 'excesses' in sport,[7] and lastly, economic stakeholders (media and journalists – namely pay-TV channels, sponsors, professional clubs, sporting goods manufacturers and sport industrialists). Football is obviously dominating in the European area of publicised sports. This area thus consists of all the stakeholders affected by the changes that sport undergoes at the European level. Convinced of the transnational importance of sport, these stakeholders come together, co-operate or come into conflict with each other about the issues that affect them, which are related to the missions and values of the institutions to which they belong: the free circulation of football players, the state aid to clubs, doping, corruption, stadium violence, the transfer and recruitment of extra-European minor athletes, discrimination and sexism, television broadcasting of sport images, the defence of sporting values.

These stakeholders stand out from others through the volume and nature of the capital they possess and how they benefit from it, in order to take action in the European football area: economic capital, reputation capital, social capital, political capital and European institutional capital. Besides, one has to account for the strength of their commitment in the game and their interests, often related to the socio-economic sector to which they belong (private commercial sector, non-commercial private or public sector). In this sense, we call the most committed 'sport entrepreneurs of Europeanization'.[8] These entrepreneurs can also be distinguished by their position within these institutions: on the one hand, permanent specialised stakeholders such as officials and European institution officials or permanent employees of European sport organisations; and on the other hand, irregular or occasional stakeholders such as athletes, advocates of the sport cause or sports clubs and sports federations managers.

Conclusion

The construction of a European sport area does not result from the voluntarist action of Europe as a community or from any other post-WWII great political project, but rather from increasingly significant exchanges between stakeholders from civil society at first, then between professional sport bodies established as institutions, and finally between European institutions. The European construction would not meet sport, and especially football, before the 1980s. Far from being apolitical, football takes over the field of soft power at the European level.

It appears clearly that sport does not escape the larger political issues of the European Union. The European construction is indeed the result of a largely unplanned process determined by the three logics it involves, which are sometimes contradictory, sometimes complementary: the strategies of states, the inherent dynamic of institutions and the organisation of both collective and individual interests. It is the interaction of these elements which makes the European construction an incomplete political process by nature.

Notes

1 For example the fight against doping and corruption, or the promotion of the educational values of sport.
2 See the file 'Constructions européennes', *Actes de la recherche en sciences sociales*, n° 166–167, 2007; see also Gasparini, W., 2011, 'Un sport européen? Genèse et enjeux d'une catégorie européenne', *Savoir/agir*, 15, pp. 49–59.
3 Bourdieu, P., 1993, 'Esprits d'État. Genèse et structure du champ bureaucratique', *Actes de la recherche en sciences sociales*, 96–97, pp. 49–62.
4 Radaelli, C., 2000, 'Whither Europeanization? Concept stretching and substantive change', *European Integration online Papers* (EIoP), 4 (8).
5 Gasparini, W., Polo, J-F., 2012, 'L'espace européen du football: dynamiques institutionnelles et constructions sociales', *Politique européenne*, n°36, pp. 8–21; Gasparini, W., 2017, *L'Europe du football. Socio-histoire d'une construction européenne.* Strasbourg: Presses universitaire de Strasbourg.
6 See Gasparini W., 2015, 'Sport', in Lambert Abdelgawad E, Michel H. (eds), *Dictionary of European Actors*. Brussels: Larcier, pp. 359–363.

7 For example the European networks FARE (Football Against Racism in Europe), European Gay & Lesbian Sport Federation, as well as the association 'Sport and Citizenship'.
8 In reference to Baisnée O., Pasquier R. (eds), 2007, *L'Europe telle qu'elle se fait*. Paris: CNRS.

Bibliography

Digennaro, S., Gasparini, W., 2013, 'La costruzione di una Europa sociale dello sport', *Rivista di Scienze dell'Amministrazione*, n° 1, pp. 27–44.

Eurobarometer, EU Commission, 2018,ec.europa.eu/public_opinion/index_en.htm.

Gasparini, W., 2017, *L'Europe du football. Socio-histoire d'une construction européenne*. Strasbourg: Presses Universitaires de Strasbourg.

Gasparini, W., Polo, J.-F., (eds), 2012, L'espace européen du football: dynamiques institutionnelles et constructions sociales. *Politique européenne*, n°36.

7 The organisation of sport and sports policies in Germany

Michel Koebel

Introduction

The evolution of sport in Germany must be understood in the light of its historical legacy, and especially the Nazi era. Germany would indeed use sport to glorify and strengthen its supremacy over the world, as would other totalitarian dictatorial regimes throughout the 20th century (such as Italy or the Soviet Union). This period – and in particular the way power was gained and exercised during the 1930s – has had a lasting impact on the making of the fundamental laws that have been governing Germany ever since. They have shaped the organisation and funding of sport, as well as other areas of the social, economic and political life. These dark days had to be left behind and prevented from ever happening again. Consequently, federalism was established in order to create an entity and ensure that the state would not become too powerful. In this way, *Länder* play a significant role in the German federal state, especially when it comes to establishing a regional government, provided that the national legal requirements are met: each *Land* possesses its own constitution, head of government, ministries and parliament. Similarly, the freedom to create companies or associations – provided that their objectives and actions do not go against the public order or the principle of understanding between peoples (Article 9 of the Fundamental Law) – contributes to the promotion of sport, although indirectly since organised sport is essentially associative.

The principle of subsidiarity that governs state intervention guarantees the relative independence of local authorities. The desire to break away from the way the Nazi regime used to treat part of the German population on religious, sexual or political grounds found expression in an effort to guarantee every human being fundamental rights, as detailed in the body of the same text – and not in the introduction as is often done – and also to guarantee the existence of political parties, including opposition ones (provided that the latter do not jeopardise the constitution). In the same way – despite the German history of direct democracy allowed in municipalities, yet hardly applied outside the smallest ones (Wollmann, 1999) – there is no referendum process at the national level, because of the way it was misused by the Weimar Republic and

Hitler when he was in power. Over the last decades, this type of governance has been increasingly adopted at the local level, and we will see its impact on sport policies, particularly on the refusal to host certain major sports events.

Since a reform enforced in 2006, the central government has acquired more important prerogatives than the mere traditional sovereign functions, and especially in the areas of education, research and environment. The issue of sport was still not integrated into the Fundamental Law (*Grundgesetz*),[1] despite the regular demands of some political and sports figures: for instance, representatives of the sports movement in 2006, shortly before the football World Cup hosted by Germany and right as the two historic federations merged (their strategy consisted in taking culture into account in their request to integrate sport into the Fundamental Law, as the German Council for Culture had long tried to do with the promotion of culture, in vain); the liberal-democrat party (FDP) in 2009 and social-democrat party (SPD) in 2012, both with the support of the German Olympic and Sports Confederation – Deutscher Olympischer Sportbund (DOSB) – although this integration may have impeded the independence of the sports movement.[2] As of now, none of these attempts has been successful. Constitutional law experts have looked into this issue, numerous adversarial debates have taken place, both in academies and in the media, providing an opportunity to introduce a somewhat contrasted overview of sports practices and the organisation of sports events.

The political promotion of sport at the local level

Although sport has not made its way into the German Fundamental Law, the promotion of sport is enshrined in virtually all of the *Länder*'s constitutions (with the exception of the *Land* of Hamburg, although it was Germany's official candidate for the 2024 Olympic and Paralympic Games). Most often, the support and promotion of sport is rather mentioned than detailed, in a short sentence that yet manages to draw links with municipalities and associations of municipalities. Sport is often associated with art and culture (sometimes with science and education). Some of these constitutions address the need for a universal access to sports facilities in more detail.

Besides the inscription in the constitution, the political expression varies from a *Land* to the other: behind the traditional support to universal sport, grassroots sport and high-level sport, the maintenance of sport facilities and the necessary efforts to include people of foreign origin or people with disabilities, a brief analysis of the *Länder*'s institutional communication based on their web portals reveals links between the emphasised themes and the political affiliation of the ministers in charge of sport as well as of the heads of governments.[3]

First of all, it is interesting to observe that sport is attached to the ministry of the interior, public works and homeland at the national level. Sport falls within home affairs, but is not unrelated to patriotism. On the ministry's website, sport is one of the ten issues addressed and presented. There is a clear focus on elite sport, a prerequisite to ensure the international recognition of Germany

('Germany's reputation across the world') and bring the rest of sport (the basis) in its wake. All of the three main aspects developed in this 'sport' theme are related to this goal: maintain its position on the international sport stage. The head of this ministry is Horst Seehofer, who has been heading the Christian Social Union (CSU) since 2008, a party allied with the CDU in power in Bavaria since 1962, of which Horst Seehofer himself was the president from 2008 to 2013 (which earned him, to occupy for one year, the position of president of the federal council, with an annual rotating presidency). Prior to this, he was alternately Minister of Labour, Minister of Health, Minister of Agriculture, and even acting federal president of Germany. This CSU minister in a CDU/SPD/CSU 'great coalition' government sets the tone for his idea of sport, an idea very similar to the one all CDU-led *Länder* (or CSU in Bavaria) adopt, since elite sport and organised sport are the themes almost systematically put forward. Sport is consistently placed under the authority of a representative from the same party as the head of government (this is noteworthy as all *Länder* were led by coalitions at the time of the survey): in six out of the seven relevant ministries, sport is incidentally attached to the ministry of home affairs. The situation is very different – and more contrasted – in the seven *Länder* led by a coalition with an SPD majority. For instance, in the Rhineland-Palatinate *Land*, health-sport and well-being-sport are put forward (in the general presentation, high-level sport is not even mentioned). In Brandenburg, the values of sport, and especially its educational virtues, are advocated. In Lower-Saxony, it is the quality of life that is put forward, in Mecklenburg-Western-Pomerania, it is physical activity, before the associative network is mentioned. It is also in these *Länder* that the existence and importance of non-organised sport are mentioned most often. In Thuringia, where die Linke is the majority party, the minister in charge of education, youth and sport firstly supports high-level sport, but also integrates non-organised sport. The only *Land* where the ministry of sport is not headed by the majority party of the coalition is Baden-Württemberg, dominated by the Grüne (although they are allied with the CDU, which is a rare case) and whose minister in charge of culture, youth and sports is a member of the CDU.

Thereby, the way the ministries in charge of sports design sport and prioritise measures to support and promote it may vary from a *Land* to the other, although they may follow partisan logics. However, sport is not supported or promoted only by national and regional policies: most municipalities and associations of municipalities are also active in this area, relying on the principle of subsidiarity that is supposed to define everyone's responsibilities.

Supporting sport based on the principles of subsidiarity and participation

Subsidiarity is a societal and political principle based on individual responsibility for public action. The state's obligations must first and always be assumed by the lower level, especially in case of doubt: the region instead of the state, the district (or community) instead of the region, the municipality instead of the district. The higher levels must withdraw in front of the competences of the lower levels (yet they must take their capacities into account and avoid overloading them). More generally, the public intervention of the higher level is required only when the lower level is incapable of assuming the relevant political project on its own. This principle does not apply only to the political-administrative levels: it also encompasses the economy, religious communities, trade unions, associations and even the citizens and families. It is a pluralist view of society. The provisions of the Fundamental Law regarding the sharing of responsibilities between the federal government, *Länder* and municipalities (and associations of municipalities)[4] are important for the constitutional situation of sport, even if sport is not explicitly mentioned – and precisely *because* it is not mentioned.

One of the consequences of the principle of subsidiarity is that no city, district or municipality will develop a direct sports policy if a private local organisation can take care of it. In this case, the corresponding council must give the latter the means to meet the objectives set by the council. If there is no one to manage the sports policy, the relevant local administration must take the necessary measures to meet its goals (or resort to the intervention of the higher levels if it is unable to do it on its own, provided that they share objectives with the higher levels).

This principle has been discussed numerous times and has often created confusion: sports associations and clubs saw it as a real chance to demand that public authorities provide them with the necessary funds to carry out their activities. This principle being acknowledged, the analysis of local public sports policies in Germany shows that the priority mission of municipalities is to manage and maintain sports facilities, which are generally made available to local sports associations, to facilitate the development of their activities (Eckl, Wetterich, 2007, 80). However, observations indicate that approximately 30% of German cities are starting to charge the rental of their facilities for the training of children and youth (for adults, the proportion is 50%). This tendency to rent facilities – essentially sports and gymnastics halls – is particularly pronounced in big cities and the south of Germany. This rising trend is linked to the economic and financial crises that have affected Europe since 2008 and resulted in drastic reductions in the funds allocated to sport at every level of the state's intervention (Koebel, 2013).

Some municipalities (especially in the north and west of Germany, but also in big cities) have directly entrusted local sports associations with the management of a part or the entirety of their sports facilities, especially sports fields. Public intervention can also be observed in the support to non-organised sport and physical activity, notably since traditional sports organisations have abandoned them. Anyway, when sports policies are developed at whichever level, it is because the population has expressed a need that must be satisfied, but also because there are votes to win (Daumann, 2015, 308).

Another element must be taken into account to understand the evolution of public policies, and especially sports policies. Throughout the 1960s, various protests (including that of May 1968) have led to the introduction of new forms of citizen participation: preliminary citizen consultation (*vorgezogene Bürgerbeteiligung*), with the obligation for local authorities to publish their planning intentions soon enough and to account for all of their citizens' criticisms (although the final decision remains at the discretion of the elected councils). At the same time, the local influence of political parties has induced changes: political parties (and especially minority groups) have eventually succeeded in imposing that the federal regulations of the municipal policy give local political parties and locally elected deputies an almost parliamentary level of control over elected councils and their decisions (right to information and control over the local administration and its representative). Direct democracy got a second wind after the reunification of October 1990, because of the popularity of the citizen movements that led to the fall of the Berlin wall. Two main reforms were undertaken. The first consisted in the direct election of mayors and the possibility to dismiss them through a referendum (*Abwahl*) – even if it was not adopted by all *Länder* at once. The second one was the introduction of the local referendum,[5] which can take one of two forms: 'the right [for citizens] to initiate a referendum (*Bürgerbegehren*) and the local population's decision-making power (*Bürgerentscheid*)' (Wollmann, 1999, 111). For a local referendum to have a decision-making power, the proposed reform must obtain a majority vote and there has to be a 25 to 30% quorum of voter turn-out (compared to registered voters); the popular initiative towards a referendum can only be adopted with a certain quorum, from 10 to 20% of the population eligible to vote, depending on the *Land*. The issues that can be addressed are restricted to important matters coming under the relevant local level (*Selbstverwaltung*), with the exception of all that is related to purely financial aspects. Local referendums have been on the rise since the early 2000s. According to one report on this issue,[6] the use of referendums varies from one *Land* to another: it is most widely used in Bavaria – accounting for almost 40% of the total number of referendums – but the frequency of their use increases with the size of the authorities (a vote is arranged once per year on average in each of the seven districts of Hamburg). Schools, sports facilities and bathhouses are among the issues most frequently addressed in local referendums.

However, in the area of sports, the citizens' decisions that have caused the biggest stir in German media were the successive refusals to host the Olympic Games in various German regions. After the referendum of 2011 rejected Munich's candidacy for both the Summer Olympic Games of 2018, and the Winter Olympic Games of 2022 (that could have taken place in Munich and two surrounding metropolises, the three cities having rejected their candidacy by a majority vote, including one with over 60% of expressed votes),[7] then it was the mayor of Hamburg's turn to fail a local referendum, despite the support of the Ministry of the Interior and the sports movement. Admittedly, it was a close call (51.6% against), but it was an indisputable verdict because of the population's strong mobilisation (50.1% of registered voters, which is way above most traditional consultations). The population was influenced by NOlympia – a citizen movement already active in Munich, supported by several left-wing parties (especially the Grüne) and trades unions of teachers, students and migrant workers – which led a fierce campaign, with an anti-Olympics petition that gathered over 10,000 signatures and the diffusion via social networks of a shock argumentation[8] mainly focusing on the issue of funding and its consequences in the long run.

The organised sports movement

The DOSB is the umbrella organisation of German sport. It was established in 2006 as a result of the merging of the national Olympic Committee and the German Sport Federation (DSB). From 1 January 2018, it comprised 27.4 million memberships in over 92,000 sport clubs. The way the DOSB presents its figures (the DOSB produces its own data) may lead one to think that one out of three Germans is a member of a sports club. The DOSB makes the classic mistake of implying that the number of registered licences corresponds to licence-holders,[9] which does not account for the fact that people hold multiple licences.[10] In France, one considers that a licence-holder holds 1.3 licences on average (Louveau, 2002). Let us apply this to Germany, the proportion of licence-holders drops from 33% to approximately 25%, which is close to the 23% produced by the 'sport' Eurobarometer for the practice of sport in clubs in Germany.[11] Since the Eurobarometer only concerns people aged 15 or more, a simple adjustment gives an approximate licence-holder ratio of 25% of the total German population. This figure is still very high.

This imprecision in the interpretation of the number of licence-holders, which results from the fact that multi-memberships are not taken into account, does not interfere with comparative analyses.

The first interesting piece of data addresses the evolution of the number of licence-holders over time. After a virtually uninterrupted growth phase from 1983 to 2013[12] (from 18.4 to almost 28 million licence-holders), the number of licence-holders has been stagnating since 2013. This situation varies from one discipline to another, but football is still leading (7.1 million licence-holders), followed by gymnastics (stable at 5 million licence-holders, which makes it a truly German tradition). Then come tennis and shooting (both with 1.4 million licence-holders and on the decline since 2000, a bit sharper for tennis), and the Alpine Club making it to the disciplines counting over 1 million licence-holders, with a number of licence-holders that has doubled over the last 18 years (from 0.6 to 1.2 million). Another important piece of data concerns the difference between *Länder*, and especially the low rates observed in the ex-GDR countries, which are half as high as in the rest of Germany. The clubs in this part of Germany have lost half their licence-holders since the fall of the Berlin wall, which means that, given the figures of the migration to the ex-FRG *Länder*, virtually all migrants were members of sports clubs. Besides this effect of the reunification, some *Länder* are a bit 'sportier' than others, especially in the south of Germany. As for gender equality, as in many other countries, fewer women practise sport than men, with approximately 40% of the total female population. While only 15.6% of football licence-holders are women, this proportion is still almost three times as high as in France (although the latter is experiencing a rise). The second most-practised discipline – gymnastics – is dominated by women (68%).

This strong involvement in sports clubs – also evidenced by the number of volunteers who invest their time in these clubs (6.8 million in 2005)[13] – makes Germany one of the sportiest countries in the European Union (5th place out of 28).[14] It is also the European leader in terms of the proportion of people who practise a sport on a regular basis and choose to practise it in a club.

The DOSB regularly asserts its social role and its desire to take charge of the issues expressed in the sport policies of the federal government and the governments at every territorial level (tremendous funding issues are at stake due to the principle of subsidiarity): policies for the integration of young people in difficulty, foreign citizens and people of foreign origin, disadvantaged neighbourhoods, people with disabilities, health-sport, etc. It also claims responsibility for an ambitious 'universal sport' policy, affirming that it enables people to break free from ethnic and social barriers. Behind this ideological discourse – and despite a broadened access to sport resulting from the scale of this phenomenon – lie various inequalities revealed by sports sociologists. Up until the 1980s, different sociological analyses have pointed out an over-representation of middle and upper classes in this area, especially in adults, an over-representation of men, even greater among the working class, executive positions and small clubs (Schubert, Horch, Hovemann, 2006), a decrease in the activity rate with age, and an influence of the social background on the choice of disciplines (Haut, Emrich, 2010, 315). These disparities in access to sport practice, including age, gender and ethnic inequalities, were criticised in the 2000s. Serious surveys show that, while more women and elderly people now benefit from greater access to sport, competitive sport remains extremely unequal. The traditional idea of sport – which associates sport, performance and competition – prevails in the working class, where the activity rate is the lowest (Haut, Emrich, 2010). A survey with a broader scope, based on international comparisons, shows that contrary to popular belief, 'vertical' disparities (with respect to the social and professional position, income, qualification level) are still prevalent, while 'horizontal' disparities (gender, age) are less significant when it comes to explaining the inequalities in access to sports practice (Rohrer, Haller, 2015).

New policies, new trends

Like many other industrialised countries, Germany is diversifying sports practice: sport now has a broader scope and is no longer restricted to its traditional, associative forms. It has won new fields and can now be found in private clubs from the market sector (and especially *fitness* clubs), in various institutions using sport as a tool for educational, integration, entertainment or business purposes. Together with family or friends, individuals get self-organised to practise physical activities regularly, whether alone, in pairs or in groups. These new fields can also be literal fields, since sport is also practised in places that were not initially designed for this: on the street, in parks, at the office, at home. Activities that would not be labelled as sport – walking or bike-riding to the workplace – are now integrated into policies advocating movement as a means to improve one's health. The initiators of these policies – especially the *Länder* and all local authorities – are aware that practising sport outside clubs is as important as, if not more than, the traditional ways of practising sport, and invest more and more in the development of spaces facilitating active mobilities by securing them, and increasingly fund the stakeholders who use sport as a means of integration or prevention. These new trends – implying a broader acceptance of the notion of sport – have not escaped the DOSB, which wants to convince local authorities that it is able to implement their policies at every local level and in (almost) every sector, particularly as it also allows them to win new members. This is how local sport policies and those of the traditional sports movement have evolved over the years.

This evolution is particularly perceptible in the fields of integration through sport and of the development of social and sports activities.

A survey conducted in Baden-Württemberg on local sports policies has demonstrated that, at every territorial level, actions targeting young people – in the sense of prevention – are a priority. However, the survey shows that this priority is more often planned than realised (Eckl, Wetterich, 2007). Local policies often remain limited to supporting the traditional sports movement, maybe because the sports administrative executives themselves are pure products of this sector and/or former sports champions (Koebel, 2013).

However, policies for the integration of marginalised populations through sport (*Integration sozialer Randgruppen*) were developed in many sectors, targeting migrants, deviant young people, girls and women, homeless people, prisoners and drug addicts, among others. Various activities have been used to meet these objectives of integration, prevention or empowerment: certain traditional sports (such as football, basketball or martial arts), climbing, slackline, self-defence, but also artistic activities or dancing. Over the years, the sectors of sport and of social work have gradually come together, the integration of immigrants having played a major role (Koebel, Stahl, 2013). A partially autonomous organisation of the DOSB named Deutsche Sportjugend (DSJ) is behind this work, initially called 'the social offensive of sport' (Nippe, 2000), which welcomes all audiences without any formal membership.[15] Sport is even legally recognised as a social work tool since 1991, thus securing significant funding for the organisations that take these actions (Seibel, 2007; Michels, 2007). In 1989, a programme is implemented at the federal level, first named 'Sport for all – sport with repatriates' and renamed 'Integration through sport' in 2001, to account for the broadening of the programme to all populations of immigrant background. More recently, it has also been including refugees.

As in France, social workers have long resisted using sport as a prevention tool, because of the ideology of performance, competition and elitism associated with it, but also because of the authoritarian nature of the sports organisations. This resistance has gradually faded. In the 1990s, most social educators were willing to use sport in their educational and prevention activities. These methods have even been integrated into their training curriculum (Seibel, 2007). As for the traditional sports associations that enter the programme of integration through sport, they frequently resort to social workers in the framework of their actions targeting marginalised people.

Conclusion

Germany is one of the most sport-oriented countries in Europe, as evidenced by the high number of memberships in clubs from the traditional sports movement, supervised by a single organisation and largely funded by public authorities at all local levels, in compliance with the principle of subsidiarity, although there are slight variations depending on the political orientation. However, sports practices now include other modes that partly escape this hegemonic organisation: sport is increasingly seen as a tool to support health policies and integrate marginalised populations, involving a growing range of stakeholders. Despite a growing number of people practising sports and an ever-improving access for women and elderly people, sport practice remains socially unequal.

Notes

1 The *Grundgesetz* has been serving as a constitution since 1949, although it does not bear this name and has never been ratified through a referendum.
2 These attempts are certainly not unrelated to the fact that Thomas Bach, the first president of the DOSB (from 2006 to 2013), and appointed president of the International Olympic Committee (IOC), had been politically active in the liberal-democrat party (FDP) for over forty years and would see obvious connections between sport and the liberal values that he would politically defend. It must be noted that the intricate links between sport and politics, especially under the Vichy regime, have set the stage in France for the emergence of the ideology of apolitical sport after 1945, which facilitated the construction and autonomy of the French sports area (Defrance, 2000). In Germany, the need to preserve the autonomy of the sports movement has followed another path.
3 This work was carried out in December 2018.
4 Each *Land* (possessing its own parliament and government) is subdivided into districts (*Landkreise* or *Kreise*, depending on the *Land*) headed by a council, with a few cities being independent of the district system (*Kreisfreie Städte*), which have their own council. Each district comprises municipalities (*Gemeinde*), which are also headed by a council. The principle of self-administration of the various levels has increased their autonomy since 1949, especially the communal level, previously regarded as a mere administrative (not a political) level responsible for the application of federal guidelines (Wollmann, 1999).
5 Baden-Württemberg is an exception since this *Land* introduced the local referendum and direct election of the mayor in the 1950s.

6 *Bürgerbegehrensbericht 2018*, Mehr Demokratie e.V., in Kooperation mit dem Institut für Demokratie- und Partizipationsforschung der Bergischen Universität Wuppertal und der Forschungsstelle Bürgerbeteiligung und direkte Demokratie an der Philipps-Universität Marburg.
7 Depending on the cities, a mere 10 to 20% of voter turn-out is required for the referendum to have a decision-making power (unlike France where this threshold is set at 50% of registered voters).
8 NOlympia, *Argumente fur ein NEIN zu Olympia*, n.d.
9 The publicly available statistical document (DOSB, *Bestandserhebung 2018*) introduces a great deal of data on licences. The mistake appears on page 12, where the licence-holders ration is calculated in relation to the corresponding population (per age category and gender). The overall rate that is presented only reaches 28.9%, because the data this calculation is based on only accounts for the licence-holders counted in each *Land* (in other words, 23.9 million out of 27.4 million in total).
10 At the demand of the DOSB, Boris Rump has produced another executive summary on the diachronic analysis of licence-holders. He has admitted and explained this error, without trying to measure it. He considers that, while the way these figures were produced is questionable, his analysis is still valid over time: DOSB (2017). *Mitgliederentwicklung in Sportvereinen* 2000 bis 2015. Bestand, Veränderungen und Perspektiven.
11 European Commission (2017). *Special Eurobarometer 472* (Sport and physical activity Report) (p. 48).
12 Data on the sport practice of Germans (including outside clubs) have been available since the 1970s, but it differs widely depending on the way surveys are conducted
13 Out of these 6.8 million, 2.1 occupy specific positions (including nearly 1 million trainers) and 4.7 million are occasional volunteers (Schubert, Horch, Hovemann, 2006, 3).
14 Special Eurobarometer 472, op. cit. (p. 48), reworked.
15 If this youth organisation has adopted this new perspective, it is also because it was deprived of the organisation of high-level sport in the early 1970s, because the success of the FRG in sport had become a national political issue and the objective was to counter GDR's use of sport as a tool for the international legitimisation of the communist regime (Teichler, 2010; Koebel, Stahl, 2013).

Bibliography

Daumann, F., 2015, *Grundlagen der Sportökonomie* (2. Aufl.). Konstanz/München: UVK-Verl.-Ges. & UVK/Lucius.

Defrance, J., 2000, La politique de l'apolitisme. Sur l'autonomisation du champ sportif. *Politix*, Vol. 13, no. 50, pp. 13–27.

Eckl, S., Wetterich, J., 2007, *Sportförderung und Sportpolitik in der Kommune*. Berlin: LIT Verlag.

Haut, J., Emrich, E., 2010, Sport für alle, Sport für manche: soziale Ungleichheiten im pluralisierten Sport. *Sportwissenschaft*, Vol. 41, pp. 315–326.

Koebel, M., 2013, La territorialisation des politiques sportives dans les villes moyennes: une comparaison franco-allemande. *Revue juridique et économique du sport (Jurisport)*, Vol. 136 (novembre), pp. 42–45.

Koebel, M., Stahl, S., 2013, Die Entwicklung der Sportsozialarbeit in Frankreich und Deutschland. Zwischen lokaler Integration und nationaler Identität. *Revue d'Allemagne et des pays de langue allemande*, Vol. 44, no. 4, pp. 501–522.

Louveau, C., 2002, Enquêter sur les pratiques sportives des Français: tendances lourdes et problèmes méthodologiques. In: Mignon, P. (et al.), *Les pratiques sportives en France*. Paris: INSEP-Éditions, pp. 135–154.

Michels, H., 2007. Hauptsache Sport. *Sozial Extra*, no. 9/10, pp. 13–16.

Nippe, M., 2000. Die 'Soziale Offensive des Sports' fing in der Sportjugend an. In: Deutsche Sportjugend (eds.), *50 Jahre Deutsche Sportjugend. In einem Jugendberghaus fing es an*. Frankfurt/Main: Hofmann.

Rohrer, T., Haller, M., 2015, Sport und soziale Ungleichheit – Neue Befunde aus dem internationalen Vergleich. *Kölner Zeitschrift für Soziologie und Sozialpsychologie*, Vol. 67, no. 1, pp. 57–82.

Schubert, M., Horch, H.-D., Hovemann, G., 2006, *Ehrenamtliches Engagement in Sportvereinen*. Köln: DOSB/Bundesinstitut für Sportwissenschaft.

Seibel, B., 2007, Sportbezogene Kinder- und Jugendarbeit als Aufgabenfeld der Sozialen Arbeit. In: Seibel, B. (ed.), *Sport und Soziale Arbeit*. Berlin: LIT, pp. 9–33.

Teichler, H.J., 2010. Sport und Sportpolitik in der DDR. In Krüger, M., Langenfeld, H. (eds), *Handbuch Sportgeschichte*. Schorndorf: Hofmann, pp. 227–238.

Wollmann, H., 1999, Le système local en Allemagne: vers un nouveau modèle de démocratie locale? In: CURAPP/CRAPS, *La démocratie locale. Représentation, participation et espace public*. Paris: PUF, pp. 103–116.

8 Sports organisations and policies in France

William Gasparini

Introduction

The French sports organisation model is based on the assumption that the development of sport and physical activities is an objective of general interest, supported by the state, communities and the civil society as a whole, including the sports movement and companies. Throughout its history, the organisation of French modern sport has yet gone through various configurations (Elias, 1970), with different stakeholders and organisations depending on the context, the situation and the issues of interest to the involved groups. Between cooperation and competition, the main sports stakeholders defend their own private or public interests in these historical and social configurations, seeking to secure a monopoly over the lawful organisation of sport in France. In this respect, the organisation of sport is truly a social field, insofar as sports practices are integrated into the socio-economic areas that make up and structure French society (Gasparini, 2000, 2003): amateur sports associations in the non-market private sports sector, professional sport and the sporting equipment and events business in the private market sector, physical education, school sports and the mechanisms of integration and public health through sport (Gasparini, 2008) in the public sector and lastly, 'free' sports practices in the non-organised area.

In this light, we will see that sport in France is a complex system evolving over time and involving numerous organised and self-organised stakeholders, both from the public and private sectors. As far as the organisation of sport is concerned, France also occupies a special place in Europe, since this organisation is based on a system where public organisations prevail. Over the past century, sport has indeed become an issue for public policies that have set out the framework of its organisation. At the national level, the state plays a role of coordination, control and support, namely through the Ministry of Sports and the public institutions that come under it, while the French National Olympic and Sports Committee (CNOSF) represents the sports movement.

Nevertheless, the state control and organisation of sport is a relatively recent phenomenon. Indeed, apart from the regulations related to public order (on the occasions of sports events in public spaces) and the law of 1901 on the freedom of associations, sport would not be subjected to state or legal standards until the 1930s. The French state eventually took an interest in sport in the early 1940s, and especially after WWII. However, for practical reasons, the state could not take care of all sports-related affairs: the diversity of practices, audiences, stakeholders, locations and situations would just make it impossible. Therefore, the state assigns a public sport service mission to sports federations, which organise sports activities and undertake national selections on its behalf. At the local level, together with sports clubs, local authorities (cities and community of municipalities) provide physical and sports activities to amateur athletes and populations wishing to engage in a physical activity.

The organisation of sport in France: a legal framework and historical legacy

The organisation of sport in France is rooted in history. Compared to Anglo-Saxon countries, the history of the French society and nation is more closely linked to that of the state and dates back to the establishment of a centralised monarchy in the 13th century. Moreover, the historians specialised in French history have demonstrated how the intervention of the state in economic and social matters reached a peak during the Great War (1914–1918). Sport and athletes are also affected by this long-standing trend and by the interventionist context of the first half of the 20th century. The organisation of sport makes its appearance in France towards the end of the 19th century with Olympism and the institutionalisation of competitive sports. The creation of federations and unions of clubs results from the need to organise games or club meetings based on common and consistent regulatory frameworks (Defrance, 1995). Various committees and leagues are established, in an effort to promote physical and sports activities, essentially in the context of high schools, colleges and after-school clubs. Indirectly, these initiatives also aim, for parts of the economical and socio-political elites of the time, to support the youth.

The French sports scene is occupied by three main organisations at the time: *the Union des sociétés de gymnastique de France* (UGSF), the Union des sociétés françaises de sports athlétiques (USFSA) and the patronages of the Fédération gymnastique et sportive des patronages de France. The USFSA was established in 1887 under the initiative of athletes from the social elite. Baron Pierre de Coubertin, a young Anglophile aristocrat and pioneering advocate of educational sport, will be its Secretary General until 1891. The Union will play a major role both as an organisation centre and a think-tank. In the wake of WWI (1919–1920), the USFSA is divided into several specialised sports associations. The football division is the first to leave with the creation of the FFF on 7 April 1919. The Popular Front shows some interest in developing grassroots sport. However, the Vichy French State was be the first to establish a legal framework with the Sports Charter of December 1940.

In France, sport is also organised according to the importance the various heads of the government give it, be they Ministers, Ministers' Deputies, State Secretaries, or High Commissioners, as was the case of Maurice Herzog in 1958.

It is not until Léon Blum's government, on 4 June 1936, that a Deputy State Secretary for Leisure and Sports is appointed for the first time (Léo Lagrange).

Up until 1940, the French sports movement was an almost autonomous entity, without regulations or structure. In 1940, the French state partakes for the first time in the organisation and operation of sport through laws and regulations voted by the Parliament. Since then, numerous bills have been passed, allowing sports institutions to adapt to their social context.

The first of these bills is the law of 20 December 1940, also called 'Sports Charter'. The government led by Marshal Pétain wanted to exercise control over the national federations, in a sort of nationalisation that no longer accounted for the freedom of association outlined in the law of 1 July 1901. The ruling of 2 October 1940, called the 'Ruling of Algiers', then repeals the law of 20 December 1940, by restoring the law of 1 July 1901 in its entirety, thereby giving back the sports movement its lost autonomy and independence. Associations enjoy a factual independence (law of 1 July 1901), yet are under the control of the state, which subsidises them. The ruling of 28 August 1945 outlines the general conditions for the organisation and development of sport in France: it is the state's exclusive responsibility – via its Minister in charge of sport – to organise competitions and carry out the selection of athletes (individuals and teams), although the state delegates its authority to federations so that they organise competitions on its behalf. The state nevertheless intervenes in sports administration matters (statutory rules, geographical territories of leagues and committees, nature of the activities).

This ruling institutes the state monopoly over the issuing of national titles and the formation of French national teams. This monopoly is simultaneously delegated to federations that have yet to include mandatory provisions in their statutes. These new concepts of authorisation and delegation of authority set out the new foundations of the relations between the state and French sport. The current organisation of sport is a legacy of the French sports model established in the wake of WWII.

The nation's urgent need of reconstruction yet overshadows the state's interest in sport until 1960, when the under-performance of French athletes at the Rome Olympic Games (no gold medal, 25th in the ranking of nations) results in a rude awakening.

The welfare state in support of the planning of sport

The 1960s mark a turning point in the history of French sport and have shaped its originality on the European stage.

In 1958, General De Gaulle becomes President of the Republic. He wants France to regain a certain power and greatness on the international stage. To do so, the training of athletes, and especially high-level athletes, must be promoted. Sports performances and international competitions are widely used for diplomatic purposes and to assert a nation's superiority over the other. This is all the more true in the Cold War context. General De Gaulle entrusts Maurice Herzog, a prestigious mountaineer whose achievements include the ascent of the Annapurna, with the mission of putting French sport back onto the right tracks.

A series of three nationwide programme laws enables France to catch up in terms of national sports facilities. From then on, no school is to be built without both outdoor and indoor sports facilities. As early as 1960, the state creates a corps of technicians specialised in sports competitions (sports technical advisers and national technical directors who are at the disposal of each and every state-approved federation). Dedicated to taking a bottom-up approach to sport, they represent the agents of French sports policy with a mission to put France back up to its due rank. A law of 1963 rules the trade of physical educator and establishes national sports instructors' certificates (BEES), leading to the creation in 1972 of a national certificate in three stages for each sport specialty. This is a first in Europe, where professional sports instructors have to pass a state degree.

May 1968 also affected the organisation of sport in France. In its effort to promote international competition, the state has overlooked a great portion of the youth who aspire to practise non-competitive leisure physical activities. Besides, municipalities are best positioned to develop a sports policy that fits the territorial specificities and inhabitants' aspirations, with a view to making sport accessible to all. However, instead of following these cultural trends, the sports law of 1975 is to confirm the role of the state, while the latter withdraws its financial support from 1970 onwards. The law of 29 October 1975, called 'Mazeaud', maintains the role of the state and Ministry of Sports with regards to the organisation of sport in France. A gap can be observed between state-controlled, high-level competitive sport and leisure or maintenance sport, which are increasingly caught in a vice, between local authorities and the market.

Between public service and the sports market: the evolution of sport in France since the 1980s

Law Mazeaud is replaced in 1984 by a new text that establishes a public service for physical and sport activities, at once delegated to the sports movement. The law of 16 July 1984, called 'Avice' law (named after the Minister of Sports) updates the principles of organisation and development of physical and sporting activities in the context of the transformation of sport in France. It brings innovations, namely by taking into account the separation between the two ministries that used to work together up to that point (the Ministry of National Education for physical education and the Ministry of Youth and Sports for sport), as well as the French law on decentralisation. The law on decentralisation confers new sports competences to local authorities, such as the construction, operation and maintenance of sports facilities for municipalities.

Since the 1990s, sports policies fall within inter-ministerial action (City, Employment, Solidarity, Defence, Education, Interior, Health): intervention in suburbs, sport-employment plan, disability sport, fight against obesity. As for sport of the highest level, faced with the financial power of the media, advertisers, and professional leagues, the state is limited to a regulatory role: safety regulation in sports arenas, stock exchange listing of professional clubs, public-private partnerships for the construction of large stadiums and arenas, authorisation of online sports betting.

Yannick Noah's victory at Roland-Garros in 1983, together with Platini and his teammates at the Euro 1984 football championship, paved the way for the concept of 'winning France'. Many others will ensue, including David Douillet's world and Olympic gold medals in 1996 and 2000, the 1998 football World Cup won by the 'Bleus', Amélie Mauresmo's world leadership in tennis or Laure Manuadou's in swimming from 2004 to 2007, or the triple World, Olympic and European titles of the 'Experts' in handball between 2008 and 2010. A kind of partnership is gradually established with regards to the sharing of responsibilities, positioning France at the crossroads between liberal sport and state sport (public service).

The law of 13 July 1992, called 'Bredin' law, partly amends the 'Avice' law so as to account for the professionalisation of sport and adapt the sports trades to the evolution and diversity of sports practices, as well as to ensure the safety of spectators during sports events (the Furiani and Heysel incidents). The law of 6 July 2000, called 'Buffet law', also amends the law of 16 July 1984, by specifying that all stakeholders (be they public, non-market or market private ones) contribute to the promotion and development of physical and sports activities.

The law of 1 August 2003, called 'Lamour law', makes amendments regarding the supervision of professional sport, allowing clubs to own their brands and giving them audiovisual exploitation rights. The law of 1 February 2012 for the improvement of sports ethics and athletes' rights includes several mechanisms to fight against the deviations sport is confronted with (supporters' violence, doping, fixed competitions, etc.). Finally, the law of 1 March 2017 aims to ensure sports ethics are adhered to and to fight against the fixing of professional sports competitions, to improve the competitiveness of professional clubs and the professionalisation of their stakeholders, but also to promote the development and media coverage of women's sport.

Today, the legal framework of the French organisation of sport is determined by three legal sources:

- the law of 1 July 1901 on associations (called Waldeck-Rousseau Law), which is the common law legal document for associations.
- the French and European common law documents, which constitute the set of legal rules that are to be applied to every situation that is not subjected to

specific or particular rules. For instance, the application of the French public community law for the construction of sports facilities, the Public Health Code for the safety on bathing sites (1951, 1978, 1981), the employment code for sports employment; the application of the Bosman ruling in the Member States of the European Union, in compliance with the regulations for the free movement of workers of the Rome Treaty.
- the Sport's Code, ratified in 2006–2007, the legal part of which largely takes the provisions of the 1984 Avice law[1] on sport, as well as all the amendments that have been voted on ever since.

The Sport's Code allows for the gathering within a single document of all the legal and regulatory documents on sports activities that were scattered among various sources up to that point. The legal and regulatory parts, together with a 'decree' part, are now included in the Sport's Code.

It mainly contains the provisions included in the amended law of 16 July 1984 on the organisation and promotion of physical and sports activities and the provisions included in the Education Code and Public Health Code. Also, Article 1 is a reminder that

> physical and sport activities are key components of education, culture, integration and social life. They contribute to fighting school drop-out and reducing social and cultural inequalities, as well as improving health. The promotion and development of physical and sport activities for all, especially for people with a disability, are of public interest. The equal access of men and women to sport activities, of all kinds, is of public interest.

The key sports stakeholders in France

As demonstrated above, two key stakeholders have been sharing the responsibility of organising sport in France for over 50 years: state services and the sports movement, the latter being itself structured on the federal system that is specific to each sport and its shared representation, through the French National Olympic and Sports Committee. Since the 1980s, two other key stakeholders have been intervening in sports affairs: local authorities (especially municipalities) and companies.

As in every complex organisation, these key stakeholders work together while competing for their own interests. These can be gathered into three socio-economic sectors:

- the *non-market private sports sector* (also called 'non-profit sector') includes a multitude of associations and federations governed by two legal frameworks: the law of 1901 on the French associative status and the laws on sport included in the Sport's Code.
- the *market private sports sector* includes a great variety of *companies* whose main activity is either to specifically provide sports services or sports counselling, manufacture of sports goods, or companies whose

main activity is unrelated to sport, although they use sports activities as flagship services (for example a hotel proposing fitness or aquafit sessions to its clients).
- the *public sector* essentially comprises *state administrations* and *territorial administrations*. These organisations can have different legal statuses (central administration, devolved services or decentralised administration) and various geographical and administrative situations. Their mission is to control, run and/or supervise physical and sports activities from a public service approach. Given both by their line ministry (mainly the Ministry of Youth and Sports, the department of social cohesion and health, and the Ministry of National Education) and the national or local sports policies, their missions are carried out by services and their officials: 'external services' of the Ministry of Youth and Sports (local and regional offices of the Ministry of Sports), secondary schools (in the case of compulsory Physical and Sport Education, but also voluntary sport), university services for physical and sports activities proposed to university students, regional, departmental, intercommunal and municipal services.

The state

In France, sport is a public service mission. Sports activity is a public activity serving the public interest, as determined and defined by the national collective (Art. 1 of the law of 16 July 1984). Therefore, everyone should be able to enjoy this activity as a user. In the interests of equal treatment, everyone should be provided with the same service, either by the state or a local authority. The cost of this service should be modest (related to the real cost) in order to ensure (in principle) that it is accessible to all. If the public service of the state or local authority cannot provide the activity, then it this one can be delegated to a market or non-market private entity, yet under the control and supervision of the public service. Such is the case in France for competitive sports activities, the organisation of which is delegated to sports federations. For example, the French state, via the Ministry of Youth and Sports, delegates the organisation of football and its competitions to the French Football Federation, which organises football in France on behalf of the state. The same applies for athletics, judo, volley-ball, etc.

The national sports policy is presently structured around four components: the development of sport for all, especially for people who have little access to sport practices; the organisation of high-level sport; prevention through sport, the protection of athletes and fight against abuses such as doping, cheating, violence, racism and discriminations; the promotion of sports trades and the development of sports employment.

In order to implement these policies, the ministry in charge of sport relies on a central administration (the Ministry of Sports) and national or regional public institutions. This network comprises the National Institute for Sports, Expertise and Performance (INSEP), based in Paris, 17 Centres for Resources and Expertise of Sport Performance (CREPS) at the regional level, and offices in charge of sport, youth and social cohesion across regions (one office per region). It also incorporates 1,600 agents (CTS) whose task is to provide federations with technical counselling in sport, while around 800 sports teachers and sports development counsellors (CAS), working in regional and departmental offices, operate across territories, especially in support of sports associations, with a view to promoting sport for all. These stakeholders work together with local authorities such as regions and departments.

Besides its central administration in Paris and its regional offices, the Ministry of Sports also established a National Centre for the Development of Sport (CNDS) in 2006. This centre is a public institution placed under the authority of the Ministry of Sports, which has taken over from the National Fund for the Development of Sport (FNDS). Its missions are to promote the development of sports practice among all audiences, contribute to land use planning and support the major international events taking place in France.

With a halved overall budget, its missions were redirected in 2018 towards social and environmental innovation through sport, the accessibility of sport to all audiences, and a greater support to deficient territories (Priority Neighbourhood as defined by the City policy, rural areas, French Overseas Territories). The CNDS allocates equipment grants to local authorities, their groups, authorised sports associations, and public interest associations and groups operating in the field of physical and sports activities. The Minister of Sports has declared that she wanted to devote 50% of the CNDS budget to priority neighbourhoods, especially to promote women's sports practice.

With the 2024 Paris Olympic Games approaching, the French government has opted for a shift in its sports policy, by gradually withdrawing from its control over sport in France. In this perspective, the Minister of Sports has announced the suppression of the CNDS and the creation in 2019 of an agency with a view to fund and support high-performance sport and develop sports practices. It will gather the four key French sport stakeholders (the state, the sport movement, local authorities and companies) to determine a common strategy and coordinate operations in the French territory.

The creation of this agency marks the gradual end of the state's predominance in sport policy-making in France. This new organisation will comprise two hubs: one focuses on high performance with the upcoming Olympic Games, while the other focuses on the development of sport for all, everywhere and throughout people's lives along two lines: federations (and clubs) and the main public policies such as health-sport, corporate sport, sport as social remediation or the fight against discriminations in sport. The agency is also dedicated to supporting the stakeholder-initiated projects across territories.

The sports movement

The sports movement gathers licence-holders, volunteers and the sport associations affiliated with the French sport federations, themselves part of the French National Olympic and Sports Committee (CNOSF).

The CNOSF was created in 1972 as a result of the merging of the French Olympic Committee and the French National Sports Committee. It aims at promoting the fundamental principles and core values of Olympism, as well as gathering the French sports federations. It also has numerous powers: it organises and manages the French delegation at the Olympics and competitions held by the IOC. It also represents the Olympic movement in France and is the sole agent of the French sports movement at international level.

Federations are private-law groups with a public service mission. This means that the state delegates some of its authority to these federations, so that they can administer and organise a sport. In the case of football, the FFF has created both a professional football league and an amateur football league at national, regional and departmental levels, as we will see further down. The support of the state takes the form of subsidies and the paying of technical sports counsellors (national technical directors, national trainers, regional technical counsellors). There are currently 120 sports federations in France. Some highly depend on the state (subsidies and CTS), like the FFA (athletics), while others such as the FFF (football) are highly independent from the state. The Sport's Code also makes a distinction between two kinds of federations: the authorised ones, which 'contribute to the implementation of a public service mission pertaining to the development and democratization of physical activities', and the delegated ones, such as the FFF, which have the power to organise sports competitions and define the technical and administrative rules, among other things.

The authorised federations take part in the implementation of a public service mission. In this respect, they are responsible for promoting education through PSAs, developing and organising these activities, training and improving their volunteer executives, issuing licences and federal titles. They are state-controlled and have to adopt statutes including certain mandatory provisions, as well as a disciplinary rule in compliance with model regulations.

As for the delegated federations, they are directly responsible for implementing a public service mission and organising various sports activities from a social, educational and corporatist perspective. To this day, over 70 federations are delegatees (for example, the Fédération Sportive et Gymnique du Travail – FSGT; the Union Française des Œuvres Laïques et de l'Education Physique – UFOLEP; the fédération française handisport – FFH; the fédération du sport adapté).

Local authorities

Local authorities are French administrative structures, distinct from the state's administration, which take charge of the interests of a particular territory's population: regions, departments, intercommunal bodies (community of municipalities or metropolis) and municipalities.

The local authorities' commitment to sport, and particularly to sport for all and physical education, dates back to the 1930s. Their activity has mainly consisted in funding communal infrastructures and subsidising clubs. The decentralisation laws of the early 1980s have given them more authority to develop local policies as part of their general 'jurisdiction clause': even if municipalities are responsible for the construction, operation and maintenance of sports facilities, sport remains an optional jurisdiction at the discretion of each authority. A local authority (municipality, department or region) may also choose to create a local sport public service, if deemed necessary to meet the population's needs. In other words, sports policies fall within global ones, with their own purposes and issues. Each local authority is free to engage in this area depending on its executives' policy choices. However, it should be noted that local authorities contribute 30% of the overall sport expenditure. They own 80% of sports facilities. In addition to providing clubs and associations with free access to sports facilities, municipalities take on most of the government's efforts.

Today, local sports policies differ widely from one city to another. This disparity results from the lack of regulations requiring the communities' intervention in the area of physical and sports activities.

However, they spend over €10 billion each year on local sports policies and sports facilities. Their task is to build, operate and make sports facilities available; support local stakeholders (clubs) through subsidies or the organisation of sports events, for instance; supervise sports practices in schools or clubs, for example. They have been representing a significant portion of public expenditure in sport since the 1980s. The majority of public sports expenditure falls to municipalities: the municipalities' expenditure accounts for 66% of the overall expenditure.

In the future, the actions of the French local authorities in the area of sport should be the object of 'gradual specialisations' decided during the sport conferences held in each region, in order to define a local sports project per region.

Table 8.1 Sports competences of French local authorities

Local authorities	Sports competences
Region	High-level sports support, support to the construction of sports facilities, land use planning for tourism
Department	Promotion of grassroots sports practice, support to the construction of sports facilities, organisation of areas and paths for outdoor sports
Intercommunality (community of municipalities, metropolises)	Construction of large intercommunal sports facilities (swimming pools, stadiums), shared management of public sport services
Municipality	Construction of sports facilities, support to local sport associations

Private companies

In the area of sport, companies play the role of sports event organisers, investors, advertisers or sponsors.

To retain customers and create groups, some sporting goods companies (such as Décathlon) make physical activity/sports fields available for free in the vicinity of their stores. These are open to all citizens and clubs, and some even provide the services of supervisory staff. In the same way, many gyms are opening and diversifying their range of services.

The world of work (companies, associations, administrations) has long been a place where physical activities were practised, namely *via* inter-company competitions. Works councils (CE) play a significant role in this area for companies with at least 50 employees, offering them sports activities in the workplace or in the vicinity, subsidising their employees' activities, for instance by facilitating their employees' attendance at sports events. Large companies now benefit from a lever in the form of corporate social responsibility (CSR), which refers to the set of actions taken by companies to comply with the principles of sustainable development. *Via* the RSE, these companies are able to provide a sport activity offer adapted to all, with a view to improving health. In France, among the people aged 15 or older who declare that they practise a sport at least once a week (a bit less than half of the people from this age group), 17% declare that they do so in their workplace (Gleizes, Pénicaud, 2017).

The sports press, sports communication and counselling agencies, sports medicine, and television channels are also more or less involved in the sports sector. Despite their diversity, it is possible to gather these organisations together in three main categories:

Companies providing sports services

There are two kinds of companies providing sports services, depending on how specialised their sports offer is: the first kind comprises companies whose main activity consists in providing physical and sports activities (fitness clubs, martial arts centres, dance schools, squash centres, thalassotherapy centres, nautical stadiums, agencies proposing sports stays or adventures, etc.); the second kind comprises companies that do not belong to the sports sector, yet organise activities or provide spaces to practise sports (as a flagship service) in order to attract or retain customers (spa resorts, hotels, holiday clubs, etc.).

Companies organising sports events

This category includes both professional clubs (particularly football and basketball clubs) and companies specialised in the organisation of sports-related shows (for example, the various 'sport shows' held at Pierre-Mauroy stadium or certain tennis tournaments). Since 2000, professional clubs (essentially football clubs) have a company status (limited company under ordinary law)

Companies manufacturing and distributing sporting goods

According to the INSEE, the number of sports and leisure stores has doubled over the last 25 years. Their turnover has increased by 25% in five years. Whether they are companies and large stores specialising in distribution and manufacturing, or professional football clubs selling derivative products ('merchandising'), all of these entities belong to the sports and leisure retail sector. Adidas France (Strasbourg), Décathlon (Villeneuve d'Ascq), Go Sport (Sassenage), Skis Rossignol SA (Voiron), Lafuma SA (Anneyron), Aigle International (Paris) are the main manufacturing and distribution companies based in France.

Sport in France, between organisation and self-organisation

Sport in France is typified by a paradox: today, there is an unprecedented number of private, associative or public structures in charge of organising sport than ever (clubs, associations, fitness centres) yet sport is more than ever practised outside those structures. Indeed, only a proportion of athletes are concerned by the organisation of sport in France, for even if sport represents the largest associative activity in France, only a minority of athletes are members of sports clubs.

According to the latest statistics (Gleizes, Pénicaud, 2017), 50% of French people declare that they practise a physical activity on a regular basis, with only 42% of them practising more than once a week. Moreover, only 20% of French people aged 15 or older practise a physical or sport activity at least once a week in a club.

Sport represents 317,200 associations, i.e. 24% of all French associations (a stable ratio over the last 10 years). France boasts around 13 million members of sports clubs, 160,000 associations and 1 million sports volunteers.

Between 2000 and 2015, the number of sports memberships has increased from 13.7 million to 16 million. The difference between the number of members (13 million) and the number of memberships (16 million) can be explained by multiple practices: numerous members, especially men, hold two or even three sports licences. Club members are mostly young people. In 2015, 17% of women having practised a regular physical or sports activity over the past 12 months, in a club or association, had participated in a sports competition.

Leisure walking is by far the most practised physical activity in France (53% of the French population), ahead of leisure swimming (24%) and leisure cycling (22%). Football is the most practised associative activity in France, ahead of tennis and horse-riding.

As for sports facilities, there were 270,000 on 1 July 2016, that is to say a 1% increase from 2014. While there is a slight decrease in the construction of playing fields (football and rugby, for instance) and tennis courts, the number of equestrian facilities and urban facilities designed for physical and health-sport activities is on the rise.

Conclusion

Unlike other Member States of the European Union, sport in France is considered as a public service and its organisation is closely linked to the state. However, since the 1980s, this model has evolved and the French state has been withdrawing, as a result of the development of a private sports market, of the decentralisation and of the new demand of audiences moving away from competitive sport to practising 'health-sport' and open-air recreational sports within cities (namely, walking and cycling in urban areas).

Despite advances, it must be noted that the organisation of sport remains male-dominated. While two-thirds of French licence-holders are men, men and women are not given the same opportunities to access executive positions in sports clubs and federations (only 6% of presidents of federations are women) or sports employment (only 15% of French sports instructor's certificate holders are women). The analysis of the positions occupied by women in sports organisations demonstrates a persistent gender division, but also a male domination. Despite recent voluntarist policies against gender discrimination, sports practices, responsibilities and employment are still determined by a male-centred vision of the world of sport organisation.

Note

1 Edvige Avice was the Minister for Sport under François Mittérand in 1984.

Bibliography

Bayeux, P., 2013, *Le sport et les collectivités territoriales*. Paris: PUF.
Callède, J.-P., 2000, *Les politiques sportives en France. Éléments de sociologie historique*. Paris: Economica.
Elias, N., 1970, *Was ist Soziologie?* München: Juventa. (Published in English as *What is Sociology?*, London: Hutchinson, 1978).
Defrance, J., 1995, *Sociologie du sport*. Paris: La Découverte.
Gasparini, W., 2003, *L'organisation sportive*. Paris: Revue EPS.
Gasparini, W., 2000, *Sociologie de l'organisation sportive*. Paris: La Découverte.
Gasparini, W., Vieille Marchiset, G., 2008, *Le sport dans les quartiers. Pratiques sociales et politiques publiques*. Paris: PUF.
Gasparini, W. (ed.), 2007, *L'institutionnalisation des pratiques sportives et de loisir*. Paris: Le Manuscrit.
Gasparini, W., 2007, 'Domination masculine et division sexuelle du travail dans les organisations sportives' in Causer, Pferfferkorn, Woehl (eds), *Métiers, identités professionnelles et genre*. Paris: L'Harmattan.
Gleizes, F., Pénicaud, É., 2017, Pratiques physiques ou sportives des femmes et des hommes. *INSEE Premières*, no. 1673.
Ministère des sports, 2017, *Les chiffres-clés du sport en France*. Paris. Retrieved from www.sports.gouv.fr/accueil-du-site/a-la-une/article/Les-chiffres-cles-du-sport-2017.

9 Sport and welfare in Britain

Ivan Waddington

Sport and welfare in Britain: general considerations

Within Britain sport has never been formally considered as part of the welfare state. However, some writers have suggested that, since the 1970s, sport has been elevated to near equivalence with the constituent elements of the welfare state. Coalter has noted that from the 1970s one can identify the development of what might be called 'recreational welfare', with a 1975 government White Paper, *Sport and Recreation*, defining recreational facilities as 'part of the general fabric of the social services' (cited in Coalter, 2007: 10).

Since that time, those who have argued for governmental support for sports development have sought to locate their arguments within the context of the contribution which, it is claimed, sport can make to public welfare, broadly defined. The development of this policy of 'sport for good' (Coalter, 2007: 8–24) was particularly significant after the election of the Labour government in 1997, which placed sport more centrally within the spectrum of social policy, largely because of the wider social benefits which, it was claimed, were associated with sporting participation.

The claimed external benefits of sport are many and varied and include improved health, both physical and mental; improved psychological well-being via improved self-esteem/confidence; reducing social exclusion and breaking down barriers of class, ethnicity and gender; reducing crime, delinquency and drug use among young people; fostering community integration and renewal; fostering national identity and prestige; and personal development through benefits such as developing tolerance, co-operation, respect, trustworthiness and the development of social skills.

These are ambitious claims. Donnelly and Harvey (1996: 5) have noted, tongue-in-cheek, that 'the numerous, almost miraculous claims for the benefits of physical activity lead one to wonder why it has not been patented by an innovative company'; more seriously, they point out that the disparate nature of these claims should serve as a warning against a too easy and uncritical acceptance of these claims and that the context of the claims needs to be examined carefully.

In a wide-ranging review of different kinds of 'sport for good' schemes, including sport and social regeneration, sport-in-development, sport and educational performance and sport and crime programmes, Coalter (2007: 172–3) has noted 'the limitations of much research evidence for the wider impacts of sport ... In most areas there is an increasing acknowledgement of such limitations and the associated lack of robust evidence for many of the claims about sport which underpin sports-related policy'. In a separate systematic analysis of sport-for-development schemes in Africa and elsewhere, Coalter (2013a: 183) notes that 'despite certain tendencies in the data, there was no clear and systematic "sport-for-development" effect' and he argues that academics 'need to bring a degree of informed scepticism to the claims of sport-for-development' (Coalter, 2013a: 185).

A systematic analysis of sport and crime prevention schemes for young people by Nichols (2007: 199) similarly noted that there is 'limited evidence' that sport diverts young people away from crime and 'little evidence that sport offered a direct alternative to a sense of excitement derived from crime' (Nichols, 2007: 204). The case studies also 'did not reveal particular boosts to self-esteem from sports participation' and there was 'little evidence that sport itself offered new peers and that these peers were any less likely to be involved in offending'. Nichols noted that there may be some benefits associated with participation in some sports schemes, but these benefits may be no greater than in schemes built around car or motor bike maintenance, fishing or art work (Nichols, 2007: 199–202).

Waddington and Smith (2004) also reviewed a number of sport and crime prevention schemes and concluded that 'there is little evidence of the effectiveness of such schemes in reducing crime or drug use'. They added:

> A major problem in this regard is that relatively few "sport in the community schemes" have built in techniques for monitoring their impact on levels of crime or drug use: as a result, it is difficult to be sure about what impact, if any, they have on rates of crime and drug use. Moreover, the absence of any clearly articulated theoretical rationale for these schemes means that, even where success is claimed, it is unclear what specific aspects of the schemes account for that claimed success. (Waddington and Smith, 2004: 294)

A recurring theme in many academic studies of sport in the community schemes is the lack of systematic monitoring of the impact of such schemes, and there is also substantial agreement about the reasons for this. Numerous authors (Dunning and Waddington, 2003; Coalter 2007, 2013a, 2014; Nichols, 2007; Waddington, 2000; Waddington and Smith, 2004) have all pointed out the need, as Nichols (2007: 198) has put it, to understand 'the value judgements wrapped up in the use of sport'. In this connection, Dunning and Waddington 2003: 359) have argued that:

> one possible reason for the absence of systematic monitoring may be that such schemes are, all too often, premised not on a relatively detached

analysis of the characteristics of sporting culture but on a one-sided perception of sport which amounts almost to a statement of faith in its effectiveness to achieve desired social outcomes.

Coalter (2014: 163) has similarly noted that:

> A fundamental problem in undertaking research in sport-for-development is that the policy area is dominated by a mixture of interest groups, sports evangelists and conceptual entrepreneurs ... who offer an apparent economy of remedies to deep-rooted problems via focusing on a single concept – "sport". This produces a potent mixture of self-interest, faith and a general lack of intellectual rigour ... believers talk to believers, minimise exposure to ideas that run contrary to their own beliefs and adopt a selective perception of data and information by ignoring less than supportive research findings.

And, perhaps most worryingly, Coalter adds elsewhere (Coalter 2013a: 184) that 'some academics also seem to work within the normative and affective perspectives of the evangelists'.

In order to illustrate these problems it may be useful briefly to examine what is perhaps the most frequently claimed benefit of sports participation: improved health. The idea that sport is good for health is very widely and generally uncritically accepted in many societies. In Britain, the idea that sport is health-enhancing is one which is frequently stressed by those involved in promoting sport; a typical example is the claim by Sport England (2008: 8) that sport can 'promote better health and well-being for all'. In its policy document, *Sporting Future*, the British government similarly claimed that 'evidence for sport's impact on physical and mental health ... is well established' (Department for Culture, Media and Sport [DCMS], 2015: 72). How valid are such claims?

In Britain, the Department of Health (2009, 2011) and Public Health England (2014) have repeatedly emphasised that regular physical activity contributes to the prevention and reduction of non-communicable diseases including cardiovascular and especially coronary heart disease, high blood pressure, some cancers, obesity, liver disease, type 2 diabetes, and that it helps to control body weight and improves bone health, while the Academy of Royal Medical Colleges (2015:2) has described physical activity as one of the 'best buys' in public health.

At first glance, such studies might seem to suggest that the health-based arguments in favour of sport and exercise are overwhelming. However, it is important to note that almost all of those studies which are cited to support the claim that sport is good for health relate *not* to sport but to physical activity or exercise. But, as has been pointed out elsewhere (Waddington, Malcolm and Green, 1977; Waddington, 2000; 2010; Waddington and Smith, 2018), sport and exercise are *not* the same thing. Physical activity or exercise might involve walking or cycling to work, dancing, gardening or walking upstairs rather than taking the elevator. None of these are sport. There are several important differences between sport and physical activity or exercise, perhaps the most important being that while competition is not central to most forms of physical activity, sport, in contrast, is inherently competitive. The high level of competitiveness of modern sport means that, unlike most people who take part in non-competitive physical activities, those who play sport are, especially at the elite level, frequently subject to strong constraints to 'play hurt', that is, to continue playing while injured 'for the good of the team' with all the associated health risks that this entails (Roderick et al. 2000; Malcolm, 2017).

It is also important to remember that many sports – and not just the obvious combat sports – are mock battles in which aggression and the use of physical violence are central characteristics. In this context, we might note that many sports have, in present-day societies, become enclaves for the expression of physical violence, not in the form of unlicensed or uncontrolled violence, but in the form of socially sanctioned violence as expressed in violently aggressive 'body contact'; indeed, in the relatively highly pacified societies of the modern West, sport is for many people the *only* activity in which they are regularly involved in aggressive physical contact with others. The close association between sport, aggression and violence has long been noted by many authors (Elias and Dunning, 1986; Dunning and Sheard, 2005; Messner, 1990). Writing of professional sport, Young (1993: 373) noted:

> By any measure, professional sport is a violent and hazardous workplace, replete with its own unique forms of "industrial disease". No other single milieu, including the risky and labor-intensive settings of miners, oil drillers, or construction site workers, can compare with the routine injuries of team sports such as football, ice-hockey, soccer, rugby and the like.

But it is not just elite sport which involves health risks for, even at the local level, sport participation involves a high cost in terms of injuries. Community studies in Europe suggest that every sixth unintentional injury is associated with leisure-time physical activity, mainly sports, and that 50% of people participating in team sports sustain one or more injuries over a season (Hardman and Stensel, 2009: 250). Large scale, national studies of sports injuries are rare, but the only national study in Britain estimated that in England and Wales there are 19.3 million new injuries and a further 10.4 million recurrent injuries each year, with sports injuries causing the loss of 11.5 million working days each year (Nichol et al. 1993, 1995).

In 2003, the editor of *Physician and Sportsmedicine* referred to 'the increased physical, financial and emotional costs of injuries resulting from sports' and to the 'growing body of evidence documenting the enormousness of the sports injury burden'. He added: 'exercise … clearly promotes health, but competitive sports often may not. We need to own up to that fact, and shape our practices to address it' (Matheson, 2003: 2). Two years later he returned to the same theme, arguing that physicians should 'emphasize, for our patients' sake, the difference between sport and exercise. Sports value winning and dominating, while exercise favours health and enjoyment' (Matheson, 2005: 2). While it is clear that there is overwhelming evidence that regular exercise has considerable health benefits, the often taken-for-granted relationship between sport and health is much more problematic.

Having examined some general aspects of the relationship between sport and welfare, the two following sections focus on the central importance of a key intervening variable – social inequality – in relation, firstly, to welfare and, secondly, participation in sport.

Social inequality and welfare

The publication of *The Spirit Level: Why Equality is Better for Everyone* (Wilkinson and Pickett, 2010) was a landmark in our understanding of the relationship between social inequality and welfare. Research by sociologists, epidemiologists, educationalists and criminologists has, of course, long since indicated that social inequality is closely related to a variety of social problems, including illness and reduced life chances, educational underperformance and crime. But what gave *The Spirit Level* its landmark status was, firstly, the huge mass of data which the authors gathered on a variety of welfare issues and inequality in relatively affluent countries and, secondly, the way in which these data were theorised into a compelling argument about the relationship between inequality and welfare.

Wilkinson and Pickett (2010: 5) recognise that for 'thousands of years the best way of improving the quality of human life was to raise material living standards'. However, they note that economic growth, 'for so long the great engine of progress, has, in the rich countries, largely finished its work', for in affluent societies, measures of well-being have ceased to rise with economic growth. Among more affluent countries, getting richer does very little for health and welfare, for, as Marmot has noted, 'other things are more important' (Marmot, 2018:39). Central among these 'other things' is the degree of inequality within the society.

Wilkinson and Pickett compared data on inequality and welfare from a large number of relatively affluent societies, including 14 Member States of the European Union and several countries outside the European Union, among them Japan, Norway, Canada, Switzerland, Israel, New Zealand, Australia and the USA. As a measure of inequality they used the ratio of the income received by the top to the bottom 20% of the population within each country, a measure which is provided independently by the United Nations. Among the most unequal societies were the USA, Portugal and the UK, in all of which the richest 20% received between seven and ten times as much as the bottom 20%. The least unequal societies were Japan and the Scandinavian countries Finland, Norway, Sweden and Denmark, in all of which the top 20% receive around four times as much as the bottom 20% (Wilkinson and Pickett, 2010: 15–17).

Wilkinson and Pickett developed an Index of Health and Social Problems, based on an analysis of as many aspects of welfare for which there are reliable data; these include rates of mental illness (including drug and alcohol abuse), infant mortality, life expectancy, adult and child obesity, children's educational performance, teenage birth rates, homicide rates, rates of imprisonment, conflict between children (bullying, fighting etc.), and social mobility rates (Wilkinson and Pickett, 2018: 19). Their consistent finding, in relation to all these dimensions of welfare, is that how a country scores on the Index of Health and Social Problems is *not* related to how wealthy the country is, as measured by average Gross National Income per head, but *it is strongly related to the degree of inequality within the society*. Thus less wealthy countries with a relatively equal distribution of income have higher levels of welfare and fewer social problems than countries which are richer but more unequal. For example, the USA is one of the richest but also one of the most unequal countries, and it has consistently poor scores for almost all dimensions of welfare, including the very worst scores in the study for infant mortality rates, obesity, rates of mental illness, teenage birth rates, homicide rates, violent conflict between children and rates of imprisonment. Other countries with very high levels of inequality also scored badly on the overall index of welfare, whether they were very wealthy (e.g. the UK) or among the less affluent of European countries (e.g. Portugal). By contrast, the countries which consistently exhibited the fewest social problems and the highest levels of welfare were the Scandinavian countries and Japan, which were also the countries with the most egalitarian patterns of income distribution. In summary, the data in *The Spirit Level* showed that people living in societies with bigger income gaps between rich and poor are – independently of the wealth of the countries – much more likely to suffer from a range of health and social problems than those living in more equal societies. In a recent follow-up book, *The Inner Level* (2018), Wilkinson and Pickett documented in copious detail the relationship between inequality within a society and lower levels of stress and better mental illness and mental well-being.

It may be appropriate to examine in a little more detail, and specifically in relation to British data, the relationship between inequality and health because not only is health a key aspect of well-being but it is also an aspect of well-being which, as we noted earlier, is often claimed to have a close relationship with participation in sport. A past President of the World Medical Association, Sir Michael Marmot, has recently documented the health gap between rich and poor in Britain. He notes that the difference in life expectancy between rich and poor parts of Glasgow – and indeed, the difference in life expectancy between rich and poor parts of a single London borough, Westminster – is no less than 20 years (Marmot, 2018: 25). On the national level, life expectancy at birth in the most deprived areas is around 72 and in the least deprived areas, around 81. The social gradient in disability-free life expectancy (DFLE) – disability is defined as any limiting long-standing illness – is even steeper. DFLE in the most deprived communities is just 51 years whereas in the least deprived areas it is around 68 years. Marmot describes this as 'adding insult to injury: the more deprived people spend more of their shorter lives with "disability"' (Marmot, 2018: 27). Put succinctly, 'Inequalities in health arise from inequalities in society' (Marmot, 2018: 37).

Having briefly outlined the relationship between inequality and health, let us now turn to an examination of the relationship between inequality, as expressed in class, ethnicity and gender, and participation in sport and exercise.

Social inequality and participation in sport

Before discussing data on participation in sport, it should be noted that it is difficult to compare absolute levels of activity between different studies at different points in time, since different studies have used different criteria to define active participation (e.g. how many times/hours per week/per month) and different studies have also used different definitions of social class. However, this need not concern us too much here, for we are not concerned with whether the British population as a whole is becoming more active; rather, our concern is with gender, social class and ethnic differences within these studies.

In recent decades there has been a reduction in – though not an elimination of – the gender gap. A major study covering the period 2005–2009 indicated that 61% of men and 46% of women had taken part in sport in the previous 12 months (DCMS, 2011); the most recent data, for 2017/2018, found that although men were still more likely to take part in sport, the gap was much smaller, with 65% of men and 61% of women described as 'physically active' (Sport England, 2019a). However, these figures mask significant differences in the patterns of sport/exercise, with the bulk of the increase in women's participation being focused on indoor sports, especially swimming and keep fit/gym/aerobics, while men's participation is more widely spread across a range of activities. As the DCMS (2011: 14) report noted, 'Specific sports have their own sex profiles'.

Social class differentials in participation have changed little over the last 30 years. Data from 1990 indicate that 79% of professional workers and 71% of managerial workers had participated in at least one activity in the previous four weeks, compared with 55% of semi-skilled and 46% of unskilled manual workers (Sports Council, 1994). The DCMS study (2011) found that 63.7% of those in professional or managerial occupations participated in sport compared with 42.3% for those in semi-routine jobs. The most recent data from Sport England (2019a) indicate that large class differentials remain. 72% of those in professional and managerial occupations took part in sufficient sport/physical activity to be classified as 'active' compared with 54% of those in routine or semi-routine work and, significantly, the latter (33%) were twice as likely as the former (16%) to be classified as 'inactive'.

Moreover, just as specific sports have their own sex profile, so each sport has its class label. Coalter (2013b) has noted that, in a study in Scotland, of the 30 sports for which robust data were available, the two lowest social classes were under-represented, in relation to their proportion of the population, in 28 of the sports, the exceptions being fishing/angling and snooker/billiards/pool. By contrast, the two highest classes were over-represented in 22 sports, proportionately represented in seven and under-represented in just one – fishing/angling. These class labels serve as a useful reminder that those who take part in sport do so within the context of a wider society in which social class divisions remain important, and that the dynamics of class relations continue to privilege some groups and disadvantage others in the context of sporting activity.

Finally, it is clear that members of the non-white ethnic minority communities have patterns of participation in sport which differ significantly from those of the general population. A study of sports participation and ethnicity by Sport England (2000) found that, for ethnic minority groups overall, the participation rate in sport was 40% compared with a national average of 46%. For ethnic minority males the participation rate was 49% compared with a national average of 54%, while for ethnic minority females the rate was 32% compared with a national average for all women of 39%. Special concern was expressed about the low participation rates among the Black Caribbean (39%), Indian (39%) and especially the Pakistani (31%) and Bangladeshi (30%) populations. The most recent data from Sport England (2019a) indicate that the black and South Asian communities continue to have participation rates well below those of the general population.

How, then, do these data feed into our discussion about sport and welfare? This question is examined in the conclusion.

Conclusion

It was noted earlier that, although many claims have been made for the wider social benefits of sport, there is growing recognition by researchers that there is little systematic evidence to support most of those claims. However, as Coalter (2007: 173) has noted, the absence of robust supporting evidence does not constitute 'disproof' – i.e. that sport does not have wider benefits and he suggests that the Scottish legal verdict of 'not proven' is appropriate in relation to the claims of the wider social benefits of sport. This is an appropriate conclusion. Sport *may*, under certain circumstances, have wider benefits, though such claims should not be accepted at face value but should be carefully examined with an informed scepticism. This is, for example, the approach which underpinned the above analysis of the relationship between sport, exercise and health, in which it was argued that it is essential to differentiate between exercise and sport because they are different kinds of social activities and these differences give rise to significant differences in terms of the likely health consequences.

But if there are benefits associated with sport, it is clear that these benefits can only be generated insofar as people actually participate in sport. It is in this context that we need to revisit the data on participation. What, then, do these data tell us about the relationship between sport and welfare?

What is clear is that the complex network of interdependency centred on class, gender and ethnic relations locate people in relatively advantaged or disadvantaged positions, and that these positions of relative advantage and disadvantage relate to many areas of social life, including sport. The British data suggest that, though there are specific exceptions (e.g. black and ethnic minority people are more likely than white people to play cricket and basketball; see DCMS, 2011: 22), in general people in these disadvantaged groups – the working class, women and ethnic minorities – experience in relation to sport the same kind of limited access that they experience in relation to income, employment, housing and other goods and services. Commenting on the most recent data from the Sport England survey, the chief executive Tim Hollingsworth noted that 'stubborn inequalities remain' and he argued: 'It isn't right or fair that people on a low income, women and black and South Asian people are still less likely to be active' (Sport England, 2019b). Sporting opportunities within Britain remain unequally distributed and in this respect it might be argued that the organisation of sport mirrors, rather than challenges, patterns of inequality within the wider society. In this regard, the relationship between sport and welfare is problematic.

It may be appropriate to conclude by locating this discussion within the context of the analysis set out in *The Spirit Level*. As we saw earlier, Wilkinson and Pickett (2010) provide a plethora of data indicating that levels of welfare are strongly associated with the degree of inequality within a society. If this analysis is correct then it has important implications for sport; as Coalter (2013b: 16–18) has noted, 'it points to fundamental limitations on the ability of sports policy interventions ... to address social issues in any meaningful way' for the analysis in *The Spirit Level* suggests that problems such as crime, drug use, social cohesion and obesity 'are the price to be paid for such extreme and increasing levels of inequalities'. Moreover, even if sport does provide some degree of amelioration for some of these problems, this is likely to be very limited for, as Wilkinson and Pickett point out (2010: 26), 'our societies are endlessly re-creating these problems in each new generation'

Finally, and in the context of the analysis by Wilkinson and Pickett, it should be noted that a recent analysis of income distribution in the UK from 1961 to 2015 noted that from 1977 until 1991 there was a long sustained period of continually rising income inequality, with a further increase in income inequality between 1996 and 2009, in which year income inequality was higher than at any time since 1961 (Institute for Fiscal Studies, 2019). Given this degree of inequality, it would seem unlikely that sport could make a significant contribution to improving welfare in Britain.

Bibliography

Academy of Royal Medical Colleges (2015), *Exercise: The Miracle Cure and the Role of the Doctor in Promoting It*, London, Academy of Medical Royal Colleges.

Coalter, F. (2007), *A Wider Role for Sport: Who's Keeping the Score?*, London, Routledge.

Coalter, F. (2013a), *Sport for Development: What Game are We Playing?*, London, Routledge.
Coalter, F. (2013b), '"Game Plan" and 'The Spirit Level': the class ceiling and the limits of sports policy?', *International Journal of Sport Policy and Politics*, 5(1), 3–19.
Coalter, F. (2014), 'Researching sport-for-development: the need for scepticism', in A. Smith and I. Waddington (eds), *Doing Real World Research in Sports Studies*, London, Routledge, 163–178.
Department of Health (2009), *Be Active, Be Healthy: A Strategy to Get the Nation Moving Again*, London, Department of Health.
Department of Health (2011), *Start Active, Stay Active: A Report on Physical Activity for Health from the Four Home Countries' Chief Medical Officers*, London, Department of Health.
Department for Culture, Media and Sport (2011), *Adult Participation in Sport*, London, DCMS.
Department for Culture, Media and Sport (2015), *Sporting Future*, London, DCMS.
Donnelly, P. and Harvey, J. (1996), 'Overcoming systematic barriers to active living', Discussion paper prepared for Fitness Branch, Health Canada and Active Living Canada.
Dunning, E. and Sheard, K. (2005), *Barbarians, Gentlemen and Players* (2nd ed.), London, Routledge.
Dunning, E. and Waddington, I. 2003, 'Sport as a drug and drugs in sport: some exploratory comments', *International Review for the Sociology of Sport*, 38(3), 351–368.
Elias, N. and Dunning, E. (1986), *Quest for Excitement: Sport and Leisure in the Civilizing Process*, Oxford, Blackwell.
Hardman, A. and Stensel, D (2009), *Physical Activity and Health* (2nd ed.), London, Routledge.
Institute for Fiscal Studies (2019), *Living Standards, Poverty and Inequality in the UK: 2019*, London, IFS.
Malcolm, D. (2017), *Sport, Medicine and Health*, London, Routledge.
Marmot, M. (2018), *The Health Gap: the Challenge of an Unequal World*, London, Bloomsbury.
Matheson, G (2003), 'Sports: hazardous to your health?', *Physician and Sportsmedicine*, 31(2).
Matheson, G. (2005), 'Sports gone wild. Part 2: regaining proper perspective', *Physician and Sportsmedicine*, 33, 2.
Messner, M. (1990), 'When bodies are weapons: masculinity and violence in sport', *International Review for the Sociology of Sport*, 25, 203–218.
Nichol, J., Coleman P. and Williams, B. (1993), *Injuries in Sport and Exercise: Main Report*, London, Sports Council.
Nichol, J., Coleman P. and Williams, B. (1995), 'The epidemiology of sports and exercise related injury in the United Kingdom', *British Journal of Sports Medicine*, 29, 232–238.
Nichols, G. (2007), *Sport and Crime Reduction: the Role of Sports in Tackling Youth Crime*, London, Routledge.
Public Health England (2014), *Everybody Active, Every Day: An Evidence-based Approach to Physical Activity*, London, Public Health England.
Roderick, M., Waddington, I. and Parker, G. (2000), 'Playing hurt: managing injuries in English professional football', *International Review for the Sociology of Sport*, 35 (2), 165–180.

Sports Council (1994), *Trends in Sports Participation: Fact Sheet*, London, Sports Council.
Sport England (2000), *Sports Participation and Ethnicity in England*, London, Sports Council.
Sport England (2008), *Healthier Communities. Improving Health and Reducing Health Inequalities through Sport*, London, Sport England.
Sport England (2019a), *Active Lives Adult Survey November 17/18 Report*, London, Sport England.
Sport England (2019b), Record numbers more physically active. https:/www.sportengland.org/news-and-features/news/2019/april/11/record-numbers-of-people-in-england-are-getting-active/, accessed 19/8/2019.
Waddington, I. (2000), *Sport, Drugs and Health*, London, Spon.
Waddington, I. (2010), 'Attività fisica, movimento, sport e salute. Qual è il messaggio corretto per la salute pubblica?', La comunicazione per lo sport e la salute, *Sociologia e Politiche Sociali*, 13(2), 13–27.
Waddington, I., Malcolm, D. and Green, K. (1977), 'Sport, health and physical education: a reconsideration', *European Physical Education Review*, 3(2), 165–182.
Waddington, I. and Smith, A. (2004), 'Using 'sport in the community schemes' to tackle crime and drug use among young people: some policy issues and problems', *European Physical Education Review*, 10(3), 279–298.
Waddington, I. and Smith, A. (2018), 'Physical activity, sport and health: what is the appropriate public health message?' in G. Russo (ed.) *Charting the Wellness Society in Europe: Social Transformations in Sport, Health and Consumption*, Milan, FrancoAngeli, 35–49.
Wilkinson, R. and Pickett, K. (2010), *The Spirit Level: Why Equality is Better for Everyone*, London, Penguin Books.
Wilkinson, R. and Pickett, K. (2018), *The Inner Level: How More Equal Societies Reduce Stress, Restore Sanity and Improve Everyone's Well-Being*, London, Allen Lane.
Young, K. (1993), 'Violence, risk and liability in male sports culture', *Sociology of Sport Journal*, 10, 373–396.

10 Welfare and sports policies in contemporary Italy

Nicola R. Porro

1   The grassroots movement, inserted in the traditional system of competitive sport but at the same time expression of forms of in-group sociability and reinforcement of identity (the social bonding model).
2   The citizenship dimension that operated in the bridging perspective, producing experiences aimed at socialisation, education, integration (towards migrants), solidarity campaigns and the exploration of post-materialistic needs.
3   A system of sport for all that aimed to satisfy both non-competitive sports activities and physical education practices (fitness, wellness and health-care).

The Italian sports environment: an overview

The Italian sports system is composed of four major social agents, which displays autonomy and different organisational structures. These four social agents are:

(i)   the *Olympic performance-led activities* which are publicly funded and, because of the significant contribution of the Army and Police, sports groups have contributed to four-fifths of the medals gained by Italy at the Olympic Games (summer, winter and Paralympic) in the 20 years that elapses between the Summer Olympics in Atlanta of 1996 and the latest Winter Olympics held in of PyeongChang in 2018;

(ii) the *For-Profit Sports sector*, identifiable with the professional clubs of major team sports games and with individual sports (namely cycling, boxing and motoring), which in terms of revenues have yielded between 1996 and 2018 four-fifths of the whole economic turnover of the Italian sports sector;

(iii) the *Amateur Non-Profit sector*, which is composed of 63,517 competitive and non-competitive[1] associations (2018), and which are involved in delivering 'sport for all'. From 2002, these associations can access normative and fiscal benefits from the state thanks to their legally recognised social function. These associations represent four-fifths of the organisations affiliated to the Italian National Olympic Committee (CONI) as amateur one-sport or multi-sport clubs;

(iv) the area of '*DIY*' *sports enthusiasts*; they do not have any links to the three sectors mentioned earlier. In Italy, just as in the other major EU countries (France, Germany, Great Britain and Spain), the proportion of sporting nationals falling into this category is a little lower than four-fifths of the total of sport participants.[2]

The four-fifths rule applies to the share held by each of the four social agents in relation to the following key result indicators: the number of Olympic medals won, the sports sector sales turnover, the number of active sports associations and the demographic consistency of the active sporting participants.

The longitudinal studies commissioned by the Italian Olympic Committee (CONI) and produced by the National Institute of Statistics (ISTAT) in the time frame between 1995 and 2016 indicate a constant but non-linear growth of sports practice. The CONI-ISTAT report 2017 states that 17.7 million citizens are consistently sports active. Overall, males are more active (56.7% of participants) but females are significantly present among 15–25-year-olds. The data published in December 2018 estimate that 34 million Italians are sports active (60% of the reference population). These values are closer to the average of the EU countries than the past surveys of the Eurobarometer which, in the 2013 census, the European population aged over 15 disappointingly indicated that in Italy only 40% of the population were sports active (better: not completely sedentary).[3]

Moreover, according to the CONI-ISTAT report, there is an increase of consistent sports participants and occasional participants in the 'post-agonistic' population range between 35 and 44 years old increasing from 27% of the population (1995) to 33.4% in 2013. Those among the 45–54-year-olds increased from 17.3 to 27% while the older sports participants (55–59 years old) almost doubled, from 12.6 to 22.3%. The percentage of people regularly involved in sport remains significantly higher in the central-northern regions, where more than one-third of the citizens are active, than in the southern ones, where just over a fifth of the population is not sedentary. The propensity to practise sport is strongly correlated to age and locality of residence, significantly decreasing in locations of under 2,000 inhabitants, where the average age is higher. On the other hand, the number of women who continue sporting activity after school age is growing. Graduates are almost twice as likely to engage in sport than the less educated, but are less prone to consistent sports practice. Family socialisation strongly influences the likelihood for children to practise sport: almost four-fifths of people under the age of 24 were sports active if both parents were engaged in sport. The number drops to 68.4% among those who have only one sports active parent and drops further still to 42.2% among children of the sedentary. Since 2013, sports participants aged 36 years and over exceed those aged between 18 and 35 years old.

Over a million Italians were being identified by the CONI-ISTAT report (2017) as 'Sports Operators' (CONI management and Sport Federations executives, coaches and referees). There was a growth by one-third compared to data of 2003. The football sector has almost 1.1 million members from the Italian Football federation to football clubs in all football divisions. Among other sports it is possible to find a growth in memberships in volleyball (366,000 members), basketball (314,000) and in individual sports such as tennis, athletics, sports fishing, swimming, motorcycling and gymnastics.

The Italian sports model: strengths and weaknesses

At first glance, the data gathered seem to reflect the dynamics of contextual de-sportisation of sport and sportisation of European society identified by social research since the early 2000s (Steenbergen, De Knop and Elling 2001). However, the Italian milieu is peculiar if compared to other EU countries because of social and institutional actors such as CONI and national Sports Federations which monopolise the governance and representation of both competitive and organised amateur sports. This is an anomaly in Europe that makes the Italian sports milieu a conflictual space, crossed by interests, negotiations and instability factors, similar to the political arena described by Schein (1985).

In the second decade of the millennium, the non-profit sports sector still has as its main objective the expansion of the demographic perimeter of the practice. Incentive strategies and proselytising campaigns aim to establish sport as a right of citizenship, according to the traditional philosophy of Sport for All. It promotes equal opportunities, solicits programmes financed by the state and opposes the ideology of 'winning at any cost' that pervades the for-profit sports sector.

Sport for all adds to traditional sport the task of promoting inclusion in school curricula and strategies to tackle unequal access to sports activities targeting socially disadvantaged groups such as the elderly, young children, disabled people, and immigrants. Sport is also considered as a valuable health promotional tool for a better quality of life, against the menace of doping and all forms of discrimination.

Sport, following this philosophy, can be conceived as 'merit goods', capable of producing wide-ranging collective benefits despite an estimation in the short term that their social effects may be challenging (Mishan 1981). The Sport for All objectives have been pursued with greater or lesser success for three decades in almost all the countries of the European Union; however, in Italy they were thwarted by a controversial conflict of competences between policies and/or organisations such as CONI promoting sport as competition and those promoting sport as a right of citizenship. In this framework the vision of a specialised and strongly structured body like CONI has almost always prevailed. Thus it has actually surrogated roles and functions traditionally carried out by government in other countries via Ministries.

Since the 1990s, however, there has been a new and original sports participation/experience trend namely, to join sports practice with environmentalism and the promotion of rights and solidarity.

Their main organisational diffusion route is represented by the non-profit sports sector, often in connection with voluntary organisations and their networks, particularly active in urban centres and the central-north regions of the country. From this point of view the social rooting of amateur sports associations reproduces the salient features of civic culture as described in numerous researches dedicated to the Italian case (Almond and Verba 1963, 1980; Putnam 2004), which has both a secular and Catholic matrix (Porro 2013, Martelli and Porro 2018).

In the post-war period, in accordance with the model of organisational collateralism, specialised mass organisations were created that belonged to the major political, religious and even entrepreneurial networks. These organisations in principle supported the reasons for innovation. But they disagreed on the issue concerning the role of CONI, by some conceived as the reassuring guardian of the national sports system, while others denounced its hegemonic inclinations and the lack of attention to the emerging issues of social sport.

Between the 20th and 21st centuries a mobilisation took shape for the reform of sports institutions inspired by the values of welfare and the Scandinavian model of sport citizenship.[4] However, the scenario began to be crowded with actors who interpreted the social mission of sport differently from the competition system. They demanded a radical reform of the CONI structure or an autonomous statute that would assign responsibility for sport for everyone to social policies and educational agencies. This change of paradigm should have mainly concerned the amateur sports sector.

The emerging sport for all philosophy however appeared ambiguous and culturally elusive in the eyes of the defenders of the Italian sport power system status quo. Leisure sport reflected what the works of Lasch, Inglehart and Bourdieu have associated since the end of the 1970s with the culture of narcissism, the individualism of mass, the production of specific *Habitus*. Sport for all was more and more related to an active style of life which does not aim to extend so much participation in itself but to use sport as a tool to tackle the pathologies of ageing in an increasing elderly population or to use sports programmes as a tool of social inclusion in favour of at a population of immigrants which has grown in the country significantly between the 1990s and the second decade of the millennium. Hence the Italian interpretation of sport for all aimed to tackle social malaise, loneliness, and social exclusion focusing on disability, poverty and the prisons population: the abandoned people which the Italian welfare state was unable to help. At the same time unprecedented demands about quality of life and expressive experimentation were flourishing (Eichberg 2010). They had little or nothing to do with the institutional mission and the organisational culture of CONI and of the historical Italian sport promotion agencies themselves.

The sedentary lifestyle, favoured by computerisation, is opposed by a demand for adrenaline that is expressed in 'no limits' activities and so-called extreme sports. They are almost never competitive and, in some cases, simply extravagant. The competition governed by rules and procedures is replaced by a kaleidoscope of biodegradable activities, while affirming a rich range of mind games or competitive simulations regulated by digital algorithms.

Since the early 2000s, the transformations of Italian sport represent the exemplary case of a controversial transition. Moreover, since the early 2000s, Italian sport experiences a sociologically evocative dialectic between cultural paradigms, concrete material interests (fitness market, wellness marketing) and organisational logics that are increasingly distant and less compatible. Italy represents the fifth Olympic power in the medal standings of all time, but it shows levels of sports practice among the lowest in Europe. The system is still governed by the Olympic Committee (CONI) which concentrates powers and resources while the institutional actors responsible for social policies (Ministries, local authorities, educational institutions) do not yet seem entirely capable of effectively promoting sport as a social resource.

The Italian Sports Federations constitute a goal-oriented system, efficient in recruiting and enhancing competitive talents but inadequate to satisfy requests for wider sports participation, inclusion and solidarity. Sport for all logics cohabit with those inspired by the social democratic compromise that inspired the philosophy of the welfare sport during the second half of the 20th century.

Despite this, the survey carried out by CONI-ISTAT 2017 documented the existence of 90,000 non-profit sports institutions, two-thirds of which were fully affiliated to a federation. With well over a million volunteers – one-third of the whole Italian voluntary action system – and 88,000 employees, the voluntary sports system alone was producing an economic turnover of €5 billion.

Heritage and history: the Italian sports promotion model

Effective in ensuring the results of high-level sport, but much less in supporting physical activity as a tool for social inclusion, CONI has operated since the 1950s a continuous negotiation of interests with state institutions and various social actors. In the 1970s important areas of sport were assigned to the newborn *Regioni* within the framework of a semi-federalist reform of the state. In the following two decades the alliance between sports organisations, heirs of post-war political flanking (*enti di promozione*),[5] and the vast Third Sector network took shape. Strong of prerogatives never being officially included in legislations, CONI administered 'sporting power' by not allowing innovations that were not reduced to modest administrative adjustments. In 1992, the collapse of the so-called 'Republic of the political parties' (*partitocrazia*) by the judiciary action that brought to light an extensive system of corruption, produced effects in the official sports system too, historically close to the ruling parties. Only in the early 2000s, however, the hegemony of CONI on the entire Italian sports system, its institutional rank and the more prosaic access to public funding – first coming from general taxation and then directly from the state budget – began to be challenged.

In the period of the so-called Second Republic, between the 1990s and the first decade of the 2000s, a crisis of legitimacy affected the management of the sports system. Timid attempts at reform were developed and the influence of the associations that supported the philosophy of sport citizenship grew. The CONI – ending the conflict with the non-profit sports associations that had characterised the Presidency of former socialist politician Franco Carraro between 1978 and 1987 – started to have a dialogue with the vast area of organised charity organisations. CONI succeeded in remaining the centre of gravity of a constellation of subsystems, namely sports promotion organisations, volunteer associations, the schools, the Paralympic movement, all recipients and promoters of specific welfare policies.

The first lacerating crisis of the Italian post-war political system coincided, moreover, with the transition from the old welfare state model – inspired by social paternalism and Catholic solidarity of the Christians democrats (*Democrazia cristiana*) which was the main political party of the First Republic (1948–1992) – to a welfare system more sensitive to the issues of social citizenship. The *enti di promozione sportiva* became part of the new governance of public policies established by law 383 of 7 December 2000 by the centre-left government led by Giuliano Amato. For the first time, the sports practice was recognised as a right of citizenship.

For heterogenesis of ends, the ideological influence of political parties and mass organisations, typical of totalitarian strategies of social control, vigorously contributed to the Italian democratic rebirth, substituting in the case of sport the lack of specific public policies. In addition to political parties, other important social networks – the Catholic Church and various religious-inspired associations, trade unions and even the representative body of industrial entrepreneurs (*Confindustria*) – created structures specifically dedicated to the dissemination of mass-level sport participation. Originally called 'propaganda bodies', these organisations were recognised by the CONI in 1978, benefiting from a symbolic legitimacy and some financial resources coming from betting games.

Since the 1980s, however, the most dynamic and widespread sports bodies in the territory tended towards an autonomous organisational model from the federal sports one, still structured on competitive sport specialties. Together, there is a more radical product innovation, which concerns the sports offer to make it more suitable to intercept emerging social issues and needs. In the following decade the two major non-profit sports organisations: the Uisp (Italian Union of Sport for All), close to the left political parties, and the Catholic CSI (Italian Sports Centre) are put to the test of sport for all (Porro 2005; Pioletti and Porro 2013). The pact between sports volunteering and the Olympic system was not formally denied but opened to re-negotiation. With the 1990s, the political landscape of the Second Republic becomes more fluid and unpredictable. Silvio Berlusconi's centre-right governments, led by a tycoon with massive interests in football and in broadcasting, systematically privileged commercial sport assuming an attitude of paternalistic indifference for sport for all.

In the absence of a Ministry of Sport – like the one that neighbouring France had set out in the early Sixties – the governance of the Italian sports system did not undergo any significant transformations. The CONI remained the hierarchical node of a dense network of sport subsystems, such as the

Army-promoted sport (very efficient in winning Olympic medals) and the territorial sports districts. However, in terms of citizenship, financial support was guaranteed, as well as representation in the federal sports system and the ownership of certain institutional roles. For example, from 2001 to 2005, voluntary sports associations represented the Third Sector system within the prestigious Consiglio Nazionale dell'Economia e del Lavoro (Italian National Council for Economy and Labour).

The Italian quest for sports governance

In the early 2000s, a new legislative provision (the law 178, passed on 10 August 2002) included sport in the Italian government welfare agenda. Four years earlier, a scandal concerning anti-doping practices had invested the leadership of the Olympic Committee (CONI) and compromised the relationship with the volunteers networks passionately engaged in a free-from-doping-in-sport campaign. This scandal de-legitimised the Ptolemaic order centred on the hegemony of the Olympic Committee. At the same time a dramatic problem of financing the expensive bureaucratic apparatus of the Olympic system was made public (Cherubini and Franchini 2004). The revenues originated from the Totocalcio (football pools) decreased as new betting games became more attractive to the Italian betting market, such as the Superenalotto launched in December 1997. As the leader of the Third Sector sports movement, UISP began to openly challenge CONI's hegemony over the entire sports system. The controversy concerned above all the legitimacy of interference by competitive Federations in social policies.[6] It is important to stress that in this period, the European professional sports landscape was also facing tensions created by the uncertainty and conflicts of competence between commercial sports stakeholders and institutions. The Bosman ruling (1995), by which the European Court of Justice imposed a supranational jurisdiction in defence of professional footballers, fuelled the hope of a regulation of sport more coherent with the dominant models emerging in Europe.

In the 13th legislature, with the D'Alema and Amato centre-left governments and the delegation to cultural heritage and sport attributed to Minister Giovanna Melandri, timid attempts at reforming Italian sport took shape. However, the legislative decree no. 242, launched in 1999, was limited just to rationalising the Olympic system and to make its government structures more democratic without focusing on its functions and purposes. Only with the 15th legislature, with Romano Prodi's centre-left government (2006–2008), was government funding established to promote and support 'sport for all' bypassing CONI control. This important innovation process predictably clashed with the CONI leadership closer to the centre-right political opposition.[7] However, a part of the sports promotion agencies, fearful of losing organisational protection and the economic benefits given discretely by CONI, did not support the reform project with the necessary conviction. There prevailed an ambiguous compromise between the defenders of the status quo and the advocates of the autonomy of 'socially' led sport. In the end, the only concrete result consisted in assigning to the Ministry of Welfare instead of CONI the competences in the matter of the tax regime and financing of sports programmes with exclusive social aims. However, amateur sports clubs were officially associated with the social promotion network established two years earlier. Consequently, they were forced to enrol in the regional registers of CONI on pain of losing government contributions for recognised activities of social utility. Thus a double legal regime was created, which implicitly recognised the dual vocation of non-profit sport, the competitive amateur one and the socially oriented one. This institutional differentiation remained, however, an unfinished 'business'.

The law 242 was not even accompanied by adequate funding to promote a programme of information and qualification of the technical offer geared to the specific needs of citizenship sport as well as for supporting PE teaching programmes in schools. The economic and organisational costs of solidarity welfare sports campaigns remained to a large extent borne by the clubs and voluntary organisations. Only a few Italian Regions (mainly Emilia Romagna and Tuscany), thanks to the financial resources allowed by the semi-federal state regime, and the major municipalities – all governed by centre-left political alliances – concretely supported the experimentation of innovative and politically courageous social sports programmes. Among these social sports programmes were those aimed at inclusion and integration of migrants. At the end of the following decade, on the contrary, these sports programmes became the target of anti-migratory policies – conducted with particular aggression by the Lega politicians Matteo Salvini who will be from June 2018 until August 2019 the Minister of the Interior in the populist government led by Giuseppe Conte.

The reforms of the Italian sports model – started in the early years of the 2000s – resulted in such a way almost entirely in an infra-systemic differentiation of functions, useful for the survival of the old system.

The measures adopted by the populist government between the end of 2018 and the first months of 2019 are exemplary in this regard. The main and most controversial innovation involved the company CONI Servizi. Its skills and financial resources have been devolved to a new body called *Sport e Salute* (Sport and Health). It is a private company but owned by the government. In this way the Ministry of the Economy has incorporated all the 'instrumental' activities of the agency responsible for the financial enhancement of the patrimony and the brand.

The most suitable principles of management and control were affirmed and the cumbersome Italian federal sports bureaucracy was reduced, without however severing the 'umbilical cord' between political interests and the government of Italian sport.

The Italian Olympic system found as always legitimisation in the Olympic successes of the Italian athletes, ensured above all by the champions recruited by the Army and Police sports clubs (in 2008 at the Beijing Summer Olympic Games, 11 of the 27 Italian Olympic medals were obtained by athletes affiliated with military or paramilitary sports clubs). These, in the first decade of the 2000s, were the protagonists of an unprecedented gender-related issue, which can legitimately be associated with social policies as the unintended effect of an institutional reform. The law 332 of 2000 abolished compulsory male military service and a historic ruling by the Constitutional Court (16 July 2001) consequently imposed the abolition of any gender discrimination in the recruitment of the Armed Forces. Thus it was possible to recruit women athletes in military and paramilitary bodies, finally offering them professional status and social security and pension when they ended their athlete career.

Conclusion

In the absence of structural reforms, in the second decade of the 2000s new tensions began to agitate the sports system. In 2013 the Roman entrepreneur Giovanni Malagò was surprisingly elected CONI president, as he had been very critical of the previous CONI administrations. Malagò supported the relaunch of the Italian sporting movement using the candidacy of the city of Rome as host of the 2024 Olympics. However his strategy was blocked by Virginia Raggi, mayor of Rome and exponent of the populist Five Stars Movement, who vetoed the Olympic candidacy. After the March 2018 political elections, Italian sport was in fact erased from the government political agenda. There were frictions among the Sports Federation leaders and representatives of the government. As always, no state support was redirected to social sport programmes.

At a retrospective glance, the relationship between sport and welfare in Italy developed therefore through four periods, between the end of the Second World War and the first two decades of the 2000s. The 'mass participation in sport' period (1945–1978) was characterised by a strong political imprint: all mass organisations, mainly the political parties reconstituted after the fascist dictatorship, give impulse, in line with a top-down philosophy, to dedicated movements that combined proselytism and promotion of sport activities with social goals. In this period the hegemonic role of the Olympic movement in the governance of the Italian sports system was restored under the banner of republican democracy.

The 'sports promotion' phase (1978–1990) started with the recognition in 1978 of the sports promotion organisation as subordinate actors of the CONI. In this period, however, a slow metamorphosis of the aims and the same mission of mass sport was generated. The change was expressed in the direction of a progressive transition from the ideology of *popular* sport, often associated with political or religious flanking, to the emerging philosophy of sport for all.

The season of 'sport for all' (1990–2002) was in turn characterised by a double transition. On one hand, the sports volunteering movement accentuated the distance from its traditional stakeholders, anchored in the tradition of sports promotion and in post-war political loyalties. On the other, the representation of sport for all as a mere extension of the right to sport was gradually threatened by a different vision. It focused on the autonomy of the experience of the body and privileged wellness-oriented practices: from sport for all to sport for everybody.

After 2002, when the governance system of the sports system was partially modified, the sport for everybody paradigm began to develop successfully despite the hostility of the Olympic body and the poor incisiveness of government policies. The amateur sport organisations developed strategies of active citizenship through the experimentation of new sports practices. The intolerance for the hegemony of the sport of performance model became more and more evident in the constellation of non-profit sport organisations.

The demographic phenomena affecting Italian society, such as the noticeable growth of the older age groups and the presence of a significant immigrant community, together with the long economic crisis and the lack of incisiveness of the policies aimed at citizenship sports, do not allow easy forecasts on developments. A culturally mature and socially oriented demand is compared to an offer that is still partly traditional and not always sensitive to the social opportunities offered by the sports experience. The scenario is open to many different possibilities.

Notes

1 Report of Centre for Sports and statistical observers (CONI Servizi), December 2018.
2 The 4,703,000 members in the year 2017 represent 73.6% of the active subjects with a slight percentage growth compared to those surveyed two years before from the CONI-ISTAT report, *I numeri dello sport 2015*,www.CONI.it.
3 The data collected by Italian research institutes appear more reliable for the amplitude of the statistical sample and the measurement methodologies adopted than those elaborated on a continental scale and based on statistical standardisation criteria that are not always shareable.
4 By the date of December 2018 the bodies (*Enti di promozione*) recognised by the CONI and authorized to perform official competitive activities were 15.
5 The sports promotion bodies represented an active promoter of welfare policies through sport since the early post-war years. Their origin lies in the period of the reconstruction of democracy following the fall of fascism and the catastrophe of war. However, their model borrowed from the totalitarian regime an organisational structure that aimed to adhere to 'all the folds of society' by mobilising and representing its subjects (women, young people, factory workers, pensioners, cultural promoters, etc.).
6 Already in 1990, with the Congress of Perugia, UISP (Italian Union of Popular Sport) changed its name to 'Italian Union of Sport for All' to symbolically emphasise the end of the old political flanking and the adoption of a philosophy of sport for citizenship intended as a constitutive element of social policies. With the formula 'Rights, Environment, Solidarity', the movement also proclaimed itself as an ally of European environmental movements.
7 The former President of CONI Mario Pescante was 'sponsored' by the two Berlusconi governments between 2001 and 2006.

Bibliography

Almond, G.A., Verba, S., 1963, *The Civic Culture*. Princeton: SAGE.
Almond, G.A., Verba, S. (eds), 1980, *The Civic Culture Revisited*. Boston: SAGE.
Cherubini, S., Franchini, C. (eds), 2004, *The Reform of the CONI. Legal and managerial aspects*. Milan: FrancoAngeli.
CONI-ISTAT, 2017, I numeri dello sport 2017, www.CONI.it.
Eichberg, H., 2010, *Harnchakkham Democracy: Towards a philosophy of sport for all*. London: Routledge.
Esping-Andersen, G., 1990, *The Three Worlds of Welfare Capitalism*. Cambridge, UK: Polity Press.
Eurobarometer, EU Commission, Editions 2007, 2010, 2013, 2017. Ec.europa.eu/public_opinion/index_en.htm.
Ferrera, M., 1998, *The Welfare Traps. A sustainable welfare state for the Europe of the XXI century*. Bologna: Il Mulino.
Martelli, S., Porro, N., 2018, *Nuovo manuale di sociologia dello sport e dell'attività fisica*. Milano: FrancoAngeli.
Mishan, E.J., 1981, *Economic Efficiency and Social Welfare*. London: Unwin Hyman.
Pioletti, A.M., Porro, N. (eds), 2013, *Lo sport degli Europei*. Milano: FrancoAngeli.
Porro, N., 1997, Politics and Consumption: The Four Revolutions of Spectator Football. In: D'Alimonte, R. and Nelken, D. (eds), *Italian Politics: The center-left in power*. Boulder, CO: Westview Press, pp. 183–198.
Porro, N., 2005, Sviluppo e trasformazioni del non profit. Il caso dello sport per tutti. *Relazioni solidali*, 1, pp. 71–85.
Porro, N., 2013, *Movimenti collettivi e culture sociali dello sport europeo*. Acireale-Roma: Bonanno.
Putnam, R., 2004, *Capitale sociale e individualismo. Crisi e rinascita della cultura civica in America*. Bologna: Il Mulino, Bologna.
Schein, E.H., 1985, *Organizational Culture and Leadership*. San Francisco: Jossey-Bass.
Steenbergen, J., De Knop, P., Elling, A.H.F. (eds), 2001, *Values and Norms in Sport: Critical reflections on the position and meanings of sport in society*. Aachen: Meyer & Meyer.
Titmuss, R., 1986, *Saggi sul Welfare State*. Roma: Edizioni Lavoro.

11 Physical activity and sport in Spain

Juan Antonio Simón Sanjurjo

Introduction

In 1967 the FOESSA Foundation (Fomento de Estudios Sociales y Sociología Aplicada), pertaining to the Cáritas Española organisation, published its *Informe sociológico sobre la situación social de Madrid* (Sociological Report on the Social Condition of Madrid). This document highlighted the alarming situation that the Spanish capital had found itself in with regard to the provision of sporting infrastructures. More specifically, 81% of the parishes in the city of Madrid that took part in the survey indicated that there was no infrastructure in place to practise sport in their neighbourhood, while 89% also mentioned the complete lack of swimming pools in their area. Of the 323 parishes that were surveyed, only 19% had sports pitches, and only 4% of those were free to use. In relation to swimming pools, it is interesting to highlight that in 1966 only three of these facilities were free of charge across the whole city of Madrid. This study also carried out a survey of 1,147 housewives, asking them for information about the provision of sports fields, pitches and children's playparks in their respective neighbourhoods. Their response clearly defines the situation that Spain was experiencing in the 1960s, with only 185 of these mothers stating that they considered their neighbourhood to be adequately provided with sports pitches, and only 25% thought the same about children's play areas and fields (Fundación FOESSA, 1967: 225–226).

Another later report from FOESSA, with information corresponding to three years before the death of Franco, indicated that the average number of working hours per week in 1972 had been 44, although 36% of workers did more than 50 hours. As such, leisure time was considered 'a goal that was as yet unreached by current Spanish society'. When analysing sports practice amongst Spaniards, the increase in the number of federal licences stood out, showing that it had risen from 701,808 in 1963 to 2,553,904 in 1973. Hunting and fishing, alongside sports such as football, handball and basketball seemed to be the most-practised sporting activities in this era (Fundación FOESSA, 1978: 548).

This data presents a desolate picture that clearly defines the failure of Franco's sporting policy, a policy which was used as a tool for the development of the socialisation of the practice of physical and sporting activity in

Spain. From 1937 onwards, Francoist authorities tried to implement a model of sporting policy based on the totalitarian models of Italy and Germany. At the hands of the sole ruling party, the *Falange Española Tradicionalista y de las JONS* (FET y de las JONS), a clearly politicised sporting system was developed, but before long it began to give clear signals of its evident limitations. The lack of adequate investment and necessary political will ended up reducing sport to an empty rhetorical discourse and a propaganda instrument at the service of the state, without managing to achieve mass access to sports practice.

The implementation of sporting policy during the Franco dictatorship fell to the Delegación *Nacional de Deportes* (DND-National Sports Delegation), an organisation created in 1941 and dependent on the *Movimiento Nacional*, the apex of the political structure (Santacana i Torres, 2011). While it is true that from the mid-1960s onwards we start to see a small transformation – with campaigns such as *Contamos contigo* ('We're counting on you') which aimed to promote the diffusion of physical activity and sports amongst Spanish citizens – we have to wait until the beginning of the transition to democracy in 1975 before we start to see substantial improvements in these areas. This chapter will cover the process of the democratisation, decentralisation and expansion of sport which has taken place throughout Spain; at the same time it will look at the time period from 1975 until the present day, analysing the evolution of popular sport, or sport for all, with regard to the development of the welfare state and the social, political and economic transformations that this country has undergone in the last few decades.

The first phase in the process of the democratisation of Spanish sport

The death of the dictator Francisco Franco in 20 November 1975 marked the start of a phase of democratic transition, which would conclude/be brought to a close years later with the victory of the Spanish Socialist Workers Party (PSOE) in the general elections that took place in October 1982. Sport also went through its own transition process. The aforementioned lack of public sporting facilities had been a constant throughout the Franco regime, and one of the huge objectives which the sporting authorities had to tackle during the transition. While in 1968 only 12% of the population practised some sort of physical or sporting activity (Llopis-Goig, 2017), the results of a study carried out by the ICSA-Gallup Institute in 1975 highlighted the growing interest amongst the Spanish people in sporting practice, represented in the more than half a million federal licences held at that time and the 22% of Spaniards who took part in some type of sporting activity. With regard to this information, Spanish society continued to demand a higher number of sporting facilities and real commitment to this process from the political authorities (García Ferrando, 1982).

Tomás Pelayo Ros was named the national delegate to the DND in 1975 and held the post until September 1976, when Benito Castejón took over and became the true driving force behind the sporting transition. Pelayo Ros was confronted with great difficulties when trying to start a process of reform, fundamentally due to the instability of Arias Navarro's government. However, Benito Castejón was able to take the first steps towards the development of a real plan for the restructuring of sport. In his takeover speech he made clear what would be his primary lines of action, highlighting the undeniable political transcendence of sport, the importance of both short- and long-term planning on a sporting level, 'without falling into the political opportunism of shiny medals'. He also communicated that some of his primary objectives would be to achieve 'the spread of sport' amongst the Spanish people and the promotion of physical education – in short, a profound restructuring and democratisation of the country's sporting policy. In 1977 the first step towards the democratisation of Spanish sport was taken, on a legislative level, with the approval of the Royal Decree Law 23/1977 on 1 April, which allowed the state administration to take back control of sport. From this moment on, the DND was dissolved and the task of coordination between regions of the ensemble of common competencies throughout Spain fell to the recently created *Consejo Superior de Deportes* (CSD, National Sports Council).

The arrival of democracy inspired a large number of social changes, which in the sphere of sport allowed for the expansion of the pillars of popular sport, the increase in sporting facilities and the re-evaluation of the practice of physical education and sport in schools. The Spanish Constitution of 1978 clearly specified in Article 43 Number 3 the responsibility that the state had in the promotion of sport, noting that 'public powers will promote sanitary education, physical education and sport'. The promotion of sport and its diffusion to the Spanish population fell at this moment in time to public organisations. The constitution clearly speaks to the European Charter on Sport for All, which had been signed in Brussels in 1975, which specified that 'in a modern society, in which industrialisation, urbanisation and automation can denature man's living and working conditions, the overall objective of Sport for All is to allow all people – regardless of sex or age – to maintain their physical and mental capacities' (Consejo de Europa, 1975). The process of administrative decentralisation that Spain was undergoing, and its relation to sport, was also reflected in Article 148 Number 19, in which it is stated that 'the Autonomous Communities can take over the following responsibilities: the promotion of sport and the appropriate use of leisure time' (Constitución española, 1978). From this point onwards, Spain's autonomous communities would take control of sporting matters by means of their respective autonomy statutes, and taking on the task of promoting sports. The state administration, Comunidades Autónomas (autonomous communities) and Local Administration would, from this point onwards, have shared responsibilities in the specific public function of sporting matters.

The Spanish Constitution put in place the groundwork so that a few years later the National Sports Act 13/1980 of Physical Culture and Sport, which stated in its first article that its objective was 'the promotion, direction and coordination of physical education and sport as essential factors in the formation and comprehensive development of the individual. We recognise the right of every citizen to the knowledge and practice of sport'. The implementation of this law highlighted the importance of the development of physical education within the educational system, drawing attention to the importance of increasing the sports facilities in schools. This law tried to give a definitive push towards the promotion of sporting practice in Spain, stating that urban authorities would be entrusted with setting, 'in accordance with the legislation concerning land and town planning, the minimum space that would be allocated for the use of sport on urban and building land, according to the previous report from the Competent Sporting Organisation'. These measures prompted the increase in this period of sporting facilities in Spain, from 19,418 in 1975 to 48,723 in 1986, an increase of 60%, alongside the 32% of schools that now had access to these facilities (CSD, 2005).

The organisational structure of Spanish sport

The organisation of Spanish sport is based on a mixed system, with collaboration between the public and private sector to deal with the duties of the encouragement, promotion and development of sport. The public sector has been characterised since 1978 by demonstrating a decentralised structure which distributes its duties at a local, regional and national level. In contrast, the private sector can be divided into the commercial for-profit private sector, and the associative non-profit private sector.

With regard to the public sector, the structure of Spanish sport divides the duties carried out by the CSD, an autonomous organisation of an administrative nature, affiliated with the Ministry of Culture and Sport. The CSD directly carries out the actions of the state administration in the sphere of sport, in compliance with the constitutional mandate which establishes that public powers will be responsible for the promotion of physical education and sport. The second-in-command of the public sporting entities are the autonomous communities' Directorates-General for sport. The respective autonomy statutes of Spain's autonomous communities establish the grouping of functions and duties that they have for the promotion and development of sporting policy in their region. Some of the duties are recognised as being of extreme importance, such as the promotion, construction and management of sporting facilities, physical education and sporting activity in schools, and the coordination, promotion and guardianship of sporting associations. Finally, there are local entities and city councils, which become the principal managers of public sporting services. Their main objective is to develop key functions for the socialisation of sporting practice, such as the task of reserving land necessary for the construction of sporting facilities within town planning, as well as the construction and management of these facilities. Furthermore, they are in charge of the development of programmes to promote sport for all ages, and to help sports clubs located in their local areas.

With regard to private sporting entities, the structure of Spanish sport recognises bodies such as the Spanish Olympic and Paralympic Committees, professional leagues, the Spanish Sporting federations and the sports associations. The Spanish Olympic Committee (COE) is a non-profit association, bestowed as legal entity, which has as its main objective the development of the Olympic movement and the dissemination of Olympic ideals. It is made up of Federations of Olympic events, and it represents Spain in front of the International Olympic Committee. The Spanish Paralympic Committee was created in 1995 as a result of the impetus that was generated by the Barcelona Paralympic Games, and out of the need to match the social advances accomplished by people with disabilities.

The National Sports Act of 1990 specified that sporting federations are private entities, with their own legal status with a national jurisdiction, and are integrated with autonomous sports federations, sports clubs, athletes, coaches, judges, referees, professional leagues and other parties interested in the promotion and development of a specific sporting model within Spain. They have a private aspect and also a public one, in which they operate under the guidance of the CSD, carrying out duties of an administrative nature, the most important of which is exercising control of the grants assigned by the sporting Associations and Entities under the conditions set by the CSD. The autonomous sporting federations are entities of a very similar nature and with very similar objectives to their national counterparts, but the difference is that they carry out their duties in their own autonomous regions, representing the Spanish Sporting federations in their respective autonomous communities

In Spain, the professional leagues are private entities with their own legal status and autonomy over their internal organisation and operation, with regard to the corresponding Spanish Sporting Federation, a federation which they form part of. They include the clubs which participate in official competitions of a professional nature and on a state level. Currently there are two leagues that are recognised as professional: the ACB (Association of Basketball Clubs) and the LFP (Professional Football League). Lastly, the private sector also has sports associations, which are private associations whose objective is to promote one or more sporting events, the sporting practice of their associates and participation of these associates in sporting activities and competitions. The National Sports Act of 1990 classifies these entities as elementary clubs, basic clubs, professional sports clubs and Sociedades Anónimas Deportivas (a special type of private limited company especially tailored to the needs of the sports market).

The evolution of Spanish sporting policy from the start of the transition to democracy until the 1990s

The arrival of the Spanish Socialist Workers Party (PSOE) to government in 1982 coincided with a clearly positive set of circumstances that had started to take place on an international level in 1975, with the aforementioned European Charter of Sports for All, and which was reflected in the diverse campaigns of 'Sports for All' which were rolled out from the mid-1980s onwards. At the same time, the push from the implementation of the National Sports Act 13/1980 clearly favoured the increase of opportunities for the practice of sport in Spanish society.

Between the general elections of 1986 and 1993, a period which we could define as the second stage of socialist government, Spain experienced a phase of economic growth which coincided with their full integration into the European Economic Community in 1986. From the mid-1980s onwards, the governing party implemented policy which gradually distanced itself from its traditional social democratic stance, in order to embrace a newer, more liberal line. Sport became an essential part of Spanish culture, in winning over the collective cultural imagination and striving for the normalisation that was so desired. Two factors are key for understanding the evolution of physical and sporting activity in Spain from the 1990s onwards: the promulgation of the National Sports Act 10/1990, which revoked the previous law, and the celebration of the Olympic Games in Barcelona in 1992.

The new legal framework was centred on aspects related to the professional regulation of elite sport. This law was created two years before the Olympic Games were held, and it caused a clear increase in investment in competition sports, Olympic sports, and high-performance and technical sports centres. Spain would go on to achieve an historic milestone, winning 22 medals. This success was due in part to the implementation of the ADO Programme (Asociación de Deportes Olímpicos) in 1988, which aimed to ensure dignified economic and training conditions for the country's best athletes. It is undeniable that, while the National Sports Act 13/1980 had focused on the democratisation and development of sporting practice, the new legal framework of 1990 bestowed much less importance on Spanish citizens and 'sport for all'. From this point onward, the task of promoting and encouraging sporting practice amongst the Spanish people fell to the autonomous communities and, above all, to the city councils. This means that, in the face of economic crisis, the financial resources provided for small- and medium-sized municipalities to carry out these tasks is drastically reduced, something which has a direct impact on society.

With regard to the development of the welfare state and the economic evolution of the country, 1990 marked the beginning of the end for the socialist programme of 1982. Despite everything, the state's investment effort – facilitated by the large scale international events that were held in the country (the Olympic Games and the World's Fair in Seville, both held in 1992) – afforded the modernisation of dilapidated and obsolete infrastructures. This was especially true in the travel sector (as much as in transport, roads, railways, ports and airports as in the provision of information), and in large urban areas (Barcelona, Seville and Madrid in particular) whose underdevelopment was preventing economic growth and the improvement of quality of life. But the economic scene would change radically in September 1992, commencing a phase of crisis, unemployment and inflation, which was accompanied by the aforementioned political decline of the PSOE. These factors meant that from the early 1990s the Spanish state had an impact on investment into high-performance facilities and in large international sports events, which in turn reduced interest in grassroots sports, schools sports and popular sports.

Between the successes of professional sport and the reduction of popular sports practice in times of economic crisis

In recent years, we have seen an interesting contradiction between the success that elite Spanish sport has enjoyed, and a much more concerning panorama with regard to the levels of sporting practice amongst the Spanish population. Alongside the triumphs of Spanish football, with the victories of the national side in the World Cup in 2010 and the European Championship in 2008 and 2012, there have also been numerous victories from Real Madrid and FC Barcelona in European tournaments in recent years, as well as plenty of singles titles for Rafael Nadal in the world of tennis, Alberto Contador in cycling, Carolina Marín in badminton, and the swimmer Mireia Belmonte, to name but a few. The phenomenon that some of the press have dubbed the 'Spanish miracle' when talking about high-performance sport loses some of its shine when we look at sporting practice data that is collected by surveys about sporting habits.

The various surveys that have been carried out since the mid-1960s indicate that sporting practice amongst the Spanish population aged 16–65 has risen from 12% in 1968 to 47% which was recorded in 2014 (García Ferrando, 1982; Puig, 1996; García Ferrando y Llopis-Goig, 2011a, 211b; Llopis-Coig, 2014). This data alerts us to the fact that sporting practice has indeed grown throughout this period, quadrupling in just five decades. But while it is true that the percentage of Spaniards practising sport has clearly risen since the Franco regime, Spain is still far behind the countries of northern and central Europe. According to data from the Eurobarometer 412, carried out in 2013, 44% of the Spanish population had never done any sport, which was two points higher than the average amongst EU countries, and miles away from the 9% recorded in Sweden, 14% in Denmark, 15% in Finland or 29% in Germany. Furthermore, as for the differences between men and women, 57% of Spanish women never or rarely practised sport, which is seven points higher than the percentage for Spanish men.

With regard to the variable of age, the percentage of men aged 25–39 who never or rarely practised sport was 37%, a figure which grew to 70% when referring to the population over 55. This indicator shows that in the case of men, the older they are, the less sport they practise – although it is also important to point out that the 64+ age band of the Spanish population is the group that has most increased their sporting practice in recent years. At the same time, and comparing with Spanish women's results, we see some worrying indicators such as the 15–24 age band, where we see 19% of men who do not do any sport, compared to 44% of women who said the same. We continue to see this increment in the 25–39 age band, with 37% of men compared to 53% of women who don't practise any sport. It is, however, interesting to note that in the 40–54 and the 55+ age groups, the percentage of men who don't do any physical activity clearly overtakes the percentage of women – 70% of men compared to 65% of women (European Commission, 2014).

Some authors have highlighted the fact that, from the 1990s onwards, the process of the commercial liberalisation of sport that has taken place in Spain as well as a large number of EU countries has had some clear negative consequences on the promotion of sport for all (Moscoso Sánchez, 2011; Rodríguez Díaz, 2018). Therefore, it seems clear that according to this data, success in elite sport has not served to encourage the Spanish people to reproduce these sporting habits.

At the same time, the great economic recession that has affected Spain since 2008 has caused huge cuts in budgets dedicated to sport. The country has had to wait a decade for the €193.2 million that the CSD had in 2009 to be matched and surpassed. At the beginning of January 2019, the minister for Culture and Sport, José Guirao presented a budget with a global provision of €204 million, the largest to date, of which €195 million would be destined for the CSD. A few weeks later, these budgets were not approved by Pedro Sanchez's socialist government and new general elections will be held in April of this year (CSD, 17/01/2019). In 2012 this very organisation had to reduce its budget to €111.37 million euros, a figure that was a long way short of the 181.1 that had been given in the 2007 budget, before the economic crisis (CSD, 2007; *Europa Press*, 3/4/2012).

A report produced by the magazine *Deportistas* in 2017 stated that the sum invested by the provincial councils into sport was placed at €5.96 per person, 4.78% less than in 2016, and held in stark contrast to the 12% rise in the lot set aside for sport in the autonomous communities. Spain's autonomous communities are showing signs of a slow recovery, while its councils have had a cumulative decline of 42.15% since the crisis began in 2008 (Deportistas, 2017a). With regard to the city councils, in 2017 the budgets set aside for sport increased by 3.57% in comparison to the previous year, which has helped to reduce the average cumulative drop since 2008 to 8.36%. This data shows the heavy impact that the economic crisis has had on local investment in sport, and that there is a slow but steady recovery in the sums of money that city councils are beginning to allocate to such activity (Deportistas, 2017b).

The economic crisis also meant that elite sport suffered the consequences. In 2013, the debts of football clubs drowned the majority of teams, while minority sports experienced situations such as the disappearance of Atlético Madrid's Handball team, the Ros Casares basketball team and the Euskaltel-Euskadi cycling club (Heras, 9/7/2013). At the same time, the CSD has tried to counteract the impact of the economic crisis through trying to ensure universal access to sporting practice for the Spanish population, shaping the Comprehensive Plan for Physical Activity and Sport, referred to as the A+D Plan. With this plan, their aim for the period 2010–2020 was to implement a strategic plan which would raise the level of sporting practice amongst the

Spanish people, achieve the generalisation of sport for school children, use sport as a tool for social inclusion and, lastly, advance equality between men and women in the world of sport. With these four grand objectives, they hoped to ensure that 'Spain would occupy, in an international context, the same place in our levels of sporting practice as we hold in the results of European, world and Olympic high level competitions' (CSD, 2010, p. 135).

Conclusion

From the beginning of the transition to democracy, sporting policy that was implemented in Spain demonstrated a strong social content, trying to correct the deficiencies generated during the Franco dictatorship and giving special attention to the improvement of public facilities and the socialisation of sporting practice. Starting with the Sporting Law of 1990 and the responsibility of holding the Olympic Games in Barcelona in 1992, this country liberalised its markets and went in for increasing investment in high level competition. Since then, Spain has stuck with the sporting policy, something which has allowed the sporting success of many Spanish athletes who have become part of the world elite. Victories in high-profile sports such as winning the football World Cup and European Championships, being the European and World basketball champions, and other athletes' individual titles, have not been reflected as expected in an increase in popular sporting practice.

From the mid-1960s onwards, the public sector was aware of the inequalities that existed in the field of sport, which is why they didn't hesitate to include this field in the elements that were deemed key to the welfare state. The democratic sporting model demonstrated a clear structural change, in which the transferral of sporting duties to Spain's autonomous communities was on the main elements, although it also gave some responsibility to public administrations in so far as promoting, protecting, financing and encouraging sport. The collaboration between public and private entities allowed for an historic increase, as much in sporting practice as in the international presence of Spanish sport; but from then mid-1990s onwards, a clear discrepancy between high-performance sport and sport for all started to establish itself.

Despite a notable change to the Spanish sporting system in recent decades, levels of sporting practice have not managed to even come close to those in other northern and central European countries. At the same time, the profound crisis that started in 2008 caused a marked reduction in the money allocated to developing sporting practice in autonomous communities and city councils. The economic crisis has had hugely negative effects on the well-being and living conditions of the Spanish people. The poverty rate in Spain is six points higher than the European average. Although in recent years it appears that the hardest phase of the economic crisis has passed, its social consequences are still being noticed. The differences in socio-economic and cultural status are still determining factors in being able to understand the slow development of the advancement of sporting activity in this country.

Bibliography

Consejo de Europa, 1975, *Carta Europea del Deporte para Todos*. Brussels.
Consejo Superior de Deportes (CSD), 2005, *Censo Nacional de Instalaciones Deportivas 2005*. Madrid: Consejo Superior de Deportes.
Consejo Superior de Deportes (CSD), 2007, Presupuesto del CSD 2007. Retrieved from: www.munideporte.com/imagenes/documentacion/ficheros/20071112192336Presentacion_Lissvetzky_presupuestos2007.pdf.
Consejo Superior de Deportes (CSD), 2010, Plan Integral para la Actividad Física y el Deporte. Retrieved from: www.csd.gob.es/csd/estaticos/plan-integral/LIBRO-PLAN-AD.pdf.
Consejo Superior de Deportes (CSD), 17/01/2019, El Gobierno destina cerca de 204 millones de euros al deporte, el mayor presupuesto de su historia. Consejo Superior de Deportes. Retrieved from: www.csd.gob.es/csd/documentacion/01GabPr/Novedades/el-gobierno-destina-cerca-de-204-millones-de-euros-al-deporte-el-mayor-presupuesto-de-su-historia/view.
Constitución española, 29/12/1978, *Boletín Oficial del Estado* (BOE), 311. 1.
Deportistas, 2017a, Los presupuestos de las Diputaciones para el deporte vuelven a bajar (-4,78%), abril-mayo, número 73, pp. 6–7.
Deportistas, 2017b, Los ayuntamientos continúan recuperando sus presupuestos deportivos (+3,57%), junio-julio, número 74, pp. 6–7.
Europa press, 3/4/2012, Política deportiva. El CSD rebaja su presupuesto de 2012 hasta los 111,37 millones, un 33,2 por ciento menos que en 2011. Retrieved from: www.europapress.es/deportes/noticia-politica-deportiva-csd-rebaja-presupuesto-2012-11137-millones-332-ciento-menos-2011-20120403143548.html.
European Commission, 2014, *Special Eurobarometer 412: Sport and Physical Activity*. Brussels.
Fundación FOESSA, 1967, Informe sociológico sobre la situación social de Madrid. Madrid: Caritas Diocesana de Madrid-Alcalá. Retrieved from: https://www.caritas.es/producto/informe-sociologico-la-situacion-social-madrid/.
Fundación FOESSA, 1978, Síntesis actualizada del III Informe Foessa 1978. Madrid: Caritas Diocesana de Madrid-Alcalá. Retrieved from: https://caritas-web.s3.amazonaws.com/main-files/uploads/1978/04/SINTESIS-ACTUALIZADA-DEL-III-INFORME-FOESSA-1978-ocr.pdf/.
García Ferrando, M., 1982, *Deporte y sociedad. Las bases sociales del deporte en España*. Madrid: Ministerio de Cultura.
García Ferrando, M., Llopis-Goig, R., 2011a, *Ideal democrático y bienestar personal. Encuesta sobre los hábitos deportivos en España 2010*. Madrid: Consejo Superior de Deportes.
García Ferrando, M., Llopis-Goig, R., 2011b, El deporte en España. Un enfoque sociológico. In: Fundación Encuentro (eds), *Informe España 2011. Una interpretación de su realidad social*. Madrid: Fundación Encuentro, pp. 3–57.
Heras, Rubén, 9/7/2013, La crisis exprime al deporte español. *RTVE*. Retrieved from: www.rtve.es/deportes/20130709/deporte-crisis/709722.shtml.
Llopis-Goig, R., 2014, *Crisis, cambio social y deporte*. Valencia: Nau Llibres.
Llopis-Goig, R., 2017, Efectos de ciclo vital, generación y periodo en la práctica deportiva de la población española. Un análisis referido al periodo 1984–2014. *Reis*, 157, pp. 85–102.

Moscoso Sánchez, D., 2011, Los españoles y el deporte. Del pódium al banquillo. *Panorama Social*, 14, pp. 110–126.

Puig, N., 1996, Sociología del deporte en España. In: García Ferrando, M. and Martínez Morales, J.R. (eds), *Ocio y deporte en España: Ensayos sociológicos sobre el cambio*. Valencia: Tirant lo Blanch Libros, pp. 143–164.

Rodríguez Díaz, A., 2018, La inversión en la elite deportiva versus la práctica popular. *Revista de Humanidades*, 34, pp. 173–193.

Santacana i Torres, C., 2011, Espejo de un régimen. Transformación de las estructuras deportivas y su uso político y propagandístico, 1939–1961. In: Pujadas, X. (ed.), *Atletas y ciudadanos: historia social del deporte en España, 1870–2010*. Madrid: Alianza Editorial, pp. 206–232.

12 Sport and welfare in Central and Eastern European countries

Simona Kustec and Simon Ličen

Introduction

Sport has long played an important role in the societies and politics of Central and Eastern European (CEE) countries. Sport and physical activity, especially in the past also frequently referred to as 'physical culture', have served as symbols of national identity, indicators of state power and international visibility, as well as important tools for education and social integration in public education systems.

After World War II, CEE countries adopted socialist or communist regimes. They regarded the provision of welfare and social services as a crucial duty of the state. These services were codified through an array of public social, health, education and cultural, as well as sport policies. After the dissolution of socialist and communist systems of government, distinctive normative solutions and policy implementations emerged in these countries, resulting in unique forms of welfare states.

This chapter reviews the characteristics of sport and its role *in* and *for* welfare systems and practices in CEE countries. We open by surveying their broad political and social landscapes, and then examine the historical and ideological development of sport and physical activity policies in the region. We conclude with a review of popular perceptions and current normative and institutional policy frameworks. Throughout the review, we cite legal, political and policy documents, fiscal and statistical data, and selected academic and expert studies on welfare and sport systems in the region.

A note on naming is in order before we delve into the subject. In this chapter, we shall focus on the 11 former socialist or communist countries that are considered part of the CEE region and are members of the European Union (EU) as of 2019. These countries may be grouped into four regions based on geographic and cultural criteria: the Czech Republic, Hungary, Poland, Slovakia (the Visegrád Group); Estonia, Latvia, Lithuania (the Baltic states); Romania, Bulgaria (South-eastern Europe); and Slovenia and Croatia (former Yugoslav countries).

Political and welfare state overview of CEE countries

Outside observers often perceive CEE countries as monolithic or at least very closely related. This is due to their historical and former ideological commonalities and the importance they assign to welfare state principles. (Similar names, flags and languages do not contribute to their distinctiveness, either.)

Before the democratic transformations that occurred in the late 1980s and early 1990s, the political systems of CEE countries were based on totalitarian or self-management single-party models. Economies were centrally planned, and social welfare arrangements were crucial sources of regime legitimisation (Cerami and Vanhuysse, 2009). The state (i.e. the Communist Party) was the exclusive financer and provider of public social services. The right to employment was guaranteed by the constitution, meaning it was the state's duty to create jobs for those able and willing to work[1]

People were granted pensions and social security in old age, paid sickness and disability leave, and free health care and education through to the tertiary level. The state also supported cultural and sports development: these were national identity policies rather than welfare policies.

Many political, economic and social policies collapsed after the fall of communist and socialist regimes. They were replaced by democratic constitutions based on a respect for human rights, the rule of law and multi-party systems and elections. Although capitalist economies replaced state planning, political leaders in the newly democratic systems remained committed to maintaining the previous welfare state model (Offe and Fuchs, 2007; Boje and Potůček, 2011).

A comparison of welfare models and policies between CEE and Western European countries, as well as among CEE countries, reveals significant differences. Despite their welfare state legacies, CEE countries today are less generous and effective than some Western countries in addressing citizens' social needs. They often offer less promising economic and financial environments. Reasons are manifold: in some cases, there is a lack of institutional and managerial capacity to run the system. This is counter-intuitive, given the size and efficiency of former state apparatuses, and is perhaps a consequence of the dismantling of established systems of long-term planning and staffing, as well as of foreign intervention into national politics and economies. Some countries lack efficient policies and programmes to respond to new and on-going effects of the market economy. Inadequate and insufficient responses resulted in several problems, including changes of labour force demand, increased inequality in income distribution, low wages, increased unemployment, social exclusion and poverty, marginalisation of vulnerable social groups, homelessness, and lower quality and access to health and educational services (Eurostat, 2017). A generation after the collapse of communism and the economic, political and social transformations that followed, it is not clear whether these changes have truly resulted in the new social policy equilibria they sought (Potůček, 2008).

Accession to the European Union has only partially improved the situation. The EU does not adopt a single social policy,[2] many structural reforms have not been undertaken, and the new financial and economic policy models have not proven successful for these realities. Most CEE countries rank below average in GDP per capita and other financial and economic indicators. Minor exceptions are the Czech Republic, Slovenia, Slovakia, and Estonia (Eurostat, 2017), which developed individual approaches towards social welfare restructuring. A key distinction derives from the choice between public and private provision of social welfare: Estonia and other Baltic countries adopted a private model, Visegrád countries (especially the Czech Republic and Slovakia) opted for a public–private combination, and Slovenia has, thus far, retained a predominantly public welfare system. The different routes pursued by each nation complicate learning from others' experiences. Differences between different policy domains inside the same country complicate matters further (Potůček, 2008).

CEE countries have retained social policies high on their political agendas to honour the commitment made to their citizens to maintain a broad welfare state, even after the collapse of communism and socialism. However, political responses to contemporary social needs and problems have thus far been insufficient. Crucial questions include how to resolve current policy issues and how to adjust political and public service institutions. Answers to both are key to achieving social stability in the modern democratic welfare state. When considered part of the welfare state, sports policies suffer from similar issues as other policies and institutions that were not adequately transformed after the adoption of a democratic model (Sobry, 2012). There are two main types of policies, each addressing one realm of sport. First are policies that regulate the role of the state in relation to elite sport. These are typically designed to reinforce national identification among citizens and promote the country on the international athletic, political and economic playing fields. Second are policies that connect sport, public education and, since recently, health systems. These policies view sports programmes as a component of the welfare state.

Historical and ideological development of sport policy in CEE

The success of communist states in international sports after World War II has intrigued many students of sports politics and policy. Multiple factors contributed to these accomplishments. While some were of dubious virtue (though neither limited to communist lands nor just the Cold War era), the nurturing of physical culture among the general population was a strong priority.

Success in elite sport is a tool of soft power. To this end, the countries in the Soviet sphere of influence and Yugoslavia provided sport with direct normative and financial support. Additionally, public education systems allowed talented youth athletes to combine schooling and the pursuit of competitive sport. Communist countries were actually the first to introduce physical education into general school curricula. Once only the domain of aristocratic boys (Bonnamaux, 1918), physical education was extended to students of all social classes and genders after the socialist revolutions that started in 1917. This formed the origins of the democratisation of physical activity and the conception of sport as a right rather than a privilege (Anthony, 1981).

Fuelled by the Marxist ideal of an interrelated development of mental and physical states, the Soviet Union was the first nation to introduce 'a national fitness program for virtually all age groups and free access to the means of pursuing sport' (Riordan, 1981, p. 15). This promoted the equality of all people, furthered the country's military needs, and later contributed to modernising what had been a traditional folk culture. To accomplish these goals, the All-Union Physical Culture Council – the country's de facto ministry of sport – was inaugurated in 1930 (Riordan, 1981).

The systematic organisation of physical activity dates even further back in Czechoslovakia. The Prague *Sokol* ('Falcon'), a gymnastics association that promoted physical fitness in connection with national independence from Austria-Hungary, was founded in 1862. (Women were admitted in 1869). *Sokol* instructors often worked as physical education teachers, facilitating the expansion of content and educational approaches into academic curricula (Kostka, 1981). The link was so strong and efficient that some gymnastics and physical activity routines devised by *Sokol* are still used today in school and sport programmes. Language, cultural proximity, and oppression by the same monarchy facilitated the spread of the *Sokol* movement to Slovenia and Croatia: the *Južni Sokol* ('Southern Falcon') society was established in 1863, one year after it was inaugurated in Prague (Pavlin, 2013).

The Soviet Union was eager to prove the superiority of the Marxist model in all aspects of society, including competitive sport. Therefore, it joined the Olympic movement soon after World War II. To comply with the requirement for athletes to be amateurs, the existing system of athletic talent development was further intertwined with schools and other institutions to allow athletes to pursue paths as students, servicemen or physical education teachers. Dedicated sports schools combining the regular curriculum with sports training also emerged (Riordan, 1981).

Other CEE countries, including Czechoslovakia and Yugoslavia, were less driven to succeed on the international competitive playing field; however, they still adopted physical education as an integral part of the school curriculum. The purpose was to promote physical and moral development, educate pupils about health and hygiene, and prepare them for life, labour and defence. Syllabi encouraged all-around development through gymnastics and rhythmic exercises, competitive team games and sports, and (in higher grades) skiing and athletics. School sports clubs complemented the general PE curriculum until about age 11, and offered opportunities for specialisation and competition to older pupils. Periodic 'sports days' promoted leisure-time sports activity. Notably, compulsory physical education also applied to university students.

For adults, physical activity was encouraged through the provision of opportunities in the workplace (e.g. recreational leagues, gatherings and competitions sponsored by labour unions) and the establishment of popular 'sport for all' organisations. At the local level, gymnastics and other sports organisations managed gymnasiums and sports facilities (which were owned by the state in communist countries and by the local community in socialist ones), while alpine/mountaineering associations maintained an extensive network of mountain huts. Membership in sports organisations provided free access to sports facilities.

The policy framework changed after the collapse of communism and the dissolution of multinational states held together by Marxist ideals. The new ideological framework underpinning society resulted in the state's withdrawal from many social institutions, including sport. The state's ability to financially sustain specialised programmes also declined.

In Slovenia, contemporary physical education is directed at the 'harmonious bio-psycho-social development of the young person, relaxation, neutralisation of the negative effects of prolonged sitting and other unhealthy habits' (Kovač et al., 2011: 4). Through it, pupils should learn a 'healthy lifestyle to nurture well-being, health, vitality and life optimism' (Kovač et al., 2011: 4). Curricula in other CEE countries have similar goals and sometimes more explicitly expand them with objectives related to hygiene and nurturing co-operation or teamwork.

Most states introduced mid-term (four to eight years) or long-term (10 years, or 15 in Estonia) national strategies to identify strategic and policy orientations to pursue the public interest as it pertains to sport.[3] The Slovenian document identifies four specific fields of interest: sports education (i.e. youth sport), recreation, competitive and elite sport, and disability sport. The state supports them mainly by providing funds for infrastructure and educational and professional initiatives, although not all fields are financed evenly (Ministry of Education, Science and Sport, 2014). Latvia lists the same general priorities (Ministry of Education and Science, 2014). Some countries identify priorities that are unique to their needs; e.g. the National Sport Strategy of Hungary (Hungarian Parliament, 2007) calls for special provisions for the Roma population as a marginalised group, while Romanian strategic documents call for locally responsive programmes that are sensitive to local traditions and needs (Romanian Federation Sport For All, 2001). National plans also provide a model and framework for similar strategies at lower levels of government.

National strategies for physical activity for health promotion explain in greater detail the welfare value of sport and physical activity. These strategies are developed in response to international policy guidelines published by the Council of the European Union, European Commission's High Level Group on Nutrition and Physical activity, the World Health Organization and others. They identify areas of national (content) concerns and (funding) priorities, which typically include increasing the physical activity of the population, often in an attempt to curb obesity. Other priorities include preventing chronic disease and mitigating the negative consequences of a sedentary lifestyle. Some countries also developed specific interdisciplinary policies. For example, the Czech National Strategy for Cycling Development, formally published by the Ministry of Transport (2013), aims to make cycling safer and promote it as mode of travel to school and the workplace.

Today, sports policies in CEE countries are still related to broader social welfare policies. There is still a strong link to education: this has allowed sport to become a powerful tool of social integration. (National teams in the former multi-state countries were sometimes composed on athletic, as well as national/ethnic criteria to promote integration and even development.) Legacy traits also include the support for non-governmental organisations (e.g. sport clubs; see Breuer, Hoekman, Nagel and van der Werff, 2015) and the promotion of physical activity for health. The concept of health-related physical activity (or fitness) in particular emerged relatively recently. This may be due to the new ideological underpinnings of the social system, or simply a reaction to contemporary issues: before 1991, life was considerably less sedentary.

Citizens' normative and institutional perspectives on sport and welfare policies

Welfare states and sports systems are connected in complex ways. Reasons range from unique cultural and ideological rationales (Heinemann, 2005) to the common political understanding of the 'societal role' of sport as defined by the White Paper on Sport (European Commission, 2007). The welfare benefits that individual member states reap depend on how they pursue goals and priorities through policies on sport, health and education. Also influential are the measures implemented by states to achieve social inclusion.

To assess how these normative guidelines influenced real-life policy-making, let us modify Heinemann's (2005) typology and identify three layers of the welfare character of sport. First, individual citizens and social communities should perceive sport as a pillar of their personal welfare, social security and higher quality of life. Then, state authorities should identify the historical foundation, define the ideological perception and provide argumentation for the importance of sport as a public interest. This provides the basis and legitimacy for state intervention into the field of sport (as also illustrated in the preceding section). Finally, from a procedural standpoint, institutions should produce relevant sports and welfare policy documents that can efficiently address the identified priorities and create the conditions for their implementation. (This is an aspect that Croatia is only slowly accomplishing, as indicated in an earlier footnote.) The measures that it enables should be established and active.

Participation in sport and physical activity may be driven by many motivating factors, including psychological (e.g. enjoyment, but also stress management), interpersonal (e.g. social recognition, affiliation), health (e.g. ill-health avoidance and positive health), body-related (e.g. weight management and appearance) and fitness motives (e.g. strength and endurance) (Markland and Ingledew, 1997).

The objective of the welfare state is to provide equal access to life opportunities and an equitable distribution of material goods and services to secure a minimum living standard (Heinemann, 2005: 182). To this end, supporting physical activity pursuits is warranted when these activities aim to fulfil health or interpersonal motives (specifically, social inclusion). In the past, the state supported fitness motives in an effort to develop strong workers and fit soldiers. The changing natures of work and warfare made this goal largely obsolete. Today, personal fitness is a self-actualisation, rather than welfare goal: while important, it falls outside public interest. Similarly, competitive sports are largely directed at promoting the nation among internal and external publics, and only in part to promote physical activity.

Citizens of CEE countries differ widely in their attitudes to sport and physical activity. Citizens of Slovenia and the Czech Republic rank among the most active in Europe, while those of Romania and Bulgaria are among the least active. Health improvement tends to be the most popular reason for sport participation in all CEE countries, as in most Western European nations (European Commission, 2017).

Normative settings and policy designs also differ. While all CEE countries adopted legislation regulating the role of state and local authorities in supporting sport, five (Bulgaria, Croatia, Hungary, Lithuania and Romania) even mention sport in their constitutional acts, often (though not always) in the context of ensuring citizens' health. Public interest in sport is also pursued through codified promotion and support for elite sport (especially in Visegrád and South-east European countries). This is also true for youth sport, especially in combination with the educational system (in the Czech Republic, Hungary, Baltic, and former Yugoslav countries) (Chaker, 2004; Sobry, 2012).

Institutional designs in CEE countries have largely retained centralised governmental jurisdictions used in previous systems of governance. Most regulations and policy programmes continue to be implemented from the top. As a field of public policy, sport is most often incorporated into ministries responsible for education and science (Croatia, Czech Republic, Latvia, Lithuania, Slovakia and Slovenia). In Bulgaria and Romania, it is part of the ministry of youth and sport, whereas more unique arrangements can be found in Estonia (Ministry of Culture), Hungary (Ministry of Human Resources) and Poland (Ministry of Sport and Tourism). The institutional arrangement in Poland provides perhaps the most vivid example of the different conceptions of the role of sport. Some individuals and nations see it mainly as a leisure and economic category, whereas others continue emphasising its educational and even cultivation emphasis. This is particularly prominent in states where 'physical culture' was a defining driver of nationhood. On average, CEE countries allocate around 0.1% of their national budgets to sport. Of this, about 30% is allocated from sources at the national level and 70% comes out of local budgets. Substantial portions come from lottery revenues. Frequently, local authorities and sports organisations and clubs are responsible for implementing national policies (Breuer, Hoekman, Nagel and van der Werff, 2015; Scheerder, Annick and Elien, 2017).

In addition to the institutional structure provided by state authorities, a central role is played by national Olympic committees and national federations. These are always formally organised as non-governmental organisations, even though current or former political figures often hold influential or even leading positions.

At the grassroots level, sport mainly occurs within clubs. These range from fully amateur outfits to youth sections of professional and semi-professional teams. Club sports are frequently subsidised by local governments. They are much better organised and much more competitive than school teams and inter-scholastic athletics, which exist as a complement to physical (or sports) education in schools. The contemporary CEE model thus largely reflects Western and EU models of sport (Petry, Steinbach and Tokarski, 2004; European Commission, 2007). Among adults, attitudes towards membership in sports clubs and their perceived importance as providers of participation opportunities rank from 'slightly' to 'well' below average EU rates. Thus, organised club sports are considered to be the domain of youth. An exception is adult involvement in voluntary work that supports sporting activities, in which CEE countries (except Hungary and Poland) rank among the top in the union (European Commission, 2014; Breuer, Hoekman, Nagel and van der Werff, 2015).

Although European sports policy documents emphasise the societal role of sport (European Commission, 2007), CEE countries have been slow to embrace its *communautaire* meaning and interpretation. Governments refer to the general concepts and even to the White Paper on Sport in public communications and official meetings. However, few incorporate these ideas into key national policy documents and implement them in real life. Fewer still combine sport and welfare programmes or develop practical synergistic initiatives. State and sport authorities alike focus more on supporting elite sport and less on the social benefits of physical activity and its potential contributions to societies in the 21st century. Meanwhile, citizens clearly perceive sport as valuable, especially as a means to improve health.

Conclusion

Central and Eastern European countries share some similarities yet also have many differences; the greatest parallels can be found within each of the four regional and cultural clusters that make up the group. Although all have a common 'communist' past, Marxist ideals were implemented quite differently in Soviet states, satellite states and non-aligned Yugoslavia. After the early 1990s, countries adopted different policies, resulting in uneven social and economic success. The most accomplished states – arguably the Czech Republic, Estonia, Slovakia and Slovenia – their citizens seem more concerned with the role of sport both *in* and *for* a society than other nations in the group.

Contemporary strategies and policies in Central and Eastern European countries generally identify areas of interest and concern, provide guidelines and allocate public funding for specific initiatives. National governments more or less successfully translate European and international priorities into local languages and provide funding to entrepreneurial initiatives pursuing them. This has replaced broad networks of relatively unique state-run programmes often grounded in grassroots initiatives, culture and combined with civil society organisations. Experts disagree over whether the state's withdrawal has been successful – or sufficient. Before 1990, states in Central and Eastern Europe focused on pursuing priorities they had identified; today, they focus on identifying priorities to pursue.

Notes

1 In Slovenia, registered unemployment increased from 13,964 people in 1986 to 129,087 in 1993 (Atelšek, 2016).
2 Individual Member States choose the best social policy model for them and adopt different traditions of welfare policies; hence the separate chapters in this section of the book. Esping-Andersen's seminal work provides a detailed discussion on the three worlds of welfare capitalism (1990). Welfare models in CEE countries do not readily fit any existing typology. Also, while CEE welfare states share some distinct characteristics even after transitioning to democracy, their similarities are still small compared to the parallels among 'old democracies'.
3 At the time of this writing in January 2019, Croatia was the only country without such a strategy. One (covering the 2019–2026 period) is being publicly discussed and will probably pass in 2019. Its legal basis is provided by a 2006 law (Brajdić, 2019). The Croatian Olympic committee passed an eight-year national programme in 2014.

Bibliography

Anthony, D., 1981, Introduction. In Riordan, J. (ed.), *Sport under communism* (2nd ed.). London: C. Hurst & Co., pp. 1–12.

Atelšek, R., 2016 (28 May), Zakaj je danes desetkrat več brezposelnih kot v Jugoslaviji? Siol.net. Retrieved from: https://siol.net/posel-danes/moja-sluzba/zakaj-je-danes-desetkrat-vec-brezposelnih-kot-v-jugoslaviji-417980.

Boje, T.P. and Potůček, M. (eds), 2011, *Social rights, active citizenship, and governance in the European Union*. Mannheim: Nomos.

Bonnamaux, C., 1918, The contributions of Baron Pierre De Coubertin to physical education. *American Physical Education Review*, 23(2), pp. 91–98. Retrieved from: https://doi.org/10.1080/23267224.1918.10650691.

Brajdić, D., 2019 (19 January), Predstavljen prvi hrvatski Nacionalni program sporta. Večernji list. Retrieved from: www.vecernji.hr/sport/predstavljen-prvi-hrvatski-nacionalni-program-sporta-1295520.

Breuer, C., Hoekman, R., Nagel, S. and van der Werff, H. (eds), 2015, *Sport clubs in Europe: A cross-national comparative perspective*. Heidelberg: Springer.

Cerami, A. and Vanhuysse, P. (eds), 2009, *Theorizing social policy transformations in Central and Eastern Europe*. Basingstoke: Palgrave Macmillan.

Chaker, A.-N., 2004, *Good governance in sport: A European survey*. Strasbourg: Council of Europe.

Esping-Andersen, G., 1990, *The three worlds of welfare capitalism*. Princeton, NJ: Princeton University Press.

European Commission, 2007, White Paper on Sport (COM/2007/0391). Retrieved from: https://eur-lex.europa.eu/legal-content/EN/TXT/?uri=CELEX%3A52007DC0391.
European Commission, 2014, *Sport and physical activity report: Special Eurobarometer 412*. Retrieved from: http://ec.europa.eu/commfrontoffice/publicopinion/index.cfm/Survey/getSurveyDetail/instruments/special/yearFrom/1974/yearTo/2014/search/sport/surveyKy/1116.
European Commission, 2017, *Sport and physical activity report: Special Eurobarometer 472*. Retrieved from: http://ec.europa.eu/commfrontoffice/publicopinion/index.cfm/survey/getsurveydetail/instruments/special/surveyky/2164.
Eurostat, 2017, *Key figures on Europe, 2017 edition*. Luxembourg: Publications Office of the European Union.
Heinemann, K., 2005, Sport and the welfare state in Europe. *European Journal of Sport Science*, 5(4), 181–188.
Hungarian Parliament, 2007, Nemzeti Sportstratégia 2007–2020. Budapest: Hungarian Official Journal. Retrieved from: http://njt.hu/cgi_bin/njt_doc.cgi?docid=110484.156866.
Kostka, V., 1981, Czechoslovakia. In Riordan, J. (Ed.), *Sport under communism* (2nd ed.). London: C. Hurst & Co., pp. 55–66.
Kovač, M.et al., 2011, *Učni načrt. Program osnovna šola. Športna vzgoja*. Ljubljana: Ministrstvo za šolstvo in šport, Zavod RS za šolstvo. Retrieved from: www.mizs.gov.si/fileadmin/mizs.gov.si/pageuploads/podrocje/os/prenovljeni_UN/UN_sportna_vzgoja.pdf.
Markland, D. and Ingledew, D.K., 1997, The measurement of exercise motives: Factorial validity and invariance across gender of a revised Exercise Motivations Inventory. *British Journal of Health Psychology*, 2(4), pp. 361–376. Retrieved from: http://dx.doi.org/10.1111/j.2044-8287.1997.tb00549.x.
Ministry of Education and Science, 2014, *Sporta politikas pamatnostādnes 2014.-2020. gadam*. Riga: State Chancellery. Retrieved from: http://polsis.mk.gov.lv/view.do?id=4599.
Ministry of Education, Science and Sport, 2014, *Nacionalni program športa v Republiki Sloveniji 2014–2023*. Ljubljana: Ministry of Education, Science and Sport. Retrieved from: www.mizs.gov.si/en/legislation_and_documents/.
Ministry of Transport, 2013, *Národní strategii rozvoje cyklistické dopravy České republiky pro léta 2013 až 2020*. Prague: Ministry of Transport. Retrieved from: www.cyklodoprava.cz/file/cyklostrategie-2013-final/.
Offe, K. and Fuchs, S., 2007, Welfare state formation in the enlarged European Union – Patterns of reform in the post-communist new Member States. Discussion Paper SP IV 2007-2306. Berlin: Wissenschaftszentrum Berlin fur Sozialforschung.
Pavlin, T., 2013, Sokol movement in Slovenia: 150th anniversary of Južni Sokol. *Science of Gymnastics Journal*, 5(3), pp. 5–18.
Petry, K., Steinbach, D., and Tokarski, W., 2004, Sport systems in the countries of the European Union: Similarities and differences. *European Journal for Sport and Society*, 1(1), pp. 15–21.
Potůček, M., 2008, Metamorphoses of welfare states in Central and Eastern Europe. In Seeleib-Kaiser, M. (ed.), *Welfare state transformations*. Basingstoke: Palgrave Macmillan, pp. 79–95.
Riordan, J., 1981, The USSR. In Riordan, J. (ed.), *Sport under communism* (2nd ed.). London: C. Hurst & Co., pp. 13–54.

Romanian Federation Sport For All, 2001, *Sportul pentrul toti – Romania Mileniuli III – un alt mod de viata*. Bucharest: Romanian Federation Sport For All. Retrieved from: http://sportulpentrutoti.ro/informatii-generale/.

Scheerder, J., Willem, A., and Claes, E. (eds.), 2017, *Sport policy systems and sport federations: A cross-national perspective*. Basingstoke: Palgrave Macmillan.

Sobry, C. (ed.), 2012, *Sports governance in the world II: The transition in Central and Eastern European sport*. Paris: Le Manuscrit.

13 In the homeland of sport for all
The Scandinavian countries

Irene Masoni

Introduction: a sports model for the Scandinavian countries

The following paragraphs identify the characteristics of Scandinavian sports systems with a focus on the three Scandinavian countries: Norway, Denmark and Sweden. Surely one of the most interesting aspects to be investigated concerns the way in which the culture underlying democratic social welfare systems may have played a decisive role in developing the characteristics of national sports systems. In particular, it is interesting to understand how the universalism of public policies of these countries can be linked to the high participation level of citizens in sporting activities. One of the elements that distinguishes all of the systems taken into consideration is the close relationship that exists between voluntary organisations and public institutions. As presented below, the main characteristics that link these three sports systems can be summarised in this way the result is a voluntary sport movement characterised by a huge degree of autonomy and self-regulation, combined with extensive state support based on the notion of sport as an important component of the welfare society (Ronglan 2015). This relationship is certainly a key to understanding how the sports systems of these countries have been able to encourage sports participation.

The Norwegian sports model

The current structure of the sports system dates back to 1996 when the NIF and the NOC (the Norwegian Olympic Committee) became a single organisation retaining the name of NIF (The Norwegian Olympic and Paralympic Committee and Confederation of Sports), which progressively assumed a monopoly position over the panorama of Norwegian sport.

We can divide the Norwegian sports system into two levels: on the one hand, the administrative apparatus attributed to the public administrative bodies present in the territory, and on the other the sports organisation, comprising the sports federations and their territorial branches. At the base of the structure are the clubs, represented at the local level within the local sports council.[1] The vertices of the two parts of the system instead are occupied by the sports department – located with the Ministry of Culture – and the NIF (Norwegian Olympic and Paralympic Committee and Confederation of Sports). However, the role of the state is that of sustaining activities that are performed thanks to the NIF and the volunteer organisations (clubs) that are a part of it. We can define these as two branches of the same system, one public and the other strictly characterised by organisations with a volunteer basis (Skille and Säfvenbom 2011).

Since 1982, sports policies have been under the jurisdiction of the Ministry of Culture, within which the sports department (DSP) was created, which – in place of the executive branch of the ministry – acts autonomously from the Norwegian parliament in allocating and distributing resources that come directly from the National Gambling Agency (the national gambling system). Between the national structure of the NIF and the DSP, a mutual dependence has progressively been established, because the former is dependent on government transfers to carry out its own activities, while the latter needs the NIF in the policy implementation phase.

As far as the expertise of the local administrations is concerned, if the counties have a marginal role, the role of the municipal governments turns out to be more than relevant: in each of these, if more than three clubs are present, the creation of a *local sports council* is envisioned. The *local sports councils* give representation to the members of the club and are the point of contact between these and the municipal governments. Among its primary tasks is the job of discussing questions concerning the availability and the allocation of infrastructure, including from a programmatic perspective (Skille and Säfvenbom 2011).

Statistical surveys confirm that Norway is a virtuous country in terms of the diffusion of sports participation among the population. Taking the data published in 2016 concerning the membership of sports clubs, there were a total of 1,887,342 members (the data refers to the end of 2015): among these, the percentage consistently accounted for by women was close to 40%. When we consider that the Norwegian population is about 5 million, the percentage of the total population with membership card holders is over 40%.[2]

The data related to what we can define as physically active citizenship are also significant: according to Norsk Monitor data (2015),[3] more than 75% of Norwegian citizens attest to practising physical or sports activity at least once per week, while for those who practise physical activity three or more times per week the number is close to 40%.[4]

The other central topic of Norwegian sport is the resources available. The existence of a constant allocation of resources coming from revenue derived from the gambling system not only represents a guarantee in terms of quantity but it is also perceived as a great example of transparency in the use of these funds by the state at the same time, which are destined – as previously mentioned – to sustain the creation of sports facilities in a prevalent way.

The entire system is fed by a financial mechanism that largely rests on the revenue derived from gambling (Norsk Tipping), of which Norway has yet to start liberalising. This is certainly not an aspect to be underestimated considering that keeping the financing system of sports (and culture) anchored to that of gambling guarantees an influx of constant and certain resources to the entire system. Added to this source of funding, there are the contributions made by local entities, municipal governments in particular. These are public contributions that – in the majority of cases – are destined create and maintain sports infrastructures.

The total revenue derived from the betting and gambling system is subdivided in a particular way to sustain sports, with 64% allocated for sports purposes, 18% for cultural purposes and the other 18% for social and humanitarian organisations not affiliated with the Norwegian Sports Federation or the Norwegian Olympic and Paralympic Committee (NIF).[5]

More than €250 million[6] – to which the resources that come from the territorial institutions are added – is invested by the Sports department of the Norwegian Ministry of Culture. This is a number that must be put into perspective with the current territorial population, which gives us a per capita expenditure of about €40.

The resources that derive from betting are only a part of the total amount: to these resources that pass through the Olympic Committee, the resources of the municipal governments are also added. The municipalities' resources not only sustain the creation of infrastructure but also create – albeit to a lesser extent – specific projects destined to particular targets and the support of activities carried out by the local sports clubs (Bergsgard and Norberg 2010).

This data should obviously be approximate and used only to give us an order of magnitude with which to compare the two national systems. Precisely from the perspective of comparison, it is also necessary to refer to the absolute figures that correspond to the resources invested in the sector, the differences in national wealth and the different cost of living (the Norwegian per capita GDP is about €67,000).[7]

A final note concerns the goals and instruments declared in the two White Papers on Norwegian sport: both the 1999 and 2012 White Book of Norwegian (Kulturdepartementet 2012, 1999) sport underlined the need for sports activity to be founded on the values of leisure, sharing and well-being and that the actions of government and local entities can find legitimacy based on these elements. However, according to official documents, public action in the sports sector appears more connected to the theme of infrastructure. This aspect clearly emerges, in the 1999 White Book of Sport, as the moment at which the creation of structures for sports activity becomes identified as the main instrument capable of supporting sports for all (Seippel and Skille 2015).

The Danish sports model

The Ministry of Culture is at the top of the system, although its activities are limited to 'responsibility for forming and adapting legislation on sport and also for drawing up general agreements with the main sports organisations' (Ibsen 2017).

On the other hand, the municipalities have the most direct responsibility in this area, since they provide financial support for building and maintaining sports facilities and are the point of reference for local sports organisations. The system of public administrations responsible for the sports sector is complemented by the sports system – in the strict sense of the term – comprising non-governmental players.

The main characteristic distinguishing the Danish system is attributable to the existence of three national umbrella organisations to which the sports organisations, present in the national territory, belong. The existence of this subdivision can mainly be traced back to historical-cultural reasons that led to the establishment of three different points of reference within the Danish sports system. The Danish Gymnastic and Sport Associations (DGI) have developed in the rural areas of the country, and the Sport Confederation of Denmark (DIF) has developed based on the bourgeois sports movement and has its roots in the urban areas of the country. By contrast, the latest organisation – the Danish Association for Company sport (DFIF) – is closely linked to the workplace communities (Ibsen et al. 2016).

Although it may seem that these three organisations carry out activities in a competitive situation, in practice the majority of sports clubs (about 60%) are linked to both of the main organisations (DGI and DIF) (Ibsen 2017). The two main national organisations promote activities that can be considered in some way complementary: elite sport is mainly related to the activities carried out within the DIF, while grassroots sports activities are mainly part of the mission of the DGI.

As mentioned above, municipalities are strongly involved in supporting sports activities. In 1969, the 'Leisure Time Act' obliged municipalities to support the sports activities that they promote within the framework of voluntarily organised sport. Support to the clubs materialises through support regarding the expenses connected with infrastructure and to a lesser extent in the form of direct support for the activities carried out by the clubs and addressed to young people. Sports facilities are the primary tool through which public institutions support sports activity (Rafoss and Troelsen 2010).

The data on sports participation published in 2014 in the Eurobarometer report (European Commission 2014) confirm that Denmark is one of the countries whose citizens are the most active. According to the survey, about 68% of citizens practise physical or sporting activity at least once a week.

The data, referring instead to participation in sporting activities as members of clubs, are more complex, precisely due to the absence of a monopolistic structure and the presence of three federal umbrella organisations.[8] According to the latest data published in the document *Idrætten i tal* (Fester 2018), the members in 2017 were as follows: DIF 1,924,213; DGI 1,586,378 and DFIF 348,192. Obviously, it should be remembered that these data do not consider the possibility of double membership. Although these values can certainly be over-estimated, the levels of sports participation among a population of just under 6 million inhabitants are quite significant, even taking into account the data relating only to the members of DIF organisations.

Regarding the sources of funding for the Danish sports system, funding from both the central and local level should be taken into account. Revenue from the betting system is shared at the national level between the federal organisations. In addition to these resources, there are funds invested directly in the sports sector by the municipalities, which are mainly used to maintain the infrastructure or reduce clubs' rental costs. The data reported by Ibsen et al. (2016) identify €122 million from the betting system being transferred mainly to DIF and DGI in 2013. In addition, about €425 million was invested in the sector by municipalities.

The Swedish sports model

Like the two sports systems described above, the Swedish system is also characterised by the central role of voluntary sports organisations.

The structure of the Swedish sports system can be traced back to the European pyramidal system, at the top of which there is a single organisation (the Swedish Sport Confederation), to which the various sports federations belong. The organisation of the sports system – as explained by Fahlén and Stenling (2016) – follows two paths: on the one hand, the geographical articulation, and on the other, the sports articulation (with a subdivision by disciplines that correspond to each federation).

The tools used by the Swedish state to promote sports activities have changed and developed over time. The first concrete initiative in the sports sector dates back to 1930, with the introduction of a national plan for the building of facilities dedicated to sports activities. Progressively, the national resources were flanked by local resources with the provision of funds specifically dedicated to supporting the activities carried out by sports organisations. In particular, since the 2000s, the central government has launched specific projects dedicated to sports organisations and aimed at improving public health, lifelong learning, adult education, urban and education policy (e.g. 'The Handshake', 'The Sports Lift') (Osterlind and Wright 2014).

Therefore, as we have seen in other systems, public support for sports activities is mainly directed towards voluntary sports organisations, which are supported by a dual channel comprising national and municipal resources. Government support is directed towards the activities of voluntary sports organisations through the SSC, while infrastructure is a municipalities' competence. An annual government grant of €210 million goes to voluntary and membership-based club sport and also municipalities support the sector with €490 million (€360 million to facilities and €130 million to activities) (Fahlén 2015).

With regard to data on sports participation, these are in line with those shown for other Scandinavian countries and even better. In 2014 the Eurobarometer report (Special Eurobarometer 412 – Sport and Physical Activity) shows Sweden as the country whose citizens are the most active. According to the survey, about 70% of citizens practise physical or sporting activity at least once a week. 3,145,000 are citizens who are members (Centrum för idrottsforskning 2015) of a sports club.

Conclusion: the link between welfare systems and sports systems

Norway, Denmark and Sweden are all countries belonging to the social-democratic welfare model. According to the most common classifications, these countries are characterised by protection against social risks of a universal nature, which means that rights are enjoyed because the individual is a member of this community and does not derive from his/her work position. Added to this is a strong investment in active politics and gender equality, as reflected in the dynamics of the labour market (Esping-Andersen 1990; Hemerijck 2013).

Although this relevance of volunteering within systems where access to services is guaranteed directly by public institutions may seem contradictory, in reality the role of these organisations seems to be perfectly in line with the key principles of social-democratic culture. In this framework, it is therefore relevant to reflect on the role of non-profit and voluntary organisations that represent the main players in supplying sports services, as well as the redistributive role of public institutions (Enjolras and Strømsnes 2018).

The literature speaks of the existence of an implicit contract between the world of sport and the state, according to which the latter supports the sporting activities carried out within independent organisations, traceable to civil society, and these promote shared values that in turn strengthen according to mechanisms of circularity (Bairner et al. 2016). The idea of community, cooperation and social solidarity are therefore the basis of the redistributive action of the state but are also characteristic of the activities carried out within civil society organisations. A broader analysis of the characteristics of the social-democratic welfare model suggests that we consider not only public provisions but also the emphasis placed by these systems on the need to promote trust or social capital. This approach translates into the promotion of active participation within the organisations of civil society within which it is possible to strengthen not only the spirit of belonging but also that of equality and integration (Svendsen and Svendsen 2016).

Civil society organisations – like sports ones – have increasingly become 'an arena for socializing and the pursuit of personal interests – very positive things, of course – but to a decreasing extent as intermediary structures between the citizen and the political system' (Selle and Wollebæk 2010: 12). The same authors refer to a second relevant feature that can explain the wide involvement of citizens in voluntary organisations, namely that membership has its base in a political and social culture in which everybody, everywhere should be included (Selle and Wollebæk 2010).[9]

As suggested by Enjolras (2008: 779), non-profit sports organisations are particularly able to mobilise resources especially based on reciprocity norms:

Volunteer organisations are seen as governance structures that reinforce the norm of (generalised or balanced) reciprocity, making the pooling of resources possible according to the reciprocity principle and, because of these features, facilitating collective action oriented towards public or mutual interest or advocacy. (Enjolras 2008: 779)

Ibsen and Seippel (2010) describe the role that volunteers play in sports clubs in Denmark and Norway: 'associations are absolutely dependent on member generated-resources – partly in the form of members' dues and income from activities organised by volunteers, and partly in the form of voluntary work'. It is clear that reciprocity is the main form of integration among Scandinavian sports organisations. The offer of service is clearly based on 'a circulation of goods between groups and individuals that can only take shape when all participating parties are willing to establish a social relationship' (Evers and Laville 2004: 18). The organisations' activities seem strongly connected to the human relations within the local context. Sports practice can be considered part of a community lifestyle and the clubs are places where all members are able to make a concrete contribution according to their capability and available time.

This aspect influences not only the characteristics of each sports organisation but also the characteristics of the entire sports system: if the practice is a daily activity within a community, the principle of competitiveness could be said to be overshadowed or at least stand side by side with the principle of participation. Accordingly, multi-sport community-based clubs have certainly contributed to the inclusive character of sport.

The redistributive role of the state is instead substantiated mainly through financial support for the construction of sports facilities. Public institutions chose this strategy with a specific aim, whereby more facilities equates to more opportunities for citizens and organisations. Indeed, the cost of building a sports facility is difficult to bear for non-profit organisations. If we look at the Scandinavian systems, public intervention (with the investment of local and national resources) permits them to create uniform standards throughout the entire country.

Sports organisations carry out their activities thanks to public support, which derives from general taxation but also (especially in the Norwegian case) a specific funding channel: the gambling system. The resources that arise from a gambling system are granted at the national level and are mainly invested at the local level in building facilities.

Moreover, in the discussion about the features of sports systems, sports participation and the welfare models, the amount of public resources invested in the sports sector must be considered, however indirectly used. Investment in the sector has been driven in these countries by the conviction that it could be identified as a means of contributing to the well-being of the population. The focus of public policies has long been projected towards 'sport for all', with the objective that this activity could effectively participate in the creation and dissemination of citizens' well-being (Carlsson et al. 2011).

The decision to invest mainly in sports facilities for organised activities makes it possible to support an activity that is considered to be a public responsibility. At the same time, this approach makes it possible to protect the independence of sport and its non-governmental character (Norberg 1997).

Therefore, the Scandinavian sports model – characterised by the co-existence of redistributive mechanisms combined with strong ties of reciprocity within voluntary sports organisations – has allowed the practice of sport as an activity that is accessible to all. Even if the instruments adopted are peculiar (collaboration between the governmental and non-governmental apparatus), public policies have obtained a universalistic nature over the years.

However, this model is faced with challenges that must necessarily be addressed. The relationship between the state and voluntary organisations has certainly been the main driving force in the development of sports systems and contributed to the practice of sport among citizens. The commercialisation of sport and the de-structuring of spaces, the spread of individual physical practices can however challenge the privileged relationship between public institutions and voluntary sports organisations. Another important aspect to be discussed is the role of initiatives linked to specific policy objectives. In fact, we need to understand if we can really talk about the independence of the sports sector, with respect to political power, in the way in which public policies encourage, through specific funding, sports organisations to promote activities more focused on non-sporting outcomes (Coalter 2010) and tagged towards specific groups (e.g. disabled, migrants). The introduction of public policies based on the building of facilities makes it possible to maintain a clear separation between the sports system (which carries out its activities independently) and the public system. According to Norberg (2011), the emphasis placed on the capacity of the sports system to produce welfare and to achieve politically defined objectives has made the cooperation agreement between voluntary sports organisations and public institutions more formal. An increase of resources dedicated to specific projects could threaten this partition, but could be seen as a response to the needs of a more fragmented and less homogeneous society.

Notes

1 The Local Sport Councils are representative bodies of the sports clubs. They are created by the municipal government and are the connecting bodies between the sports system (the clubs) and the local public administration (the municipality) (Masoni 2017).
2 One should also consider that the total population includes children and the elderly.
3 Data contained in the Norsk Monitor Report 2015/2016 (Rapport utarbeidet for Norges Idrettsforbund og olympiske og paralympiske komité Erik Dalen og Jørgen Holbæk-Hanssen, oktober/november 2016). Web site: https://www.idrettsforbundet.no/globalassets/idrett/voksenidrett/2016-voksenidrett-rapport-ipsos-mmi-fysisk-aktivitet-i-befolkningen-1985-2015.pdf (2/1/2018).
4 To have a means of contrasting this with other countries (keeping in mind that it deals with different statistical methods) see the Eurobarometer data – Special

Eurobarometer 412, *Sport and Physical Activity* (European Commission 2014), which regards only EU member countries (Norwegian data is therefore not available). From a study of the Eurobarometer information can be deduced on Denmark, Switzerland and Finland, for example: for these three countries the percentage of people who claim to regularly practise sports and physical activity is just above 65%.
5 The NIF financial report is subdivided into expense sections (Article 1: Sports facilities; Article 2: National structures/special structures; Article 3: Research and development work; Article 4: Antidoping and activity against the manipulation of sports competitions; Article 5: Norwegian Sports Federation and the Olympic and Paralympic Committee; Article 6: Funding in teams and local associations) and related expenditures.
6 The exchange rate in euros corresponds to 2,422,597,000 Norwegian crowns (January 2018).
7 Source: Eurostat (2015).
8 As mentioned above, organisations can become members of all three federal organisations, creating an additional difficulty in identifying possible double membership.
9 A vast body of literature exists on the characteristics of Norwegian civil society. It is not easy to identify a universal definition of civil society from the literature and its role in Norwegian society is also quite controversial. On this topic, in addition to the recent book edited by Enjolras and Strømsnes (2018), the chapter *A social democratic model of civil society* by Selle and Wollebæk included in Jobert and Kohler-Koch (2008) is also interesting.

Bibliography

Bairner, A., Kelly, J., Lee, J.W., 2016, *Routledge Handbook of Sport and Politics*. Routledge.
Bergsgard, N.A., Norberg, J.R., 2010, Sports policy and politics – the Scandinavian way, *Sport in Society*, 13, pp. 567–582.
Carlsson, B., Norberg, J.R., Persson, H.T.R., 2011, The governance of sport from a Scandinavian perspective, *International Journal of Sport Policy and Politics*, 3, pp. 305–309.
Centrum för idrottsforsknings, 2015, Statens stöd till idrotten – uppföljning. Centrum för idrottsforsknings.
Coalter, F., 2010. Sport-for-development: Going beyond the boundary?, *Sport in Society*, 13, pp. 1374–1391.
Enjolras, B., 2008, A governance-structure approach to voluntary organizations, *Nonprofit and Voluntary Sector Quarterly*, 38, pp. 761–783.
Enjolras, B., Strømsnes, K. (eds), 2018, *Scandinavian Civil Society and Social Transformations: The Case of Norway*. Nonprofit and Civil Society Studies. Springer International Publishing.
Esping-Andersen, G., 1990, *The three worlds of welfare capitalism*. Princeton University Press.
European Commission, 2014, *Special Eurobarometer 412 – Sport and Physical Activity*. TNS Opinion & Social.
Evers, A., Laville, J.-L., 2004, *The Third Sector in Europe*. Edward Elgar Publishing.
Fahlén, J., 2015, Sport Clubs in Sweden, in: Breuer, C., Hoekman, R., Nagel, S., van der Werff, H. (eds.), *Sport Clubs in Europe: A Cross-National Comparative Perspective*. Sports Economics, Management and Policy. Springer International Publishing, pp. 343–367.
Fahlén, J., Stenling, C., 2016, Sport policy in Sweden, *International Journal of Sport Policy and Politics*, 8, pp. 515–531.

Fester, M., 2018, *Idrætten i Tal 2017 – Status på foreningsidrætten i DanmarkIdrætten i tal 2017*. Danmarks Idrætsforbund.

Hemerijck, A., 2013, *Changing Welfare States*. Oxford University Press.

Ibsen, B., 2017. Denmark: The Dissenting Sport System in Europe, in: Scheerder, J., Willem, A., Claes, E. (eds), *Sport Policy Systems and Sport Federations: A Cross-National Perspective*. Palgrave Macmillan, pp. 89–112.

Ibsen, B., Nichols, G., Elmose-Østerlund, K., Breuer, C., 2016, *Sports Club Policies in Europe: A Comparison of the Public Policy Context and Historical Origins of Sports Clubs across Ten European Countries*. University of Southern Denmark, Odense, Centre for Sports, Health and Civil Society.

Ibsen, B., Seippel, Ø., 2010, Voluntary organized sport in Denmark and Norway, *Sport in Society*, 13, pp. 593–608.

Jobert, B., Kohler-Koch, B., 2008, *Changing Images of Civil Society: From Protest to Governance*. Routledge.

Kulturdepartementet, 2012. *Meld. St. 26(2011–2012)*. Kulturdepartementet.

Kulturdepartementet, 1999. *Idrettslivet i endring-Om statens forhold til idrett og fysisk aktivitet. St.meld.nr.14(1999–2000)*. Kulturdepartementet.

Masoni, I., 2017, Cultura e Pratica Sportiva Tra Volontariato e Intervento Pubblico: Il Caso Norvegese, *Culture e Studi Del Sociale CuSSoc*, 2, pp. 9–18.

Norberg, J.R., 1997, A mutual dependency: Nordic sports organizations and the state, *The International Journal of the History of Sport*, 14, pp. 115–135.

Norberg, J.R., 2011, A contract reconsidering? Changes in the Swedish state's relation to the sports movement, *International Journal of Sport Policy and Politics*, 3, pp. 311–325.

Osterlind, M., Wright, J., 2014, If sport's the solution then what's the problem? The social significance of sport in the moral governing of 'good' and 'healthy' citizens in Sweden, 1922–1998, *Sport, Education and Society*, 19, pp. 973–990.

Rafoss, K., Troelsen, J., 2010, Sports facilities for all? The financing, distribution and use of sports facilities in Scandinavian countries, *Sport in Society*, 13, pp. 643–656.

Ronglan, L.T., 2015. Elite sport in Scandinavian welfare states: legitimacy under pressure?, *International Journal of Sport Policy and Politics*, 7, pp. 345–363.

Seippel, Ø., Skille, E.Å., 2015. Sport Clubs in Norway, in: Breuer, C., Hoekman, R., Nagel, S., van der Werff, H. (eds), *Sport Clubs in Europe: A Cross-National Comparative Perspective*. Sports Economics, Management and Policy. Springer International Publishing, pp. 309–324.

Selle, P., Wollebæk, D., 2010. Why social democracy is not a civil society regime in Norway, *Journal of Political Ideologies*, 15, pp. 289–301.

Skille, E.Å., Säfvenbom, R., 2011, Sport policy in Norway, *International Journal of Sport Policy and Politics*, 3, pp. 289–299.

Svendsen, G.L.H., Svendsen, G.T., 2016. *Trust, Social Capital and the Scandinavian Welfare State: Explaining the Flight of the Bumblebee*. Edward Elgar Publishing.

Conclusion

Established models of European sport revisited from a socio-politological approach[1]

Jeroen Scheerder

Introduction

Change is key to society as no society can exist without. Sociocultural and socioeconomic changes, among others, also affect the world of sport. Developments occurring at demographic, economic, social, cultural, technological or political level are reflected and often even enlarged in and through sport and other forms of movement culture (Digel, 1995). During the past half century sport has shifted from a rather exceptional and exclusive pastime by and for the happy few towards an almost everyday leisure-time activity of many. In other words, sport has moved from a social fringe phenomenon to the centre of daily life. Crum (1991), based on the work of, among others, Cachay (1990), Dietrich and Heinemann (1989) and Digel (1990), has aptly coined this evolution as the 'societalisation' of sport, implying that sport is no longer an island but a fully fledged part of our society. In the wake of this societalisation of sport, other developments emerged, including processes like the governmentalisation of sport (Bergsgard et al., 2007), the politicisation of sport (Grix, 2016), the commercialisation and professionalisation of sport (Slack, 2004), the globalisation and commodification of sport (Giulianotti & Robertson, 2007; Maguire, 1999), the instrumentalisation of sport (Coalter, 2007), etc. All of these developments impacted on the world of sport, both on its structuration and organisation. Also, this diversification in sport has had an influence on policy-related and managerial aspects of sport. Hence, three general key questions can be put forward, namely: (i) to what extent is the established sports sector still in a dominant position based on which they rule the world of sports; (ii) to what extent have those in power adapted themselves to new challenges and needs in society; and (iii) to what extent have new actors taken over the steering position so that they can be considered as representing the contemporary world of sport? Before we try to deal with these questions, we will first focus on the process that enabled the societalisation of sport.

Towards a de-traditionalisation of sport

The birthplace of modern sport lies in 18th–19th-century England (Guttmann, 2004; Mandell, 1984). The development of the modern sports movement is usually associated with the rise of industrial society and related processes of urbanisation, modernisation and bureaucratisation (Renson, 1975; Stokvis, 2010). In the period of the industrial revolution, the English public schools in particular transformed sports-like entertainment into modern sports activities.[2] In this regard, Elias and Dunning (1986) speak of a *sportisation* process. Characteristic of this process is the emergence of a 'team- and club-organised character' of sport (Kugel, 1977: 130–131). Permanent sports teams were established from which the first sports clubs would later emerge. Sports such as cricket, golf and rugby, but also football, hockey, athletics, rowing, badminton, horse-riding, etc., all have unmistakable British roots. In the period in which Great Britain would grow into an imperial superpower, the British subsequently exported 'their' sports worldwide (Mangan, 1986). Based on the industrial production process, rationalisation and quantification can, among other things, be regarded as important features of modern sports (see Guttmann, 1978). If athletes and teams wanted to compete with each other in the same way, it was important to put standardised rules first and to comply with them. Assessing performance and keeping records also assume a form of standardisation. It soon became apparent that there was a need for an administrative and organisational framework. This heralded the emergence of the first supra-local sports organisations, read: the first national sports federations (Stokvis, 2010). The creation of national – and afterwards international – sports governing bodies plays an important role in the above-mentioned sportisation process (Dejonghe, 2010: 12–13). National sports federations were established not only to draw up standardised rules but also to organise national competitions, to homologate results and records, to designate national champions, to select national teams based on international competitions, etc. (Stokvis, 2010: 104). The first national sports bodies were founded in Great Britain in the 19th century, such as football (1863), swimming (1869), rugby (1871), athletics (1880), tennis (1888), etc. (Demasure, 1989; Guttmann, 2004; Renson, 1975). The establishment of sports federations on the European mainland would soon follow thereafter.

Ever since its inception, modern sports sought to achieve an autonomous organisational culture without too much interference from outside. In particular, the modern sports movement has always attached importance to a high degree of independence and self-regulation (Chappelet, 2010). Szymanski (2006) states that modern sports could be developed in Great Britain precisely because since the Enlightenment the government had become less and less concerned with controlling voluntary associations. Liberal values, such as freedom, self-reliance, private initiative, etc., are central to the Anglo-Saxon organisation model. One of the basic principles on which club-organised sports is built, therefore, is the idea that sports and government should be separated as much and as far as possible. The strong drive for autonomy that characterises modern sports also largely explains the relatively long run-up to the establishment of a strong public administration with a competence in the field of sports. The self-regulating and hierarchical nature of club- and federation-related sports has also meant that, in contrast to other sectors, the sports sector has only relatively recently focused on aspects of good governance (cf. Chaker, 2004; Council of Europe, 2012; IOC, 2008; Katwala, 2000). Until the middle of the previous century, sports clubs and sports federations were almost the only players that installed and directed sports practices. The range of sports offered by these actors focused strongly on competitive sports in a club setting. In this respect, one could speak of a process of corporatisation and particularisation of sports. Central to this is the principle of self-management (Bruyninckx & Scheerder, 2009), implying that in most European countries hardly any government intervention with regard to sports existed before World War II. For example, sports clubs and sports federations initially received no structural subsidies for their operation. For more than half a century from the founding of the first national sports federations, the field of sports has therefore been a virtually entirely private matter without structural government interference. Today this situation has changed considerably as most clubs and federations are now recognised and/or subsidised by the government. After World War II, sports policy programmes run by the government have gradually developed. The process whereby governmental agencies have an increasing impact on the organisation of sports is referred to as the governmentalisation of sport (Bergsgard et al., 2007). Key to this process is the controlling function of the government. The government coordinates and directs the sports landscape. Initially, public sports policy programmes primarily focused on investments in sports infrastructure (Houlihan, 2001; 2006). Inspired by the Sport for All idea, from the 1970s onwards, the focus would increasingly be on stimulating active participation in sports.

After aerobics queen Jane Fonda had already laid the foundations for this in the first half of the 1980s, the commercialisation and commodification of sport would start in the mid-1980s. The (Western) world would increasingly become acquainted with commercially operated fitness centres, subtropical swimming pools, but also other infrastructure-related sports settings such as covered ski slopes, indoor climbing walls, bowling centres, karting racing circuits, etc. Sports, in particular fitness and health-enhancing physical activities, were given a commercial value. Active sports practice was discovered by the market, so that in addition to sports provided by voluntary associations (sports clubs) and public authorities (sports departments), a commercial sports offer (sports companies) now also emerged. The mechanism of market control is in effect here. Free market principles (supply and demand) determine the provision of sports services. During the past three decades, commercial sports initiatives have been able to capture an ever-increasing share in the sports market (Laine & Vehmas, 2017). In addition to sports clubs, sports departments and sports companies, so-called light sports communities have also gained in importance during the last 15 years (Scheerder & Van Bottenburg, 2010). Processes of informalisation and individualisation are at the very root of these sport light formulas. Light communities are characterised by more volatile, looser and/or more flexible interconnections between members than is the case in a traditional sports club (Duyvendak & Hurenkamp, 2004). Today, sports consumers seem to avoid 'greedy' and time-consuming settings. Light communities on the one hand give rise to less intense ties, but on the other hand offer the possibility of entering into multiple connections at the same time. The sports world appears not to be immune to this phenomenon of light and volatile communities. Nowadays, numerous low-threshold sports initiatives, small-scale sporting groups, as well as mass sporting events are likely to be very popular (Scheerder et al., 2015a; Scheerder & Van Bottenburg, 2010). This trend also shows up when one has a look at the popular places where people practise their sports, like fitness centres, tennis and squash courts, swimming pools, bicycle routes, mountain bike trails, ski halls, skate bowls, bowling centres, karting racing circuits, indoor climbing walls, basketball courts or recreational parks. Meanwhile, despite fierce, mutual competition, more and more forms of interaction and cooperation are developed between the different sports actors. More precisely, this involves a process of networking between sports actors from the public, private as well as third sector, and in that sense this interactive and cooperative forms are based on network control. In Table 14.1 we provide an overview of the various actors, processes and mechanisms that were discussed in this section. In particular, this table gives a picture of the

Table 14.1 Actors, processes and mechanisms with regard to the organisational and institutional evolution of modern sport

Period	Sector	Actors	Main process	Sub-processes	Mechanism
Since 18th-19th Century	Civil sports society	Voluntary sports associations	Formalisation/ institutionalisation of sports	Corporatisation/ particularisation of sport	Self-regulation
Since mid-20th-Century	Sports government	Public sports departments		Governmentalisation/ nationalisation/ collectivisation of sport	Public regulation
Since 1980s	Sports market	Commercial sports companies	De-structuration of sports	Commercialisation/privatisation/ commodification of sport	Market control
Since 1990s	Semi-formal sports sector	Light sports communities		Informalisation/ individualisation/ de-traditionalisation of sport	Light management
Since 21st Century	Inter-, cross- and trans-sectoral	Sports networks	Re-structuration of sports	Hybridisation of sport	Network control

Source: Adapted from Scheerder and Vos (2014: 114) and Scheerder et al. (2017b: 129)

changes in the organisation and structuration of sports and its institutions. We can state that sports federations and sports clubs have lost their quasi-monopoly position as providers of sport over the past decades, and that the club-organised sports sector today is in the company of public, commercial and light sports providers. From this, it may be inferred that the world of sport no longer is in the sole hands of the federated sports sector, and that therefore it can be considered that sport has undergone a process of de-traditionalisation since other, mainly non-voluntary actors entered the sports scene.

As processes of societalisation[3] and de-traditionalisation took place, the question is legitimate which actor(s) and/or institution(s) today can be considered representing and steering the world of sport. We will elaborate this topic in the following sections by focusing on three sociological levels and corresponding theories.

Level 1: The sports policy level (macro level)

Historically, in Europe, a mixed economy of welfare exists in which three sectors are embedded, namely: (i) the community (civil society), (ii) the state (public agencies) and (iii) the market (private firms). Together these sectors form the so-called 'welfare triangle' (Evers & Laville, 2004). Translated towards the field of sport, this tripolar system respectively consists of (i) voluntary sports associations (i.e. sports clubs and their umbrella organisations), (ii) public sports authorities (i.e. sports departments) and (iii) commercial sports organisations (i.e. sports companies) (Hylton & Totten, 2013; Scheerder et al., 2011a). In order to address the need for additional resources sports organisations draw upon inter-sectoral and inter-organisational relationships. According to the *principle-agent theory* (Eisenhardt, 1989; Ross, 1973) these relationships are hierarchical by nature. More precisely, it has been shown that in some European countries, national governments and national sports (con)federations might be situated in an agency relationship in which the government acts as the principle and the sports (con)federations act as agents (Scheerder et al., 2017a). This appears to be the case for, among others, Belgium, France, Lithuania, Slovenia and Spain (Willem & Scheerder, 2017). In these countries the government imposes sports policy goals and rules, while non-governmental sports bodies are expected to execute them. In accordance with the *co-governance theory* (Skelcher, 2000), however, the state is not the only actor involved with sports policy-making. As a result, so-called sports policy networks have grown in importance (Groll et al., 2010). In this multi-actor approach, public, voluntary and/or commercial actors are active and partake in shaping sports policy, based on 'governance arrangements' (Bruyninckx & Scheerder, 2009). Such a collaborative sports model, in which the government acts as a facilitator, seems to be more likely in countries with a non-interventionist sport legislation and/or a low dependency on governmental support, such as Denmark, Finland, Germany, Switzerland and the United Kingdom (Scheerder et al., 2017a; Willem & Scheerder, 2017). Here, instead of sharp cleavages between the different profit sectors, non-hierarchical interrelationships with a variety of partners occur, delivering products and

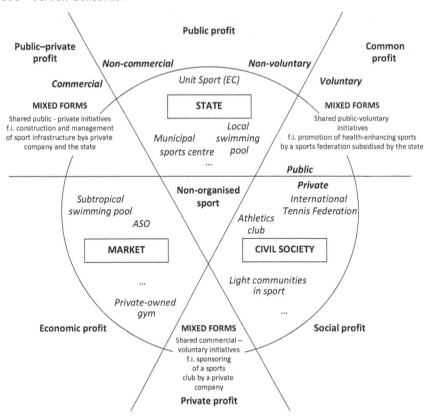

Figure 14.1 Multi-actor model of sport.
Source: Adapted from Scheerder (2007: 19) and Scheerder et al. (2011a: 6; 2011b: 104)

services that are open to a wide and diverse range of sports consumers. It should be noted that in Sport for All policies, the collaborative governance model is more frequent than is the case for the elite sport area (Goodwin & Grix, 2011: 551). In general, it seems that in European countries, top-down policies are losing ground in favour of policy-making processes in which networking, decentralisation and cooperation prevail. Although the balance between civil society, state and market can differ among European countries, it is clear that nowadays no single actor, albeit the civic, public or commercial sports sector, is yet able to monopolise the world of sport, and that the respective strengths of these different profit sectors are respected and, ideally, bundled (see Figure 14.1).

Level 2: The level of sports provision (meso level)

For decades, the overall organisational structure of the world of sport has been described and explained by means of the so-called *pyramid model of sport* (see Arnaut, 2006; EC, 1999; UEFA, 2005). The pyramidal sports model assumes a perfect coherence and mutual influence between the top and the base of the pyramid, resulting in the so-called *double pyramid theory* (IOC, 2000). This theory states that out of a pond of thousands of athletes a few Olympic champions will emerge, and that these champions, in turn, would inspire thousands of people to actively participate in sports. Hardly any consistent empirical evidence can be found for the relationship between elite sporting success on the one hand and increased levels of sports participation on the other (De Bosscher et al., 2013; Frick & Wicker, 2016; Haut & Gaum, 2018; Scheerder et al., 2012a). In contrast to the alleged role model that elite athletes would play, the supply function from grassroots sports is beyond question. Elite sports cannot exist without the supply from mass sports. However, the majority of sports participants do not need elite sports in order to be able to partake in sports themselves. Although elite sport is based on mass sport – for example, for the recruitment of potential talents – a growing part of the world of sport no longer fits into the hierarchical structure of the pyramid model (Scheerder et al., 2011a). In fact, club-organised sport is becoming a smaller part of the total mass sports picture, whereas there is a strong growth of non-club-organised sports activities (supra). Therefore, no equal or mutual influence exists between elite and mass sports. The overly hierarchical and conservative rationale behind the pyramidal sports metaphor has been criticised, and alternative, more pluralistic sports models have been proposed (see e.g. Eichberg, 2008; Heinilä, 1971; Renson, 1983; 2002; Scheerder et al., 2011a). According to these critics, the description of the world of sports as a pyramid puts too much emphasis on aspects of hierarchy and competition. Like other pyramids in history, it represents a normative, one-dimensional, centralistic and monopolistic order (Eichberg, 2008). Moreover, Eichberg (2008: 11) calls for an adequate and democratic representation, one in which the diversity and plurality of sports are included. Therefore, the pyramid model cannot be seen as a mere model of organisation and structuring, neither as a democratic system. Instead, it mainly implies a claim of bureaucratic power and political control. Describing the world of sports by applying the pyramid model neglects the existence of a rich spectrum of sports activities, among which street football, urban dance, countryside hiking, recreational cycling, gym spinning, mass running, etc. (Hoekman et al., 2011; Scheerder et al., 2011a; Van Bottenburg et al., 2005). These sports activities follow patterns that are different from a one-dimensional and hierarchical system. This is especially the case with regard to the previously mentioned light sport communities, since these informal, rather small groups of sports participants are strongly gaining in popularity (Borgers et al., 2015; 2018; Harris et al., 2017; Scheerder & Van Bottenburg, 2010). As the pyramid model of sport seems to downsize the world of sport to club-organised sport, Scheerder et al. (2011a) attempted to develop an alternative and more adequate representation of the contemporary organisation of sport by proposing the *church model of sport* (Figure 14.2).

Though club-organised sport occurs in all countries, its relative importance – as compared with overall sport – shows a large variation. Moreover,

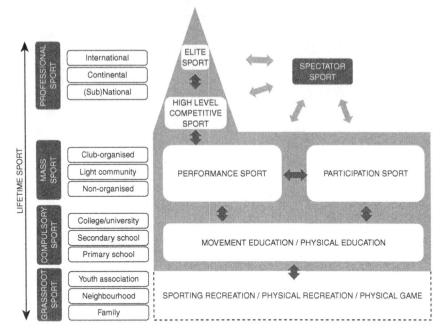

Figure 14.2 Expanded version of the church model of sport.
Source: Adapted from Scheerder (2007: 24), Scheerder et al. (2011a: 8) and Scheerder & Vos (2013: 8; 2014: 147)

as club-organised sport is not the only basis for grassroots-level sport, it is a part of the picture. Therefore, rather than following only a 'competitive' logic, as is the case with the pyramid model, also other forms of sports organisation and sports participation are included in the church model. This indicates that the church model can be defined as a pluralistic sports model. Within this model, a differentiation is made between performance sport and participation sport. Both modes of sport coexist and form the nave of the church. Or in other words, they count for the lion's share. The tower of the church represents high-level competitive sport and elite sport. As only a part of performance and participation sport can be considered as forming the basis of high-level competitive sport, the tower is built on only a limited part of performance and participation sport. As already suggested, the competitive logic is not the only possible logic. Nowadays, more and more people partake in sport for health and/or social reasons, but do not care so much about winning, setting a record or achieving high-level performances. Although the shares between the different sports modes may differ somewhat among countries, this way of representing the world of sport is more likely to be applicable to most of the European countries (Scheerder et al., 2011a; Van Bottenburg et al., 2005).

Level 3: The level of active participation in sport (micro level)

Today, in Europe, more than half of the population (54%) aged 15 and older actively engages in sports (EC, 2018). Nevertheless, it cannot be said that sports participation has been democratised as patterns of social stratification still occur. Relative to, among others, sex, age and educational status, significant inequalities in sports participation levels persist within and between European countries (Hartmann-Tews, 2006; Scheerder et al., 2011a; 2018; Van Bottenburg et al., 2005; Van Tuyckom & Scheerder, 2010). Social differences, however, not only can be noted with regard to sports participation in general but also when it comes to preferences of sports participation in particular. As Bourdieu (1978) states, the practice of sport, like any other field in society, is a site of symbolic struggle between social classes. Indeed, sociological research has empirically revealed that participation in sports activities reflects the social positions and patterns existing at large in society (see e.g. Renson, 1976; Scheerder et al., 2002; Stempel, 2005; Von Euler, 1953). In order to visualise the distinctive sports clusters, the so-called *social status pyramid of sport* has been presented (see Renson, 1976; Scheerder et al., 2002; 2013; 2015a). The rationale behind this pyramidal representation refers to the *trickle-down theory* (Fallers, 1954). This theory assumes that people on a lower position in the social hierarchy are attracted by higher status groups and their social esteem. Lower social classes try to imitate the upper classes in order to gain social prestige. Consequently, people higher up the social ladder will shift their interests and adopt new goods and lifestyle activities in order to re-distinguish themselves. Trickling-down patterns have been demonstrated for consumption goods of many kinds, for instance, fashion (Simmel, 1904), automobiles and household furnishing (Fallers, 1954), but also sports practices (Scheerder et al., 2002; Stokvis, 2010: 47–58; Van Bottenburg, 2001). The trickle-down theory, however, has proved to be useful for understanding processes of imitation and emulation when applied to a society with a relatively stable class structure (Solomon, 2007: 594). In our contemporary society, however, it seems that consumers tend to be rather affected by peers and opinion leaders who can be considered to be more similar to them. This process is referred to as a *trickle-across* effect. Here, tastes are diffused and taken over horizontally, instead of vertically, among members of the same social group. Empirical evidence shows that popular sports activities, such as fitness and running, as well as rather 'new' sports practices like mountain-biking and spinning are introduced by (upper-)middle-class people and thus not by members of the elite class (Scheerder et al., 2013; 2015a). When it comes to sports participation preferences, patterns of vertical social mobility, on the other hand, seem to have become rather exceptional nowadays. In other words, no longer appears the elite class to be dominant and decisive as new and more successful trickling trajectories show up today. Or formulated differently: no more are the upper classes conceived to be the (only) group of sports innovators.

Discussion and conclusion

According to the saying that a picture is worth a thousand words, the impact of how the world of sport is visually represented may not be underestimated. Presenting the world of sport by a mere pyramidal or triangular model implies a reduction of the realm of sport, whether through the configuration of the welfare triangle, the pyramid model of sport or the social status pyramid of sport as discussed in this chapter. The public, sports practitioners and, in particular, policy makers and sports professionals seem to be passionate about, and sometimes even obsessed with 'pyramids' and 'triangles' when visualising how they assume and perceive the structuration, organisation and management of sport. This worship, however, needs to be critically examined as its conception is mainly configured and maintained by those in power. Moreover, it may hinder social change and needed forms of innovation. The pyramidal and triangular symbol can be considered as a tool of monopolistic control in the hands of the established order. In this chapter, based on empirical evidence, we tried to demonstrate that the pyramidal and triangular configurations need to be deconstructed or at least reconstructed and refined. Since ethical aspects and principles of good governance have gained importance in the fields of sports policy and sports management, monopolies and other forms of hierarchical configuring are no longer tolerated nor deemed to be maintained. Nowadays, the world of sport is characterised by diversity and plurality, both at the supply and demand side. During the past decades, along with growing numbers of participants and providers, sport in itself has evolved from a uniform into a pluriform concept. As a consequence, a variety of actors and stakeholders should be in charge. Because new players have entered the sports scene, consequently, no single group or organisation can claim to be 'the' natural sports body. Although developments like differentiation and diversification in sport are to be welcomed, this does not imply that a process of democratisation has taken place. On the contrary, specific groups in society still seem to be underrepresented or even not represented at all, both among participants and providers. If sport is cherished as an indispensable and unmistakable part of our welfare state, it is important that the developments described here are taken into account when preparing and implementing new sports policy plans. In this way sport will truly be there for and by all.

Notes

1 Draft versions of this chapter have been presented by the author at various scientific conferences and academic workshops (see Scheerder, 2015; 2017a; 2017b; 2018a; 2018b; 2019 and Scheerder et al., 2012b; 2015b; 2017c).
2 During the previous centuries, however, the British themselves had borrowed those sport-like activities from France and Italy (Guttmann, 2004; Rijsdorp, 1977: 47).
3 Analogous to this process of societalisation of sport, simultaneously the *sportification* of society has occurred (Crum, 1991). This is evidenced by the fact that sport, in turn, has invaded many areas of society, including education, healthcare, employment, social work, spatial planning, tourism, etc.

Bibliography

Arnaut, J.L. (2006). *Independent European sport review*. Brussels: European Commission.
Bergsgard, N.A., Houlihan, B., Mangset, P., Nødland, S.I. & Rommetvedt, H. (2007). *Sport policy. A comparative analysis of stability and change*. Oxford: Elsevier.
Borgers, J., Pilgaard, M., Vanreusel, B. & Scheerder, J. (2018). Can we consider changes in sports participation as institutional change? A conceptual framework. *International Review for the Sociology of Sport* 53(1): 84–100.
Borgers, J., Thibaut, E., Vandermeerschen, H., Vanreusel, B., Vos, S. & Scheerder, J. (2015). Sports participation styles revisited. A time-trend study in Belgium from the 1970s to the 2000s. *International Review for the Sociology of Sport* 50 (1): 45–63.
Bourdieu, P. (1978). Sport and social class. *Social Science Information* 17(6): 819–840.
Bruyninckx, H. & Scheerder, J. (2009). Sport, macht en internationale politiek. Een politicologisch kader [Sport, power and international politics. A political scientific framework]. In J. Scheerder & B. Meulders (Eds.), *Sport, bestuur en macht. Wedijver in een internationale arena* [Sport, governance and power. Competition in an international arena] (Management & Bestuur in Sport 2) [Management & Governance in Sports 2]) (pp. 1–19). Ghent: Academia Press.
Cachay, K. (1990). Versportlichung der Gesellschaft und Entsportung des Sports. Systemtheoretische Anmerkungen zu einem geselschaftlichen Phänomen. In H. Gabler & U. Göhner (Eds.), *Für einen besseren Sport* (pp. 97–113). Schorndorf bei Stuttgart: Karl Hofmann.
Chaker, A.-N. (2004). *Good governance in sport. A European survey*. Strasbourg: Council of Europe Publishing.
Chappelet, J.-L. (2010). *Autonomy of sport in Europe* (Sports Policy & Practice Series). Strasbourg: Council of Europe Publishing.
Coalter, F. (2007). *A wider social role for sport. Who's keeping the score?* London: Routledge.
Council of Europe (2012). *Good governance and ethics in sport*. Strasbourg: Council of Europe/Parliamentary Assembly Committee on Culture, Science Education & Media.
Crum, B. (1991). *Over versporting van de samenleving. Reflecties over de bewegingsculturele ontwikkelingen met het oog op sportbeleid* [On the process of sportification of society. Reflections on movement culture developments with a focus on sports policy]. Rijswijk: Ministry of Welfare, Public Health & Culture.
De Bosscher, V., Sotiriadou, P. & Van Bottenburg, M. (2013). Scrutinizing the sport pyramid metaphor. An examination of the relationship between elite success and mass participation in Flanders. *International Journal of Sport Policy & Politics* 5(3): 319–339.
Dejonghe, T. (2010). *Sport in de wereld. Ontstaan, evolutie en verspreiding* [Sport in the world. Its origins, evolution and diffusion]. Ghent: Academia Press.
Demasure, M. (1989). Moderne sport kwam overgewaaid uit Groot-Brittannië. Belgische atletiek moest zich eerst van voetbaljuk bevrijden [Modern sports came over from Great Britain. Belgian athletics first had to free themselves from the football yoke]. In KBAB/LRBA (Ed.), *100 jaar Belgische atletiek* [100 years of Belgian athletics] (pp. 7–15). Reet: Vita.
Dietrich, K. & Heinemann, K. (Eds.) (1989). *Der nicht-sportliche Sport. Beiträge zum Wandel im Sport* (Texte, Quellen, Dokumente zur Sportwissenschaft 25). Schorndorf bei Stuttgart: Karl Hofmann.

Digel, H. (1990). Die Versportlichung unserer Kultur und deren Folgen für den Sport. Ein Beitrag zur Uneigentlichkeit des Sports. In H. Gabler & U. Göhner (Eds.), *Für einen besseren Sport* (pp. 73–96). Schorndorf bei Stuttgart: Karl Hofmann.

Digel, H. (1995). *Sport in a changing society. Sociological essays* (Sport Science Studies 7). Schorndorf bei Stuttgart: Karl Hofmann.

Duyvendak, J.W. & Hurenkamp, M. (Eds.) (2004). *Kiezen voor de kudde. Lichte gemeenschappen en de nieuwe meerderheid* [Choosing for the herd. Light communities and the new majority] (Kennis, Openbare mening & Politiek) [Knowledge, Public opinion & Politics]). Amsterdam: Van Gennep.

EC (1999). *The European model of sport. Consultation document of DG X*. Brussels: European Commission/Directorate-General X Information, Communication, Culture & Audiovisual Media.

EC (2018). *Sport and physical activity* (Special Eurobarometer 472). Brussels: European Commission/Directorate-General for Education, Youth, Sport & Culture.

Eichberg, H. (2008). Pyramid or democracy in sports? Alternative ways in European sports policies. www.idrottsforum.org/articles/eichberg/eichberg080206.html.

Eisenhardt, K. (1989). Agency theory. An assessment and review. *The Academy of Management Review* 14(1): 57–74.

Elias, N. & Dunning, E. (1986). *Quest for excitement. Sport and leisure in the civilizing process*. Oxford: Basil Blackwell.

Evers, A. & Laville, J.-L. (2004). Defining the third sector in Europe. In A. Evers & J.-L. Laville (Eds.), *The third sector in Europe* (Globalization & Welfare) (pp. 11–42). Cheltenham: Edward Elgar.

Fallers, L.A. (1954). A note on the 'trickle effect'. *The Public Opinion Quarterly* 18(3): 314–321.

Frick, B. & Wicker, P. (2016). The trickle-down effect. How elite sporting success affects amateur participation in German football. *Applied Economics Letters* 23(4): 259–263.

Giulianotti, R. & Robertson, R. (Eds.) (2007). *Globalization and sport*. Malden, MA: Blackwell.

Goodwin, M. & Grix, J. (2011). Bringing structures back in. The 'governance narrative', the 'decentred approach' and 'asymmetrical network governance' in the education and sport policy communities. *Public Administration* 89(2): 537–556.

Grix, J. (2016). *Sport politics. An introduction*. London: Palgrave.

Groll, M., Gütt, M. & Nölke, A. (2010). Globale Sportpolitiknetzwerke. In W. Tokarski & K. Petry (Eds.), *Handbuch Sportpolitik* (Beiträge zur Lehre und Forschung im Sport 172) (pp. 142–157). Schorndorf: Hofmann.

Guttmann, A. (1978). *From ritual to record. The nature of modern sports*. New York, NY: Columbia University Press.

Guttmann, A. (2004). *Sports. The first five millennia*. Amherst, MA: University of Massachusetts Press.

Harris, S., Nichols, G. & Tayor, M. (2017). Bowling even more alone. Trends towards individual participation in sport. *European Sport Management Quarterly* 17(3): 290–311.

Hartmann-Tews, I. (2006). Social stratification in sport and sport policy in the European Union. *European Journal for Sport & Society* 3(2): 109–124.

Haut, J. & Gaum, C. (2018). Does elite success trigger mass participation in table tennis? An analysis of trickle-down effects in Germany, France and Austria. *Journal of Sports Sciences* 36(23): 2760–2767.

Heinilä, K. (1971). Sport planning. Toward a humanistic approach. In Finnish Society for Research in Sport &Physical Education (Ed.), *Sport and leisure*. Helsinki: Finnish Society for Research in Sport & Physical Education.
Hoekman, R., Breedveld, K. & Scheerder, J. (Eds.) (2011). Sports participation in Europe. *European Journal for Sport & Society* (Special Issue) 8(1+2).
Houlihan, B. (2001). *Sport, policy and politics. A comparative analysis.* London: Routledge.
Houlihan, B. (2006). Government objectives and sport. In W. Andreff & S. Szymanski (Eds.), *Handbook on the economics of sport* (pp. 254–259). Cheltenham: Edward Elgar.
Hylton, K. & M. Totten (2013). Community sport development. In K. Hylton (Ed.). *Sport development. Policy, process and practice.* (3rd ed., pp. 80–126). London: Routledge.
IOC (2000). *Sport for All/Sport pour Tous.* Lausanne: International Olympic Committee.
IOC (2008). *Basic universal principles of good governance of the Olympic and sports movement.* Lausanne: International Olympic Committee.
Katwala, S. (2000). *Democratising global sport.* London: Foreign Policy Centre.
Kugel, J. (1977). *Geschiedenis van de gymnastiek. Leerboek voor de opleidingen in de lichamelijke opvoeding, paramedische beroepen en de sport* [History of gymnastics. Textbook for courses in physical education, paramedical professions and sports]. Haarlem: De Vrieseborch.
Laine, A. & Vehmas, H. (2017). Development, current situation and future prospects of the private sport sector in Europe. In A. Laine & H. Vehmas (Eds.), *The private sport sector in Europe. A cross-national comparative perspective* (Sports Economics, Management & Policy 14) (pp. 343–354). Cham: Springer International Publishing.
Maguire, J. (1999). *Global sport. Identities, societies, civilizations.* Oxford: Polity.
Mandell, R. (1984). *Sport, a cultural history.* New York, NY: Columbia University Press.
Mangan, J.A. (1986). *The games ethic and imperialism. Aspects of the diffusion of an ideal.* New York, NY: Viking.
Renson, R. (1975). De opkomst van de moderne sportbeweging in Groot-Brittannië. Een historisch-culturele schets [The emergence of the modern sports movement in Great Britain. A historic-cultural approach]. *Sport* 18: 97–105.
Renson, R. (1976). Social status symbolism of sports stratification. *Hermes* (Leuven) 10: 433–443.
Renson, R. (1983). Sport for All. New perspectives in text and context. In A. Van Lierde & L. De Clercq (Eds.), *Evaluation of the impact of sport for all policies and programmes* (1st meeting of the European project group; Dudzele, 1983) (pp. 121–135). Brussels: BLOSO.
Renson, R. (2002). Inclusion or exclusion? Possibilities and limitations for interaction between Sport for All and elite sport. In NOC*NSF (Eds.), *Sport for all and elite sport. Rivals or partners?* (Proceedings of the 9th World Sport for All congress) (p. 49). Arnhem: NOC*NSF.
Rijsdorp, K. (1977). *Gymnologie* [Gymnology] (Aula 464). Utrecht: Spectrum.
Ross, S. (1973). The economic theory of agency. The principal's problem. *American Economic Review* 63(2): 134–139.
Scheerder, J. (2007). *Tofsport in Vlaanderen. Groei, omvang en segmentatie van de Vlaamse recreatiesportmarkt* [Participatory sports in Flanders. Growth, size and segmentation of the Flemish recreational sports market]. Antwerp: F&G Partners.
Scheerder, J. (2015). The world(s) of sport. Three models revisited (Key note presented at the Berner Gespräche zur Sportwissenschaft Kolloquium/Universität Bern/

Institut für Sportwissenschaft; Bern; 11 May 2015). www.ispw.unibe.ch/unibe/phil human/ispw/content/e9604/e385631/e658888/e666911/TheWorldsofSport.ThreeModel sRevisited_ger.pdf.

Scheerder, J. (2017a). Church over pyramid? Busting participation in sports clubs in Europe: opportunities and challenges (Presentation at the Social Inclusion and Volunteering in Sports Clubs in Europe Conference 'Social Inclusion and Volunteering in Sports Clubs in Europe' (SIVSCE); Budapest; 30 November 2017).

Scheerder, J. (2017b). Club-organised sports in Europe. Quo vadis? (Presentation at the European Social Inclusion and Volunteering in Sports Clubs in Europe Conference 'Social Inclusion and Volunteering in Sports Clubs in Europe' (SIVSCE); Brussels; 28 September 2017). www.sdu.dk/en/om_sdu/institutter_centre/c_isc/forskningsp rojekter/sivsce/news_sivsce/europeansivsceconference.

Scheerder, J. (2018a). A tango with two or a battle with three? Sport federations and their relation with national authorities and commercial providers (Key note presented at the Social Sciences and Sport Conference; Comitato Olimpico Nazionale Italiano/Scuola dello Sport; Rome; 25 October 2018).

Scheerder, J. (2018b). A tango with two or a battle with three? Sport federations and their relation with national authorities and commercial providers from a European perspective (Presentation at the Policy/Politics in Sport Research Network Workshop (POLIS); HAN University of Applied Sciences/Olympic Training Centre Papendal; Arnhem; 30 November 2018).

Scheerder, J. (2019). Rethinking the world(s) of sport from a socio-political perspective (Key note presented at the KU Leuven – Waseda University/Faculty of Sport Sciences International Workshop; Tokyo/Higashifushimi; 7 March 2019).

Scheerder, J., Breedveld, K. & Borgers, J. (2015a). Who is doing a run with the running boom? The growth and governance of one of Europe's most popular sport activities. In J. Scheerder, K. Breedveld & J. Borgers (Eds.), *Running across Europe. The rise and size of one of the largest sport markets* (pp. 1–27). Basingstoke: Palgrave Macmillan.

Scheerder, J., Claes, E. & Willem, A. (2017a). Does it take two to tango? The position and power of national sport bodies compared to their public authorities. In J. Scheerder, A. Willem & E. Claes (Eds.), *Sport policy systems and sport federations. A cross-national perspective.* (pp. 1–17). Basingstoke: Palgrave Macmillan.

Scheerder, J., Thibaut, E., Pauwels, G., Vandermeerschen, H., Winand, M. & Vos, S. (2012a). *Sport in clubverband (Deel 2). Uitdagingen voor de clubgeorganiseerde sport* (Beleid & Management in Sport Studies 9) [Sport in associative settings (Part 2). Challenges for the club-organised sport (Policy & Management in Sport Studies 9)]. Leuven: KU Leuven/Research Centre for Sport Policy & Sport Management.

Scheerder, J. & Van Bottenburg, M. (2010). Sport light. De opkomst van lichte organisaties in de sport [Sport light. The emergence of light organisations in sports]. In B. Pattyn & B. Raymaekers (Eds.), *In gesprek met morgen* (Lessen voor de 21ste eeuw 16) [In communication with tomorrow (Lessons for the 21st century 16)] (pp. 89–120). Leuven: University Press Leuven.

Scheerder, J., Vandermeerschen, H., Borgers, J., Thibaut, E. & Vos, S. (2013). *Vlaanderen sport! Vier decennia sportbeleid en sportparticipatie* (Sociaalwetenschappelijk onderzoek naar Bewegen & Sport 5) [Sport in Flanders. Four decades of sport policy and sport participation (Social Science Research in Physical Activity & Sport 5)]. Ghent: Academia Press.

Scheerder, J., Vandermeerschen, H. & Breedveld, K. (2018). Diversity in participation reigns, policy challenges ahead. Sport for all (ages) from a European perspective. In R.A. Dionigi & M. Gard (Eds.), *Sport and physical activity across the lifespan. Critical perspectives* (pp. 45–65). Basingstoke: Palgrave Macmillan.

Scheerder, J., Vandermeerschen, H., Van Tuyckom, C., Hoekman, R., Breedveld, K. & Vos, S. (2011a). *Understanding the game: sport participation in Europe. Facts, reflections and recommendations* (Sport Policy & Management Studies 10). Leuven: University of Leuven/Research Unit of Social Kinesiology & Sport Management.

Scheerder, J., Vandermeerschen, H. & Vos, S. (2012b). Social stratification of sports. Changes in the sport pyramid between 1969 and 2009 (Paper presented at the 9th European Association for Sociology of Sport Conference; Bern; 20–23 June 2012). In T. Schlesinger, S. Günter, Y. Weigelt-Schlesinger & S. Nagel (Eds.). *Sport in globalised societies. Changes and challenges* (Book of abstracts of the 9th EASS Conference) (p. 129). Münster: Waxmann.

Scheerder, J., Vanreusel, B., Taks, M. & Renson, R. (2002). Social sports stratification in Flanders 1969–1999. Intergenerational reproduction of social inequalities? *International Review for the Sociology of Sport* 37(2): 219–245.

Scheerder, J. & Vos, S. (2013). Belgium: Flanders. In K. Hallmann & K. Petry (Eds.). *Comparative sport development. Systems, participation and public policy* (Sports Economics, Management & Policy 8) (pp. 7–21). New York, NY: Springer Science +Business Media.

Scheerder, J. & Vos, S. (2014). *De krijtlijnen van het speelveld. Organisatie en planning van sport en sportbeleid in Vlaanderen* (Management & Bestuur in Sport 7) [The outlines of the playing field. Organisation and planning of sport and sports policy in Flanders (Management & Governance in Sport 7)]. 2nd ed. Ghent: Academia Press.

Scheerder, J., Vos, S. & Borgers, J. (2017b). *Beleid en organisatie van sport* (Campus Handboek/Management & Bestuur in Sport 10) [Policy and organisation of sport (Campus Handbook/Management & Governance in Sport 10)]. Leuven: LannooCampus.

Scheerder, J., Willem, A. & Claes, E. (2017c). National sport authorities and national sport bodies. It takes two to tango (Paper presented at the 14th European Association for Sociology of Sport Conference; Prague; 14–17 June 2017). In I. Slepičková (Ed.), *The values of sport. Between tradition and (post)modernity* (Abstract book of the 14th EASS Conference) (pp. 99–100). Prague: Charles University/Faculty of Physical Education & Sport.

Scheerder, J., Willem, A., Claes, E. & Billiet, S. (2015b). The position and power of national sports (con)federations. Agency relationship or co-governance? (Paper presented at the 12th European Association for Sociology of Sport Conference; Dublin; 10–13 June 2015). In J. Connolly & P. Dolan (Eds.), *Sport, unity and conflict* (Book of abstracts of the 12th EASS Conference) (p. 153). Dublin: Dublin City University Business School.

Scheerder, J., Zintz, T. & Delheye, P. (2011b). The organisation of sports in Belgium. Between public, economic and social profit. In C. Sobry (Ed.), *Sports governance in the world: a socio-historic approach. The organization of sport in Europe: a patchwork of institutions, with few shared points* (Sport Social Studies) (pp. 84–113). Paris: Le Manuscrit.

Simmel, G. (1904). Fashion. *International Quarterly* 10(1): 130–155.

Skelcher, C. (2000). Changing images of the state. Overloaded, hollowed-out, congested. *Public Policy & Administration* 15(3): 3–19.

Slack, T. (Ed.) (2004). *The commercialisation of sport*. London: Routledge.

Solomon, M.R. (2007). *Consumer behavior. Buying, having and being.* Upper Saddle River, NJ: Pearson Education.
Stempel, C. (2005). Adult participation sports as cultural capital. A test of Bourdieu's theory of the field of sports. *International Review for the Sociology of Sport* 40(4): 411–432.
Stokvis, R. (2010). *De sportwereld. Een inleiding* [The world of sports. An introduction]. Nieuwegein: Arko Sports Media.
Szymanski, S. (2006). *A theory on the evolution of modern sport* (IASE Working Paper Series 6/30). Limoges: International Association of Sports Economists.
UEFA (2005). *Vision Europe. The direction and development of European football over the next decade.* Nyon: Union of European Football Associations.
Van Bottenburg, M. (2001). *Global games* (Sport & Society). Urbana, IL: University of Illinois Press.
Van Bottenburg, M., Rijnen, B. & Van Sterkenburg, J. (2005). *Sports participation in the European Union. Trends and differences.* Nieuwegein: Arko Sports Media.
Van Tuyckom, C. & Scheerder, J. (2010). Sport for All? Insight into stratification and compensation mechanisms of sporting activity in the 27 European Union member states. *Sport, Education & Society* 15(4): 495–512.
Von Euler, R. (1953). Idrottsrörelsen av i dag. En sociologisk studie [Contemporary sports participation behaviour. A sociological study]. In SverigesRiksidrottsförbund (Ed.), *Svensk idrott. En ekonomisk, historisk och sociologisk undersökning* [Swedisch sport. An economic, historical and sociological survey]. Malmö: Allhem.
Willem, A. & Scheerder, J. (2017). Conclusion. The role of sport policies and governmental support in the capacity building of sport federations. In J. Scheerder, A. Willem & E. Claes (Eds.), *Sport policy systems and sport federations. A cross-national perspective* (pp. 303–320). Basingstoke: Palgrave Macmillan.

Index

Page numbers in italics refer to figures. Page numbers in bold refer to tables.

2009 Stockholm Programme 13
2009 Treaty of Lisbon 69, 72

ACB *see* Association of Basketball Clubs
access to citizenship, and social integration 17
acculturation 11
active citizenship 17, 36, 38, 41, 144
active participation in sport 161
Active sports practice 155
adaptive function 15
administrative praxis 12
Adonnino, Pietro 71
'Adonnino Report' 71–72
A+D Plan *see* Comprehensive Plan for Physical Activity and Sport
aggression, violence, and sport 101–102
AGIL scheme 15–17
Alcatraz project 59
Algerian national football team, players with immigrant background in 32
All-Union Physical Culture Council 135
Alpine Club 80
Amara, Mahfoud 29
amateur sports: associations 86, 113; clubs 117; non-profit sector 110
Anglo-Saxon organisation model 154
anti-Europe insurgencies 4
Antigone 62
anti-Olympics petition 80
Arab-Muslim investments, in sports 33–34
assimilation *vs.* social integration 10
Association of Basketball Clubs 125
Asylum, Migration and Integration Fund 9
athletes 39–40, 42–43, 87–90, 92, 97, 117, 125, 129, 135, 154, 159
'Avice' law 89

Bach, Thomas 83n2
Baden-Württemberg 77, 82, 83n5
Bavaria 79
Berlusconi, Silvio 115
Beveridge model 57
Bortoletto, Nico 35
Bosman judgement 39, 71, 91, 116
bottom-up approach to sport policies 38
Brandenburg 77
'Bredin' law 90
Brexit 2, 4, 5
Bristol prison 60
Britain 4, 30–31, 104, 154
Britain, sport in: aggression and violence characteristics 102; governmental support for developing 99; health benefits of 99, 101, 103, 105; inequality in 105–106; injury risks of 102; *vs.* physical activity 101–102; policy 99, 100–101
'Buffet law' 90
Bulgaria, institutional design in 138
Buzyn, Agnès 33

Cardiff club 59
Carraro, Franco 115
case laws for sport 39
Castejón, Benito 122–123
Catholic Church 115
Catholic CSI 115
CEE countries *see* Central and Eastern European countries

Central and Eastern European countries: accession to European Union 134; commonalities of 133; financial and economic indicators 134; part of 132; PE curricula in 136; political systems of 133; regimes after World War II 132; social policies 134; sport budget allocation 134; welfare state model of 133–134, 137–139
Central and Eastern European countries, sport policy in 132; historical and ideological development of 134–137; motivating factors for 137; normative and institutional perspectives on 137–139
Centres for Resources and Expertise of Sport Performance 92
Chelsea club 59
Christian Social Union 77
church model of sport 159, *160*
citizen participation, sports policies 79–80
citizenship 1, 29, 32–33, 112, 115–116; and long-term residence 17; premium 17
civic participation of migrants 17
civil society 10, 18, 38, 86, 148, 157–158
CJEU *see* Court of Justice of the European Union
Club of Cologne 4
club-organised sport 159
CNDS *see* National Centre for the Development of Sport
CNOSF *see* French National Olympic and Sports Committee
COE *see* Spanish Olympic Committee
Collins, Mike 38
commercial sports: organisations 157; stakeholders 116
commodification 153, 155–156
Common Basic Principles 13
common law documents 90–91
communism 133–134, 136
community reintegration 59
community sports 45
companies 33, 75, 86, 91, 93, 157–158; manufacturing and distributing sporting goods 97; organising sports events 96; providing sports services 96
competences 36, 39, 70, 78, 112, 116–117, 147, 155
competitions 43, 81, 86, 88, 92, 94, 102, 112–113, 125, 129, 135–136, 159
competitive sports 92, 115

Comprehensive Plan for Physical Activity and Sport 128
concrete public policies 5
conflicts 2, 51, 56, 72, 104, 115–116
CONI 110, 111, 114; amateur sports clubs and 117; bypassing control of 116; challenging hegemony of 114, 116; demand for radical reform of 113; non-profit sports associations 115; promoting sport as competition 112; recognition of 'propaganda bodies' 115; Servizi 117; 'sporting power' administration 114
Consejo Superior de Deportes (CSD) *see* National Sports Council
Contamos contigo 122
co-operation 30–31, 36, 39, 56, 99
Correctional Institute of Parc 60
Coubertin, Pierre de 87
Council of Europe 54, 69, 71–72, 155
Court of Justice of the European Union 39
CREPS *see* Centres for Resources and Expertise of Sport Performance
crime 53, 100, 103
CSU *see* Christian Social Union
CTS 93
Czech National Strategy for Cycling Development 137
Czechoslovakia 135
Czech Republic: approach towards social welfare restructuring 134; citizen's attitudes towards sport 138

Danish Association for Company sport 146
Danish Gymnastic and Sport Associations 146
Danish sports system 145–147; DGI, DIF, and DFIF 146; funding sources for 147; Ministry of Culture at top of 145; municipalities and 146; sports participation data 147–148; and welfare systems, link between 148–150
Davids, Nuraan 33
Decathlon 33
decentralised organisational structure 46
democratic community 1
democratisation of physical activity 135
Denmark: penitentiary system of 57; *see also* Danish sports system
Deutscher Olympischer Sportbund 76; autonomous organisation of 82; licence-holders data 80–81, 84n9;

memberships in sports club 80; social role of 81
Deutsche Sportjugend 82
Developing the European Dimension in Sport 18
DFIF *see* Danish Association for Company sport
DFLE *see* disability-free life expectancy
DGI *see* Danish Gymnastic and Sport Associations
DIF *see* Sport Confederation of Denmark
disability-free life expectancy 104
disenchantment 5
'DIY' sports enthusiasts 111
DND-National Sports Delegation (Delegación Nacional de Deportes) 122, 123
DOSB *see* Deutscher Olympischer Sportbund
double pyramid theory 159
DSJ *see* Deutsche Sportjugend
Dutch prison system regulations 51

early childhood education and care 16
economic growth 1, 40, 103, 126
economic recession and Spanish sport 128
education 13, 18–19, 38–39, 58, 76–77, 90–91, 94, 110, 132–133, 136–139; outcomes 16–17; and vocational training 21
Education, Youth, Culture and Sport (EYCS) council meetings 39
elite sport 76–77, 102, 126, 136, 138, 146; success in 128, 134, 159
employability 16, 21
employment 15, 16; discrimination in labour market 15; in public sector 15
England, Gladstone Committee 51–52
England and Wales: PET 59; whole prison approach 57
English prison services, regulating 52
ENGSO *see* European Non-Governmental Sports Organisation
environmental sustainability 1
equal opportunities 1; organisations for 3
Erasmus+ Sport Programme 18, 20, 39, 72
Esposito, Maurizio 51
Estonia: approach towards social welfare restructuring 134; institutional arrangement in 138
ethnicity 20, 30, 99, 105–106

ethnic minorities, in German sports clubs 32
ethno-cultural diversities, mutual respect for 11
EU *see* European Union
EU Emergency Trust Fund for Africa2 9
European Commission 12, 128, 137–139; communication 18; community intervention programmes 69; efforts to develop European identity 71–72; *White Paper on Sport* 3
European Council 12–13; resolution 18
Europe: culture 30, 32; host society, 'guiding culture' 10; identity 70–71; integration 4; policy on migrants' integration 12; professional sports 72, 116; societies of 9–10, 18, 36, 45, 71, 112; sport practices 70; sports policy 70, 139; sports system 4, 5, 6; welfare systems 15
European football: clubs, perceived threat to identity of 34; racism and xenophobia in 33; 'scholarly' study of 70
European Institute for Statistics 13
Europeanisation of sport 4, 5, 71; challenges in empirical analysis of 70; complexity of 72; definition of 71; 'formal' and 'informal' 71; stakeholders of 72–73
European model 1, 2, 5
European Non-Governmental Sports Organisation 39–39
European Parliament 71–72
European Prison Rules 54–55
European Special Barometer Survey 44
European Sport for All Charter 38
European Union 12, 18, 30, 69–71, 81, 91, 103, 112, 132, 134, 136; challenges to 3; competency in sport field 39; efforts to remove obstacles to social integration 12–13; feeling of belonging to 2; funding for sport 39–40; impact on sport 39; legal basis to support sport 39; parliamentary elections 4; policy regulations 3; sport chapter 39–40; sport policy initiatives of 38–39; stakeholders of Europeanisation process 72; *see also* EU policies on immigrants' social integration
European Year of Education through Sport 38
Europe of citizens, ad hoc committee for 71

Index

Eurostat 13–14, 23, 37, 133–134
Eurozone 3
EU policies on immigrants' social integration 13–15, 23
EU Sport Forum 2016 19
EU Work Plan for Sport 2011–2014 (resolution) 18
EU Work Plan for Sport 2017 (resolution) 18–19
exercise 54–55, 60, 101–103, 105–108
expiation of sentence 51
extreme sports 113

federalism 75
Fédération gymnastique et sportive des patronages de France 87
federation-related sports 155
FFF *see* French Football Federation
FIFA: rules on nationality and national team eligibility 32
'Fit for Release' report 59
FNDS *see* Fund for the Development of Sport
FOESSA Foundation: report on Madrid sporting infrastructures 121; report on working hours 121
football 20, 59, 70, 72, 80, 82, 92, 94, 96–97, 97, 102, 115, 121, 154; clubs 96, 112, 128; FFF 87, 94; licence-holders 80–81; techniques, programme on 59
foreign-trained immigrants 16
formalisation, sport and physical activity 23–24
formal volunteering 37
for-profit sports sector 110
France: code of penal procedure 51; jihadists 31; outskirts cities of 31
Franco, Francisco 121–122
free-from-doping-in-sport campaign 116
French Football Federation 87, 92, 94
French National Olympic and Sports Committee 86, 93–94
French sports: as complex system 86; evolution of 89–91; federations 93–94; movement 88; nationwide programme 89; organisation 86, 87–88, 89, 90–91, 97; paradox of 97; policies 89, 90, 92, 93, 95; professionalisation 90; Sports Charter of December 1940 87, 88; sports law of 1975 89; stakeholders in 86, 90, 91–93, 94–95, **95**, 96–97; state control 86–87; state's responsibility to develop 88; trade of physical educator 89; welfare state in support of planning of 88–89
Fundamental Law 75–76, 78
Fund for the Development of Sport 93
funding 39, 75, 80, 82, 136, 145, 147

gambling system 144–145, 149
Gasparini, William 69, 86
Gaulle, Charles de 88–89
gender
gender: equality 80–81; gap, in sport participation 105–106
German Fundamental Law 76, 78
German sport: clubs, ethnic minorities in 32; data on 84n12; disparities in access to 81; evolution of 75–76; gender equality 80–81; integrated into Fundamental Law, demands for 76; integration through 82–83; at local level 77; new fields of 81–82; organised sports movement 80–81; outside clubs 82; political promotion of 76–77; as prevention tool 83; in private clubs 81; in Rhineland-Palatinate 77; as social work tool 82; 'sport' themes 77; supporting 77–78, 79; volunteers 84n13; working class representation in 81
Germany 19–20, 30–32, 44, 58, 111, 122, 127, 157; federal state 75; history of direct democracy 75–76; local public sports policies in 78; regions, refusals to host Olympic Games in 79
Gladstone Committee 51
globalisation 46
governance 1, 15, 38–39, 76, 112, 115, 118, 138
governmentalisation 155
Gozzini law of 1986 52
Great Britain *see* Britain; Britain, sport in
Grundgesetz 83n1
'guiding culture' 10
Guirao, José 128
gymnastics 80–81, 112, 135–136

The Hague Programme 12
Hamburg 76, 79
health: benefits of sport 99, 101, 106; promotion aspects 57–58; and social inequality, relationship between 104–105
Herzog, Maurice 89

Index

housing policies, and integration outcomes 17
human capital, depletion of 2
'hybrid' identity of immigrants 32

immigrants 9, 11–19, 31–32, 82, 112–113; athletes descended from 32–33; highly-qualified 16; 'hybrid' identity 32
imprisonment: measures 'alternative' to 52; psychosocial difficulty linked to 61; rehabilitative purpose of 51–52; *see also* prison
'imprisonment' syndrome 61
Index of Health and Social Problems 104
Indicators of immigrant integration (report) 13
individualisation 52
inequalities 81, 103–105, 129, 161; *see also* social inequality
infantilisation 62
inmates 51, 57, 60
INSEP *see* National Institute for Sports, Expertise and Performance
Integration durch Sport (Integration through Sport), targeted government funding for 20
integration policies 15
'Integration through sport' 82
'International Charter of Physical Education, Physical Activity and Sport' 53–54
International Olympic Committee 41–42, 94, 125, 155, 159
international protection, relocation for 9
international sport 41–43, **43**
IOC *see* International Olympic Committee
irregular arrivals 9
Islam: construction as existential threat 31; dichotomies around 29; faith 29, 30; and Orientalism 30–31; in Western/collective imagination 30–31
Islamophobia, in sport: abuses in European stadia 33; Arab-Muslim investments 33–34; Schilling's tweet 33
Italian Football federation 112
Italian National Olympic Committee *see* CONI
Italian sports: amateur sports sector 113; attempts at reforming 116; as conflictual space 112; extreme sports and 113; law 242 and 117; measures adopted by populist government for 117; non-profit sports sector 112, 113; in post-war period 113; promotion model 114–116; reform of sports institutions 113; reforms of 117; scandal concerning anti-doping practices 116; social and institutional actors 112; social sports programmes 117; Sport for All objectives and 112, 113; system 110–112, 115–118, 119n2; transformations of 114; voluntary organisations and networks 113; voluntary sports associations 116
Italian Sports Centre *see* Catholic CSI
Italian Sports Federations 114
Italian Union of Popular Sport *see* UISP
'Italian Union of Sport for All' 119n6
Italy 19; betting market 116; government welfare agenda 116; Law 354/1975 52; Olympic system 117–118; welfare state 113

job reintegration of prisoners 58–59
Judeo-Christian tradition of Europe 30

Kick It Out report 33
Koebel, Michel 75
Kustec, Simona 132

labour market outcomes 15
'Lamour law' 90
Länder's institutional communication 76
law 332 of 2000 118
law of 1 February 2012 90
law of 1 July 1901 90
law of 13 July 1992 *see* 'Bredin' law
law of 16 July 1984 *see* 'Avice' law
law of 1 March 2017 90
law of 29 October 1975 *see* 'Mazeaud'
law on decentralisation 89–90, 95
'Leisure Time Act' 146
leisure walking 97
LFP (Professional Football League) 125
liberal sport, and state sport 90
Ličen, Simon 132
life in prison 61
Lisbon Treaty 18, 38, 42
local authorities 91, 94–95, **95**; independence of 75
local political parties 79
local referendums 79
local sports: associations 78; councils 150n1; policies 82
Loi pénitentiaire of 24 November 2009 52

long-term residents 17
Lower-Saxony 77
low intensity actions, for healthy lifestyles 60

Madrid, sporting infrastructures of 121
Mandela Rules 55
marginalised populations, policies for integration of 82
market private sports sector 91–92
Marmot, Michael 104–105
Martelli, Stefano 1, 9
Masoni, Irene 143
mayors, direct election of 79
May 2019 vote 2, 4
'Mazeaud' 89
Mecklenburg-Western-Pomerania 77
Melandri, Giovanna 116
mental health 57–58, 101
migrant communities, of Islamic faith 5
Migrant Integration Policy Index 13
Migrants in Europe: A statistical portrait of the first and second generation (report) 13
migrants' social integration: dimensions of 15, 16–17; EU's efforts to remove obstacles to 12–13; 'second generation' of immigrants 12; social integration through sport and physical activity 9–10, 12, 18–21, **22**, 23–24, 82–83
migratory crisis 9
Ministry of Youth and Sports 89, 92–93
minorities, integration of 10; *see also* social integration
MIPEX *see* Migrant Integration Policy Index
modern sports movement 102, 154, 155, **156**
movement practices 9, 19–20
multi-actor model of sport *158*
municipalities 75–78, 87, 89–91, 94–95, 117, 145–147
municipal policy, federal regulations of 79
Muslim communities, demands of 29, 33
Muslim culture 30
Muslim organisations 31–32
Muslims in Europe 29, 30; sport and 31, 32, 33–34
Muslim women athletes, sports hijab products for 33

Naivasha GK Prison 60
National Centre for the Development of Sport 93
National Contact Points on Integration 12
national governance systems, profound differences in 2
National Health Service 57
National Institute for Sports, Expertise and Performance 92
national populism 2
National Sports Act of 1990 125
National Sports Act 13/1980 of Physical Culture and Sport 123, 125–126
National Sports Council 123, 124, 128
national sports federations 42, 112, 154
national sports systems 1
National Sport Strategy of Hungary 136
naturalisation 15, 17
Navarro, Arias 123
NIF 143, 144; financial report 151n5
'Nike Sport Hijab' products 33
Noah, Yannick 90
NOC *see* Norwegian Olympic Committee
NOlympia (citizen movement) 79–80
non-EU immigrants, challenges faced by 14
non-market private sports sector 91
non-organised sport 77
non-profit sports: activities 40; organisations 148–149
non-white ethnic minority communities 106
normative perspective 11–12
North African national teams, players from immigrant communities in 32
Norwegian civil society 151n9
Norwegian Olympic and Paralympic Committee and Confederation of Sports *see* NIF
Norwegian Olympic Committee 143
Norwegian sports system 143–145, 148–150
Nussbaum, Martha 53

Olympic and Sports Movement 42
Olympic Games 42, 79
Olympic performance-led activities 110
organisation: of sport 4, 37, 71, 75, 86–88; voluntary 113, 117, 143, 148
Organisation for Economic Co-operation and Development 13
Orientalism and Islam 30–31

Index 175

Pelayo Ros, Tomás 122
penalty 51, 55, 60–61
penitentiary administration 51–52, 57
personal and social development 21
Pescante, Mario 119n7
PET *see* Prisoners' Education Trust
physical activity: democratisation of 135; *vs.* sport 101–102; systematic organisation in CEE countries 135; through opportunities in workplace 135–136; and sport, in prison 53–58, 59, 60–61, 62–63; *see also* sport
physical education 29, 53–55, 86, 89, 95, 123–124, 160; as part of school curriculum 135; programmes 57–58; in Slovenia 136
physical educators 89
pluralism 23
Poland, institutional arrangement in 138
policymakers and Muslim organisations, co-operation between 31–32
political parties 75, 79, 114–115, 118
populism in politics 9
Porro, Nicola R. 1, 46, 110
Porrovecchio, Alessandro 35
post-secular society 30
poverty 20
prejudices 20
prison 5, 51–53, 55–62, 61; healthcare 57; physical activity and sport in 53–58, 59, 60–61, 62–63
Prison Act of 1952 52
prisoners, stressful circumstances experienced by 58
Prisoners' Education Trust 59
'Prisons rules' of 1964 52
private clubs 81
private sporting entities of Spain 124–125
private sports sector 86, 91
Prodi, Romano 116
professionalisation 90
professional sport 86, 90
Ptolemaic order 116
public agencies 157
public authorities 42
public institutions 86, 93, 143, 148–150
public intervention for sport 77–78
public policies 38, 51, 59, 70–71, 78, 86, 115, 138, 143
public sector 92; employment 16; of Spanish sport 124
public sports: authorities 157; policy programmes 155
pyramidal sports model 158–159

quality of life 14, 106

receiving European country 17, 20
'recreational welfare' 99
recreation volunteerism 36
referendums 79, 84n7
refugees 9–12, 14–15, 18–21, 23, 31, 82
regime sport 2
Regioni 114
'relative deprivation,' concept of 61
religion, institutionalisation of 30
religiosity, expression of 29
religious movements, revitalisation of 30
religious phenomenon in Europe 30–31
reparation 53
residence time and integration, link between 14
'restitution' 46
restorative justice, growing need for 53
Rhineland-Palatinate, health-sport and well-being-sport in 77
Ricoeur, Paul 53
Romania, institutional design in 138
'Ruling of Algiers' 88
Rump, Boris 84n10

Salvini, Matteo 117
Sanjurjo, Juan Antonio Simón 121
Santa Rita do Sapucaí prison, in Brazil 60
Scandinavian sports systems 2; characteristics of 143; Danish sports model 145–147; model of sport citizenship 113; Norwegian sports model 143–145; redistributive mechanisms 149–150; Swedish sports model 147–148; and welfare systems, link between 148–150
Scheerder, Jeroen 153
Schilling, Curt 33
Second Republic and sports system 114–115
secularism 30
Seehofer, Horst 77
self-management, principle of 155
Slovakia, social welfare restructuring 134
Slovenia 134, 136, 138
social background and education, link between 16
social capital 41, 72, 148; and volunteerism, correlation between 46
social circles, existence and setting up of 10
social citizenship 2

176 Index

social class differentials 105–106
social cohesion 10–11, 18, 33, 36, 37, 40–41, 46, 92–93
social control 62–63
'social democratic compromise' 2
social differences 161
social exclusion 10, 11, 20, 36, 113, 133
social inclusion 4–5, 13, 19, 39–41, 113–114, 129, 137–138; sociologist on concept of 11; through sport 54
social indicators on immigration 15
social inequality 14–15, 20; and health, relationship between 104–105; and participation in sport 105–106; social problems related to 103; and stress, relationship between 104; and welfare 103–105
social integration 3, 17, 36, 132, 137; anti-discrimination efforts 20; definition of 10, 11; dimensions 12; directions 11; EU efforts to remove obstacles to 12–13; as multi-dimensional process 11; perspectives about 11–12; *see also* migrants' social integration
socialisation agencies 62
socially negative climate 9
social media criticism of sports hijab products 33
social mobility 14
'social offensive of sport' 82
social policies 1, 11, 15, 18–19, 23
social practice, volunteering as 45–46
social reintegration of prisoners 52, 58–59
social resentment 2
social sports programmes 117
social status pyramid of sport 161
social welfare restructuring 134
societalisation of sport 4, 153
society structure and integration, link between 15
socio-economic background 14
Sokol ('Falcon') movement 135
solidarity welfare sports campaigns 117
Soviet Union 135
Spain 30, 111, 157
Spain, autonomous communities in 123, 124; Directorates-General for sport 124; investment in 128; Spanish Sporting federations in 125; transferral of sporting duties to 129
Spaniards, sports practice amongst: Eurobarometer 412 data of 127; federal licences 121; gender gap 127–128; rise of 127
Spanish Constitution of 1978 123
'Spanish miracle' phenomenon 127
Spanish Olympic Committee 125
Spanish Paralympic Committee 125
Spanish Socialist Workers Party 125
Spanish sport: campaigns 122; commercial liberalisation impact on 128; democratisation of 122–124; economic recession impact on 128; elite sport 128; growing interest in 122; organisational structure of 124–125; policy 121–122, 125–127; professional sport successes 127; sporting policy for socialisation of 121–122
Spanish Sporting federations 125
The Spirit Level: Why Equality is Better for Everyone 103–104
sport 3, 36, 37–49, 153; active participation in 161; activities 41, 69, 89, 91, 96–97, 118; aggression and violence, association between 101–102; balances around 3; boundaries of 1; changing way of thinking around 63; church model of 159, *160*; citizenship 2, 5, 67, 115, 117; civic inspiration of 5; clubs 20, 36, 80, 137; commercialisation of 155; commodification of 155; companies 157; competitions 41–42, 89, 94, 97; as construct of identity 4; corporatisation and particularisation of 155; de-traditionalisation of 154–157; diversification in 153; economic approach to 69; economic aspects of 40; entertainment and media, relationship between 5; ethics 90; events 44, 76, 86, 90, 95–96; facilities 31, 54, 62, 76, 78–79, 95, 97, 124, 136, 144, 146; federations 72, 87, 92, 94, 111, 118, 143, 147, 154–155, 157–158; governance 41–42, **43**, 116–118; governing bodies 154; governmentalisation of 155; health benefits of 99, 101, 106; hijab products 33; importance in EU 69; injuries 102; institutional legitimacy 3–4; institutional mechanisms 4; managers 5; market 89, 125, 155–156; movement 5–6, 41–42, 76, 79, 86, 88–89, 91, 93–94; multi-actor model of *158*; and Muslims in Europe 31, 32, 33–34; need for spaces for 54; organisational heritage 3; organisations 114–115, 136, 138, 143, 146–150, 155,

160; participation, active level of 161; and physical activity, Eurobarometer survey on 69; *vs.* physical activity 101–102; political and legislative framework of 40; practices 2, 54, 56, 61–62, 76, 81, 86, 90, 93, 111–112, 114–115, 122, 149, 161; preventive and rehabilitative value of 53–54; promotion bodies 119n5; provision, level of 158–160; pyramidal structure of 43; and religion, discourses shaping 29; services, companies providing 96; as social construction 47; social integration through 9–10, 12, 18–21, **22**, 23–24, 82–83; social role of 40; societalisation of 153; sociocultural and socioeconomic changes to 153; specificity 69; as strategic sensor 1; systems 4, 47, 114, 116, 137, 143, 146–150; volunteers 37; *see also* Britain, sport in; Central and Eastern European countries; French sports; German sport; Italian sports; physical activity; Scandinavian sports systems; Spanish sport; volunteering in sport

Sport and Recreation (White Paper) 99
Sport Confederation of Denmark 146
Sport England 37, 105–106; policy document 101
Sport e Salute (Sport and Health) 117
Sport for All 112, 123
'Sport for all – sport with repatriates' *see* 'Integration through sport'
sport-for-development schemes 99–100; problem in undertaking research in 101; systematic analysis of 100
Sporting Future (policy document) 101
sporting goods, companies manufacturing and distributing 97
sportisation process 154
'sport issue' 3
sports associations 43, 47, 59, 62, 78, 93, 125; amateur 86, 113; in EU 43–45; local 78, 95; on principle of subsidiarity 78; voluntary 116, 156–157
Sports Charter of December 1940 87, 88
sports clubs 32, 46, 57, 80–81, 87, 125, 139, 144, 146, 148–150, 155, 157–158; local 20, 43, 145; local public 78; memberships in 80–81; on principle of subsidiarity 78; school 135
Sport's Code 91, 94
'Sports for All' 125

sports non-governmental organisations for 42; organisation of international sport 42; public authorities 42; regulatory bodies 42
'Sports Operators' 111
sports policies 7, 38–39, 70, 71, 75, 76, 78, 81, 89–90, 93, 95, 132, 134, 137, 144; citizen participation in 79–80; economic growth related 40–41; English history of 38; goals 157; initiative of EU 38; initiators of 82; for integration of marginalised populations 82; international co-operation as 70; items related to 40; local 82, 92, 95; local public 78; macro level 157–158; policy approach in 38; principle of subsidiarity and 78; programmes 155; sustainable development 40
SSC *see* Swedish Sport Confederation
'Standard Minimum Rules for the Treatment of Prisoners' *see* Mandela Rules
state administrations 92
state and religion, relation between 30
state services 90, 92–93
stress and social inequality, relationship between 104
subsidiarity, principle of 42, 69, 75, 77–78, 81
Superenalotto 116
supra-local sports organisations 154
Swedish Sport Confederation 147
Swedish sports system: data on sports participation 147–148; funding sources for 147; structure of 147; and welfare systems, link between 148–150

Tampere Programme 12
territorial administrations 92
Testa, Alberto 1
TFEU *see* Treaty on the Functioning of the European Union
Thessaloniki European Council 12
Thuringia 77
Treaty on the Functioning of the European Union 39; Article 165 of 70
trickle-across effect 161
trickle-down theory 161
Turkey 30

UGSF *see* Union des sociétés de gymnastique de France
UISP 115, 116, 119n6

UK *see* United Kingdom
UNESCO 53
Union des sociétés de gymnastique de France 87
Union des sociétés françaises de sports athlétiques 87
United Kingdom 19; position on sport in prison 57–58; score on index of welfare 104; *see also* Britain; Britain, sport in
United Nations: Mandela Rules 55; 'Universal Declaration of Human Rights' 51
United States: position on sport in prison 57; score on index of welfare 104
'unpaid work' 37
USFSA *see* Union des sociétés françaises de sports athlétiques
Using EU indicators of immigrant integration (report) 13

Vichy French State 87
violence and sport, association between 101–102
voluntary action movement 5
voluntary humanitarian return 9
voluntary sports associations 157
volunteering in sport 21, 47, 148; active citizenship with 36; definitions of 37–38, 44–45; dimensions of 37, 40; dual origin of 37; EBS surveys 44; forms of 36–37, 45; growth of 46; key element of 37; main activities 44; monetary value of 44; organisational dimension of 37; for seniors and young people 36; as social practice 45–46; as social tool 36; socio-economic value of 41; status of 45; WPS 40–41
volunteer organisations 149
volunteers 84n13; economic status of 46; factors enhancing contributions of 46; quantifying work of 44, 47; in sports clubs 149–150; turnover problem 45–46

Waddington, Ivan 99
Waldeck-Rousseau Law 90
welfare 9, 107, 113, 117–118, 157; mixed economy of 157; recreational 99; and social inequality 103–105; and sport 99, 103; state model of CEE countries 133–134, 137–139; *see also* social inequality
welfare state 88, 99, 122, 126, 129, 132, 134, 138
welfare systems 3, 15, 51, 57, 61, 115, 132, 148–150
Western European and CEE countries, welfare models and policies of 133
2007 White Paper on Sport (WPS) 3, 18, 38, 40–41, 72, 137, 139
world sports institutions 42
world sports movement 42

Yugoslavia 135

Zaragoza Declaration 13
Zaragoza indicators 13, 15